Research Methods for Memory Studies

RESEARCH METHODS FOR THE ARTS AND HUMANITIES

Published titles:
Research Methods for English Studies, 2nd Edition
Edited by Gabriele Griffin

Research Methods for Law
Edited by Mike McConville and Wing Hong Chui

Research Methods for Cultural Studies
Edited by Michael Pickering

Practice-led Research, Research-led Practice in the Creative Arts
Edited by Hazel Smith and Roger T. Dean

Research Methods in Theatre and Performance
Edited by Baz Kershaw and Helen Nicholson

Research Methods for History
Edited by Lucy Faire and Simon Gunn

Research Methods for Memory Studies
Edited by Emily Keightley and Michael Pickering

Research Methods for Memory Studies

Edited by Emily Keightley and Michael Pickering

© editorial matter and organisation Emily Keightley and Michael Pickering, 2013
© the chapters their several authors

Edinburgh University Press Ltd
22 George Square, Edinburgh EH8 9LF

www.euppublishing.com

Typeset in 11/13 Ehrhardt by
Servis Filmsetting Ltd, Stockport, Cheshire,
and printed and bound in Great Britain by
CPI Group (UK) Ltd, Croydon CR0 4YY

A CIP record for this book is available from the British Library

ISBN 978 0 7486 4596 1 (hardback)
ISBN 978 0 7486 4595 4 (paperback)
ISBN 978 0 7486 8347 5 (webready PDF)
ISBN 978 0 7486 8348 2 (epub)

The right of the contributors
to be identified as author of this work
has been asserted in accordance with
the Copyright, Designs and Patents Act 1988

Contents

Introduction: Methodological Premises and Purposes   1
Michael Pickering and Emily Keightley

SECTION ONE   MEMORY AND IDENTITY

1. Autobiographical Memory   13
   Robyn Fivush
2. Oral History and Remembering   29
   Joanna Bornat

SECTION TWO   QUALITIES OF MEMORY

3. Experience and Memory   45
   Steven D. Brown and Paula Reavey
4. Between Official and Vernacular Memory   60
   Sabina Mihelj

SECTION THREE   MEDIA AND MEMORY

5. Televised Remembering   79
   Ann Gray
6. Vernacular Remembering   97
   Michael Pickering and Emily Keightley

SECTION FOUR LOCATIONS OF MEMORY

7. Memoryscapes and Multi-Sited Methods 115
   Paul Basu
8. Ethnicity and Memory 132
   Amanda Kearney

SECTION FIVE DISTURBED MEMORY

9. Painful Pasts 151
   Emily Keightley and Michael Pickering
10. Disrupted Childhoods 167
    Jo Aldridge and Chris Dearden

SECTION SIX CONFESSING AND WITNESSING

11. Apologia 185
    Cristian Tileagă
12. Testimony 200
    Jovan Byford

Bibliography 215
Notes on Contributors 247
Index 252

Introduction: Methodological Premises and Purposes

Michael Pickering and Emily Keightley

The ever-amiable Georgian clergyman, Sydney Smith, was one day walking with a friend through a narrow street in old Edinburgh when they came across two women leaning out of opposite attic windows cursing and arguing with each other. They listened for a while, after which Smith observed that it was no wonder they were in disagreement, for they were arguing from different premises.[1] This is a suitable parable for memory studies because all too often, arguments, along with their attendant suppositions, claims and statements, are joined from different premises without it being clear why those premises have been adopted. They are generally taken for granted, forming the implicit and usually undeclared ground from which a particular writer approaches and participates in work on memory and remembering. This can easily lead to confusion, or at least lack of clarity as to why this writer stands at variance with another writer.

Whether rightly or wrongly, we might expect such talking past each other when we compare neurological research on memory, or work on remembering and learning in experimental psychology, with the analysis of media constructions of public memory or national commemorative practices in critical sociology, but only because the work representative of each of these fields is obviously different (with each having its own value). Things may not be quite so obvious when different kinds of memory studies research are more closely adjacent, as in much of the work on memory and remembering done in the humanities and social sciences. The ways in which divergences in argumentation and treatment of evidence are dependent on their different, yet unacknowledged premises, may then be harder to detect. In putting together a book that primarily addresses memory studies work in the humanities and social sciences, we contend that the premises on which this work is based will become clearer if greater attention is paid to methods and methodologies and the questions and issues they raise.

As a still emergent field, memory studies accommodates wide-ranging enquiries into memory phenomena of all kinds and is multidisciplinary in quality. Its contributing streams include social psychology, sociology, history, political science, philosophy and aesthetics, drama and literary studies, and cultural and media studies. Although the work conducted within its embrace is varied and miscellaneous, a distinctive set of preoccupations and concerns has grown up. In many ways the field has developed over the past twenty years or so by proceeding outwards from individual memory and concentrating on broad dimensions of social memory and the politics of public remembering, especially those channelled through communications media. The explanatory focus has generally been on how these forms of remembering operate as collective representations of the past, how they constitute a range of cultural resources for social and historical identities, and how they privilege particular readings of the past and subordinate others. These concerns seem almost to have settled into certain defining themes, yet the range of topics and issues covered in memory studies is still broad and multifarious. As academic writing on memory and remembering continues to proliferate across its various contributing disciplines, this diversity is certainly to be welcomed. It is one index of how much memory studies is a burgeoning field of enquiry and analysis.

Despite its prodigious growth, attention to questions of method and methodology has been remarkably limited in memory studies. This is partly because much writing has been concerned with theoretical scene-setting or has taken the form of critical commentary, and partly because the many different inputs into this developing field are not always easy to reconcile or combine. It is nevertheless the intellectual promise of interaction between these different inputs which is one of the field's major attractions. What is then critical is the operational procedure through which this interaction takes place. The multidisciplinary nature of memory studies means that there are strong tendencies to enter into dialogue at a conceptual level, but these are not accompanied by any developed concern for divergent methodologies, and that lack of concern may again lead to epistemological problems – the problems of communicating across different, but unacknowledged, premises. Theoretical and conceptual dialogue needs to be accompanied by methodological dialogue. Such dialogue would make far more clear the manner in which one proceeds to produce and analyse evidence, or to produce and analyse counter-evidence in refutation of someone else's argument. Instead of this, where empirical work has been accomplished it has usually been presented with little, if any, attention to the methods that have been employed, or to the methodological implications of what has been studied in particular ways.

As a multidisciplinary field, memory studies faces a paradox: it is characterised by heterogeneous approaches to what it studies, but gives limited critical attention to potentially unifying issues of method and methodology. Without that, its movement towards creative interdisciplinarity will remain inhibited. This book appears at a time when there is increasing recognition of the need for consolidation in the field of memory studies, and increasing chances of achieving this. Our hope is that encouraging greater methodological reflexivity, and paying practical attention to how memory in its various modes and modalities may be empirically studied in the social sciences and humanities, will help considerably in the intellectual coalescence of the field. Questions of method and methodology are crucial to identifying differences and commonalities between various disciplinary approaches, along with means of combination and synthesis. Without this, the field cannot move from its current state of multidisciplinarity, where different disciplines investigate memory in parallel but disintegrated ways, to a more fertile and creative interdisciplinary exchange.

The purpose of this book is to help memory studies move from its current state of swag-bag multidisciplinarity to one of greater interdisciplinarity and more effective intellectual dialogue by focusing specifically on questions of method and methodology. It is intended to help us establish a core set of methodological approaches and techniques for memory studies; to bring a variety of methodological practices from different disciplines into productive exchange; to disseminate methodological expertise and knowledge derived from empirical and theoretical memory research; and to stimulate and set an agenda for debates about a methodological agenda for memory studies. Its aim is to provide students and researchers in the field with a set of practical guidelines to studying memory across a range of approaches, and increase awareness of the methodological issues that are attendant on these different approaches. In doing so it will throw the spotlight on various key analytical themes and so provide a forum for critical, interdisciplinary discussion of method and methodology in memory studies.

The emergence of memory studies as a distinct field is not confined to any particular country or part of the world, any more than it is to a single discipline. It has, over the past two decades, developed in a thoroughly international way. It is because the thematic content of memory studies is often international or cross-national in character that it is important to provide researchers with the skills and tools relevant to the investigation of the relationship of memory to national identities, migration, diasporic communities, exile, international and intranational conflict, and more. The provision of such skills and tools is increasingly in demand around the world as bodies funding research from doctoral level upwards require either appropriate training in research methods or explicit reference to, and discussion of, research methods and methodology in grant applications. This is becoming increasingly true of taught undergraduate and postgraduate programmes as well. Interestingly, there is an adjacent field to memory studies where recognition of the need for skills training has been quite explicit.

This is the field of oral history, one of the most innovative methods to have emerged in historical studies over the past forty years or so. Its adjacency to memory studies might suggest the potential for fruitful collaboration, yet a peculiar impasse has grown up between the two fields. It is peculiar because of the ostensible closeness of their key concerns: the one with the remembered past, the other with processes of remembering. It is true that the two fields have not developed chronologically alongside each other. Oral history has grown in importance since the late 1960s, while memory studies emerged in the late 1980s and is still moving towards active coalescence as an academic field of study. We may also note that memory studies is predominantly focused on social or collective memory, while oral history provides a notable means for producing collective memory even if this is usually confined to a neighbourhood or community context, and is obviously more concerned with autobiographical memory. Such differences do not in themselves explain why active dialogue has not occurred, and there are, in any case, certain examples of crossover which defy the broader differences. Perhaps the main reason why active dialogue has not happened is that, although oral historians have become increasingly sensitive to the hermeneutic issues involved in oral history, considered as both method and material, they have not engaged in any extensive way with the public dimension of memory and the question of how this is constituted. In turn, those involved in memory studies have failed to engage, again in any extensive way, with oral history, mainly because of a leading preoccupation in memory studies with collective 'trauma', national history and heritage, grand-scale ritualistic social practices, and macro-cultural memory, rather than with individual and small group micro-processes of remembering.

It may be the case that oral history needs to become more theoretically informed, but turning the table round, so too memory studies needs to become more practically oriented. That is why we adopt the view that greater attention to methods in memory studies will help to overcome the intellectual stand-off between oral history and memory studies.[2] With this firmly in mind, we start the book with a section on localised forms of remembering, in both autobiographical memory and group/community memory, and deliberately pair this section with one that addresses different layers of sociality and publicness in different forms of memory and remembering. This is in line with an aspiration of the book as a whole, which is that it will help bring together an empirical concern with memory in social settings with the critical question of what constitutes the public qualities of memory, and in this way also help studies of individual and collective remembering to become, if not realigned, then certainly regarded as far more directly complementary than is currently the case.

It is because of such aspirations that the book is not intended simply as a methods manual. It is certainly meant to provide guidance on how to conduct practical research and analysis of various kinds in memory studies, but conducting research and applying analytical techniques raise various critical and ethical issues, and it is the purpose of the book to address these too. It is also characteristic of the book that, while various research methods and methods of analysis will be covered, it is built on a particular methodological premise. This is that the field of memory studies includes such a diverse array of topics and concerns that it would be absurd to advocate only one approach as being suitable for each specific topic or concern. We are firm believers in taking a mixed-method approach, the main value of this being that the strengths of any one method may compensate for the weaknesses or limits in another, and vice versa. If you want to build a set of premises, you need diverse skills and techniques. Being a bricklayer, roofer or plumber is not enough in itself.

It is for this reason that the chapter titles reflect areas of research rather than particular methods. The methods used in relation to chosen topics will become clear within each chapter. The book as a whole addresses such questions as: What methods, techniques and traditions of doing empirical memory studies are there? What sort of empirical knowledge does memory studies produce? What are the problems, as well as potentialities, of interdisciplinarity, and what are the methodological implications of interdisciplinarity? What is the relationship between theory and empirical research in memory studies? What boundaries and distinctions delineate research in the field (such as the separation of research on vehicles of memory from their uses)? These examples are meant as an indicative rather than an exhaustive list. They are intended to show the kinds of issues the book will address. Among other things, it is hoped that the book will help offset somewhat a preoccupation with conceptualising and theorising memory and remembering processes, and dwelling upon the epistemological questions they raise. The pursuit of such questions is clearly valuable, but we should nevertheless strive for a better balance between methods and theory within memory studies. The concern is not only with this, however, for obviously enough, important empirical work on memory and remembering has manifestly been done. Rather, the intention is to encourage students and researchers to think more explicitly and systematically about questions of method and methodology, and bring these out in their work instead of letting them remain implicit or even buried away beneath the attainment of what they do.

The volume as a whole seeks to offer diversity in topic, method and approach while ensuring at least a degree of unity across the individual chapters. This unity is realised in the guidance provided for researching a particular topic or area of research, the reflexive considerations offered about research practice and methodological challenges, and the treatment of ethical issues and implications arising out of memory studies research. Ethics is important in this field because of the personal nature of an individual's memories, because some memories are painful and their recollection may bring discomfort or distress, and because memory and forgetting are both at times highly sensitive aspects of people's lives. There are also ethical implications in the relation of the researchers to their informants, as for example in terms of what they ask, why they ask and how they ask. Regardless of the particular area being explored, it is vital that in doing memory studies researchers are aware of the ethical dimension of what they do and are prepared to act in an ethical manner in every aspect of their fieldwork and their analytical work. The various chapters that follow deal with various ethical aspects of such work in memory studies as well as helping researchers develop their own expertise in questions of method and methodology in this particular field of enquiry and interrogation.

The book is divided into six sections, with two chapters in each. Much of the research conducted in memory studies is identifiable by a concern with either individual or collective memory, and these are clearly apparent in the first two sections. Both in these opening sections and then throughout, the book develops from a base in individual memory and alternates in diverse ways between considerations of personal remembering, group and community remembering, and public and national memory. All contributors to the book write on the assumption that all remembering is social and never purely individual, even when certain memories are regarded as private, and at the same time that it is only individuals who have the agency to recollect the past in any active or dynamic manner, even when certain forms of memory are regarded as collective. So we start with chapters which, among other things, discuss the ways in which the study of autobiographical memory may be approached, the ways in which oral historians focus upon subjectivity in the relationship between experiencing and remembering, and the ways in which we can discern the relationship between vernacular remembering and official or national memory.

While methods and methodological approaches figure throughout the book, discussion of them is always interwoven with consideration of particular topics of research. For example, one chapter discusses how social psychologists have used discourse analysis in attending to processes of remembering, showing how people co-construct the past in their interactions with each other and in their joint production of the social worlds they inhabit. They do this to a large extent through speech and language, in embodied ways in specific settings, but these means of communication can be expanded by the use of particular media, such as photographs and home videos. The products of home-mode media have become central to remembering in modern times, and clearly the methods for examining their use will be different to those used in analysing modes of remembering in everyday conversations. This becomes clear in our chapter-length mapping of such media. Certain research techniques are applied across a wide variety of research topics. This is the case with interviewing, for although it can take different forms, it is one of the most common

INTRODUCTION: METHODOLOGICAL PREMISES AND PURPOSES 7

devices for investigating a topic in any humanistic field of enquiry. Across the book we consider interviewing both as a practical procedure and as a social relationship. Discussing and critically reflecting on different methods and methodological approaches means thinking about what is involved in putting a method into action and what results from the method once we do this. So, again among other things, we look at the qualities of different types of qualitative data, and as already mentioned, argue for methodological pluralism in view of the many sources and resources for remembering in everyday life, along with the diversity of memoryscapes and the interlinkages across them that arise in any social formation.

In attending to how technologies of remembering are deployed, and how 'recorded memories' are integrated into everyday life, it is vital that we give priority to the ways in which such remembering practices are developed and assessed by their closest interpreters, the participants we recruit into our research projects. This means keeping the question of agentic capacity and power constantly in view. Human agency is a pressing question across memory studies in general, but it is of paramount importance in attending to the relationship between memory and social categories and divisions. In a chapter which looks into emergent and new forms of ethnicity, emphasis is given to seeing them as valid and legitimate means for negotiating intersubjectivity and identity in broken or wounded spaces. Spaces and spatial distinctions are of course multiple and multipliable in everyday life, and one aspect of this in how memory operates across them is that it is not only mediated by personal photography or domestic videos; it is also regularly brought into the home by the box in the corner. In a chapter dedicated to televised remembering, the methodological approach advocated requires attention to different frames of memory and different sites of investigation. Grasping the ways in which television operates along a multifaceted circuit of production, distribution, marketing and consumption should enable us to understand more fully the role of television in constructing memory across the national, familial and personal domains of everyday life in modern and late-modern societies.

Although we deal with research into personalised uses of media and into media remembering on a mass scale in different chapters, the chapters are paired, and this is intended to signal the degree of interaction between media operating on these different scales. Particular research projects have particular foci of concern, but in everyday life home-mode media and large-scale media are not hermetically sealed off from each other. It is important therefore to emphasise the need to continually bear in mind the many transactions across different contexts of memory and remembering, and as one chapter advocates, develop multi-sited methods so that a wide range of locations for interrelated forms of remembering and for storing and retrieving memory are taken into consideration. This is another reason why, in the end, the relations between individual and collective remembering are what matter most, for there are no hard-and-fast distinctions between them. Even as we identify different sites and regimes of memory, it is the traffic between them which has primarily to be accounted for.

In the penultimate section we turn to research that is concerned with memory ruptures and troubled memory, with disturbances to processes of remembering and with attempting to come to terms with painful or difficult experiences in the past. In dealing with the childhoods of those who, in the past, acted as adult child carers, research methods need to be used sensitively and flexibly in the interests of facilitating participation and recollection by informants. Specific techniques can be used in eliciting memory, as for example by taking photographs as triggers or vehicles for the remembering process. In researching painful pasts there is also a need to refine our methods so that we can better discern and analyse the gradations of difference between them, and the varying abilities of research participants to remember and talk about them. This task has been made more difficult than it needed to be because of the cavalier and indiscriminate use of the term 'trauma' to refer to more or less all painful past experiences across more or less all sorts of different scales of suffering, and because of the semantic corruptions and contradictions that have developed as a result. So thinking about methods for researching painful pasts means also developing a critique of the ways in which they have been conceived.

The final section of the book moves away from everyday life to remembering what are usually considered as exceptional or extraordinary circumstances. It is devoted to the examination of acts of confession and witnessing, as for example with public apologies for events or practices in what has subsequently come to be regarded as a regrettable, lamentable or shameful past, and with statements of testimony to acts of extreme barbarity, in this case among Holocaust survivors. Both confessing and witnessing are bound up with issues of truth and bring with them a complex set of moral issues and problems. They need to be considered as quite specific forms of discourse and representation involving quite different issues, with confession, for example, raising issues about 'image restoration' and witnessing raising issues about the distinction between accuracy and authenticity. Despite this, both chapters point to the need to address the rhetorical structures and effects of confessing and witnessing accounts, and both adopt a discourse-based approach along with attention to the broader social, cultural and political contexts in which confessing and witnessing occur.

Across the six sections of the book, we have aimed to capture some of the rich variety of concerns which feature in the field of memory studies. These range from the memory practices at work in everyday life and their role in the construction of personal identities, through to the politics of remembering the Holocaust and the iniquities of repressive political regimes. These concerns work across various scales of memory: from the individual to the collective, the private to the public, the cognitive to the social. It is by bringing together these wide-ranging areas of enquiry that we are able to build up a picture of the eclectic landscape of memory studies and establish the methodological premises on which memory studies operates. There may be different methodological premises underlying how we approach particular research questions and topics, but we shall only be able to develop our interdisciplinarity in memory studies when we are clear about why we have adopted these premises in our diverse projects and how they may be made to communicate, rather than talk past each other.

NOTES

1. For Smith's biography and samples of his writing, see Bullett (1951) and Bell (1980).
2. For one collection of essays that does seek some rapprochement between memory studies and oral history, see Hamilton and Shopes (2008).

SECTION ONE

Memory and Identity

CHAPTER I

Autobiographical Memory

Robyn Fivush

Autobiographical memory is the core of identity. To a large extent, we are the stories we tell about ourselves (Barnes 1998; Fivush 2008; McAdams 2001). Within psychology, autobiographical memory has most often been studied as an individual phenomenon, as a measure of how and what an individual remembers about their experiences, and what these memories can tell the researcher about the structure, content and meaning of personal memory (see, e.g., Conway and Pleydall-Pearce 2000; McAdams 2001; Rubin 2006). More recent psychological investigations have begun to place individual memory in a larger social and cultural context, examining how global cultural worldviews and local social interactions both reflect and shape individual memory (Fivush 2008; Nelson and Fivush 2004; Wang and Ross 2007). This approach resonates with a growing body of work on collective memory, initiated by Halbwachs (1992), and informed by cultural studies (see Erll and Nünning 2008, for an overview), that provides a more complex and nuanced understanding of autobiographical memory as a process and product of both individual and cultural construction. This emerging interdisciplinary perspective questions theoretical assumptions and methodological choices within the psychological study of autobiographical memory, and challenges researchers to examine memory both as a product of human cognition and as a process by which we construct social worlds (see Keightley 2008, for related arguments).

Whereas these debates are sometimes framed as choosing quantitative versus qualitative methods, here I argue that these approaches are not antithetical but, rather, complementary. Autobiographical memory is a socioculturally constructed narrative of one's personal life, and as such, is culturally saturated and must be understood through the subjective lens of individual meaning-making. At the same time, this thick, qualitative understanding can lead to hypotheses that can be tested in larger groups, in controlled studies, allowing investigators to draw conclusions about specific relations among variables of interest. It is only through this type of controlled experimentation that we can draw conclusions which subsume individual differences and provide the empirical basis for educational, therapeutic and forensic interventions of benefit to the greatest number of people possible.

Thus, I argue for an evolving dialectic between 'thick' and 'thin' methodological choices in the psychological study of autobiographical memories. I frame this discussion within socio-cultural theory (Vygotsky 1978), which posits that every human interaction is mediated through social and cultural frames, and that much of this framing is accomplished through language. Language, often in the form of stories, is both the process through which much of socio-cultural knowledge is communicated (Donald 2001; Nelson 1996), and language is a cultural product that shapes our thought (Boroditsky 2001). Similar to feminist theories (see Rosser and Miller 2000, for a review), socio-cultural theory posits that knowledge and memory are constructed in local social interactions that facilitate certain ways of knowing. Thus, in studying autobiographical memory, we must take seriously the idea that the research context is itself a specific socio-cultural context in which language is used to accomplish specific goals on the parts of both the researcher and the research participant, and that the memory product elicited in these contexts is framed both locally, in this specific context, and globally, within a particular historical developmental socio-cultural context. Methodological choices influence how this process unfolds within these layers of influence, and this, in turn, influence the memory product that the researcher collects for analysis and interpretation.

From this perspective, autobiographical memory becomes a site for the individual and cultural construction of truth (see Freeman 2007; Lawler 2008; and Sclater 2003, for related arguments). That is, autobiographical memory becomes a way of accounting for what happened that implies *accountability*. It is not simply that something happened, but how and why, who was the agent, and who is responsible? It is in this sense that autobiographical memory becomes autobiography. It involves the telling of a life story that is motivated and agentic (Barnes 1998), and thus has moral power. How this dimension of autobiographical memory plays out in specific research settings is not often reflectively examined within the psychological literature, so one of my goals here is to raise these issues. I first outline in more detail socio-cultural theory and how this informs our understanding of self and stories within social interactions. This switches to a discussion of the research context as a specific form of social interaction that frames participants' responses, and more specifically, leads to a discussion of voice and silence in the research context. This, in turn, leads to a more detailed discussion of the how psychology researchers choose to study and analyse narratives, and I use the expressive writing paradigm (Pennebaker 1997) as an example of the need for both qualitative and quantitative analysis strategies. Reflecting on narrative analysis inevitably begs the question of accuracy, or more appropriately, truth, and I address this issue in the context of moral authority in the final section.

SOCIO-CULTURAL THEORY, STORIES AND SELF

Human beings are born into densely cultural and social worlds, and over the course of development learn to become competent members of their culture through participating in socially structured activities (Rogoff 1990; Vygotsky 1978). Stories are deeply embedded in virtually all aspects of socially mediated activities. Stories are, quite simply, the way in which we create meaning from the environment (Bruner 1990; Fivush 2008; Ricoeur 1991). Whether they are stories about ourselves, our families, our communities or our ancestors, stories provide an evaluative and interpretive framework for understanding how and why things happen as they do. Stories move beyond chronological descriptions of what happened to include explanations, causes and consequences rife with human motivations, intentions and drama. Virtually from birth, infants are surrounded by stories (Fiese et al. 1995), stories their parents and grandparents tell them about their families and stories that are already beginning to evaluate the infant as a part of this family and as an individual (Stone 1988). Almost as soon as children begin to speak, they are drawn into these stories, participating in the telling (Eisenberg 1985). However, at this early age, it is the more competent adult, usually the mother, who structures these stories in particular ways (Fivush et al. 2006). For example, here is a mother and her young daughter talking about seeing bears at a carnival:

Mother: Were you scared?
Child: Oh, I'm not scared of bears.
Mother: No? Not even a little?
Child: No.
(a few intervening comments about the carnival)
Child: I'm scary.
Mother: You're scared?
Child: I'm scared of bears.
Mother: You're scared of bears? Well, that's all right to be scared of bears.

In this brief example, we already see how the mother is constructing a self for the child –one that is afraid of bears. Although the child at first denies that she was afraid, by the end of the joint storytelling, the daughter has accepted this definition of self. Whether she was or was not actually scared of bears at the time of the experience becomes irrelevant; she has now constructed herself through this story as a person who is scared of bears. It is in these small everyday stories that we construct ourselves (Bamberg 2006). As we tell and retell stories of our experiences with others, and others evaluate and interpret our experiences with us, we create a sense of who we are in the world (Fivush 2008; McLean et al. 2007). Thus, autobiographical memory is a fluid dynamic system that is continuously evolving.

This is not to say that there is no stability or no accuracy in autobiographical memory. There is a great deal of evidence that our memories for the experiences of our lives are reasonably accurate even over decades (Brewer 1988; Wagener and Groeneweg 1990), in that remembered details can be objectively verified and are consistently told over time. Rather, the argument is that the meaning of these stories changes according to how they are interpreted and evaluated and how they fit into the larger story of who we are. Some stories may become canonical and quite stable, and may provide for a consistent and coherent sense of self over time (Conway et al. 2004), whereas other stories may remain fluid, changing with each retelling. These ever-changing stories can be disconcerting in their discrepant evaluations. They may provide a context for re-examination of self that leads to growth (Neimeyer 2004), or they may lead to fragmentation of self. Further, individual autobiographical memories are shaped by larger socio-cultural narrative forms. At the most global level, cultures define the shape of a life, what events are most likely to occur and when. There is emerging evidence that individuals within a culture share a 'cultural life script' (Bernsten and Rubin 2004), such that they agree on the events most likely to happen to any given individual in that culture, as well as on the timing of those events (e.g., starting school, graduating from school, having a first romance, marrying, having children, etc.). Although the cultural life script can be thought of as defining a 'typical' life, it in fact defines a normative life. Cultural life scripts do not simply specify what will happen; they specify what should happen (see Fivush 2010, for full arguments). Thus an individual within a culture defines their own life experiences in relation to the cultural life script, and develops individual narratives in ways that specify conformity or deviance from this script. Evaluations and interpretations of individual life events are always made in relation to cultural expectations.

Related to cultural life scripts are master narratives. These are culturally canonical evaluative frameworks for understanding individual life events (Thorne and McLean 2003). Master narratives become increasingly important in the wake of trauma. How can something so incomprehensible become comprehensible? What cultural frames are available to create coherence out of chaos? McAdams (2006) has identified a dominant American master narrative that provides a resolution to difficult and traumatic life experiences – the redemption narrative. In this narrative structure, the individual experiences adversity, but uses this experience as a springboard to growth and redemption. For example, many survivors of sexual violence end their stories emphasizing the value of learning how supportive friends and family are, or learning how strong they are as an individual. It is not that the experience becomes positive, but that there is positive growth as a result of coping with the adversity (Janoff-Bulman 2004; Tedeschi and Calhoun 2004). Anyone who has attended or knows someone in a twelve-step programme such as Alcoholics Anonymous, or has watched the Oprah Winfrey show, knows that the redemption master narrative is very powerful in American culture. The redemption narrative does not simply provide a framework for creating meaning out of difficult experiences; it creates the narrative that only those who suffer can truly grow as individuals.

Thus, from a socio-cultural theoretical perspective, autobiographical memory is socially constructed in everyday storytelling that is itself shaped by cultural narrative frames (Fivush et al. 2011; Nelson and Fivush 2004). Critically, these stories are constructed and reconstructed in social interaction in which listeners hear the stories, contribute to the stories, confirm, validate, negate and question, in situations where there may or may not be shared social and cultural understanding of how to frame and evaluate specific kinds of experiences (Fivush 2000, 2004). Obviously, the research context is also a social interaction in which researcher and participant mutually influence each other, and the ways in which researchers choose to study autobiographical memory influence both the process of memory, as the participant narrates their past experiences to or with a researcher, and the product of memory that the participant produces for the researcher as a piece of data (Fivush 2000).

THE RESEARCH CONTEXT: PARADIGMS AND PARADOXES

A typical psychological study of autobiographical memory involves individual research participants interacting with a researcher in a laboratory environment. Whereas the majority of studies assess self-report questionnaire measures of autobiographical memory (e.g., responding to questionnaires assessing the clarity, vividness, emotionality, etc. of the recalled event), I focus here on the subset of studies that elicit narratives from participants. In these studies, the researcher asks the participants to recall certain types of events: these can be categorical types of events (e.g., a self-defining experience, a high-point experience, a traumatic experience), or a specific targeted event (individuals who have experienced of a specific event such as a sexual assault or a natural disaster). Alternatively, studies can involve a cue-word elicitation, in which the participant is presented with a word (e.g., tree) and must recall a personal event that the word evokes (e.g., the time I had a picnic under a weeping willow tree). Although many studies assessing autobiographical narratives use face-to-face interviews, some studies ask participants to write down their narratives. To date, there is little research on how these different elicitation contexts might change the type of narratives the researcher obtains, either in terms of the selection of events to be recalled or the structure and content of the narrative (but see Pasupathi 2001 for interesting research on the effects of listeners on narrative structure).

If we place the typical research study in a socio-cultural context, several critical methodological issues emerge. To reiterate, my aim is to raise these questions, which are too often not explicitly addressed in the psychological literature. In a very real sense, these questions do not have answers, but rather, these are the questions that researchers should ask themselves in order to make more reflective, explicit decisions about method and interpretation. Often in psychological studies, the underlying assumptions reflect logical positivism (see Fivush 2000; Harding 1993; Haraway 1988, for critiques): that the scientist is an objective observer who can reduce the phenomenon of interest down to its essentials and study specific isolated variables in a controlled way; that once these variables are identified, they can be put together into a meaningful whole; and that knowledge is represented in individual minds and not socially constructed within social and cultural interactions. This is, itself, a stripped-down version of logical positivism, and few contemporary psychologists would agree completely or comfortably with all of these assumptions, but these are the unexamined assumptions undergirding many of the methodological decisions psychologists make in designing and conducting experimental studies.

Postmodern, feminist, and cultural studies theories have all challenged assumptions of logical positivism (see Alcoff and Potter 1993, for a review). In particular, feminist standpoint theory has raised questions about assumptions of objectivity and control. Standpoint theory argues that knowledge is always gained from a particular standpoint, or place (Harding 1993). Being of a particular race, class and gender living in a particular historical time allows access to some ways of knowing and denies access to other ways of knowing. Standpoint relates to power, in that power allows or disallows particular individuals to assert objectivity or truth (Fivush 2000; Fivush and Marin 2007). Certainly we see this at the cultural and historical level, but we also see it in local everyday interactions. In the psychological research context, feminist theories would argue that it is the researcher who has access to power and voice; the researcher sets the agenda, asks the questions, and determines how to evaluate and interpret the data. The participant is in a position without power and, to a large extent, without voice; they can participate only in the way that the researcher will accept, by answering particular questions posed in particular ways, in a specified format and time frame. By asking every participant the exact same set of questions in the exact same way under the exact same conditions, the researcher is 'controlling' for extraneous variables and obtaining data that can be generalised across populations.

Using the scientific method in this way, and conducting controlled experiments, has yielded a wealth of data. Just a few examples within the study of memory include gaining foundational knowledge about how information is learned, retained over time, and retrieved, mapping out of forgetting functions, tracking the decline of memory and cognitive processes with age, understanding the biochemical and brain bases of memory, and investigating working memory, memory strategies and memory fallibility (see Baddeley 2010, for an overview). These discoveries have led to important educational, forensic and health-related applications. Indeed, it is quite remarkable how much we have learned about the human memory system over the last 50 years. So my point is not that the scientific method is flawed. It is not, if the researcher is asking a particular set of questions. Rather, my point is that, depending on the questions being asked, some of the assumptions underlying logical positivism and the scientific method need to be challenged in order to expand our study of memory into new arenas.

In particular, if the questions concern autobiographical memory and the creation of meaning and self-understanding through personal memories, then we may need to think in a different way about how we create the research context. For example, it matters who the participants are. Here are some questions you might ask as a researcher:

- Are the research participants all undergraduate college students taking psychology courses and participating in research for course credit?
- How might selecting such a homogenous age, educational level, and usually race and class as well, influence the research process and the type of data produced?
- If you, as the researcher, go out into the community, how do you recruit? Through churches? Through web page advertisements? Through word of mouth?
- How does this change the composition of your group of participants?
- Do you pay participants? If so, how much does this type of incentive influence who chooses to participate, and how they participate?

Related to issues of participation is what the researcher tells participants about the research when they invite them to participate. Informed consent dictates that the participants must know what they will be asked to do during the research study, but not necessarily why they are being asked to do this. So you could ask yourself:

- In studying autobiographical memory, does it matter if participants are told that they will be asked to talk about highly emotional personal events? Or that they will be asked to share personal experiences with (essentially) a stranger?
- Does this change who chooses to participate?
- When studies focus on a particular group, such as survivors of abuse or veterans, does it matter that the participants know that this is why they are being asked to participate?

THE RESEARCH INTERACTION: VOICE AND SILENCE

Underlying all of these questions is the extent to which the researcher and the participants share a world view. To what extent can, or does, the participant assume that the researcher understands what they are saying? And to what extent does the researcher assume that their own understanding of the research goals and tasks are shared by the participant? As already mentioned, within feminist theory, those in power have voice and those without power are silenced (Belenky et al. 1986; Fivush 2004). In prototypical psychological studies, the researcher has power and therefore voice. But placed in a larger socio-cultural context, this becomes more nuanced. Post-structuralist conceptions of voice and silence suggest that power does not need to be voiced – that power allows the individuals to assume shared knowledge (Simpson and Lewis 2005). From this perspective, lack of power forces voice in that individuals who do not share in the 'common' world view must provide an explanation, a defence, a justification, etc.

Returning to the idea of a life script discussed earlier, if the individual conforms to the life script, to the shared cultural understanding of how a life should unfold and how a life should be lived, then they do not need to explain themselves; it is simply understood as shared knowledge. In contrast, if one deviates from the cultural dominant life script then they must provide an explanation. In telling one's life story, one need not explain why they graduated from high school, went to college, got a job, met a heterosexual life partner, got married, had children, etc. This is the shared backdrop of cultural expectations that need not be discussed. On the other hand, if one drops out of school, or does not marry, or does not have children, and so on, then they must provide some explanation of why they deviated from the norm. This is the sense in which cultural life scripts are not simply prototypical but normative and exert moral power. This is how a life should be lived, and if one deviates, one must explain. From this perspective silence is power, in that it exists against a dominant shared cultural understanding that need not be voiced; and voice is loss of power, in that it is required to explain and justify self (see Fivush 2010, for related arguments).

This analysis changes the way researchers should reflect on the research context. For example, as a researcher, you might want to ask yourself:

- To what extent do you and the research participant share knowledge that need not be voiced?
- Is there a shared understanding of the nature and functions of research in society? Of higher education? Of notions of the common good?
- Is there suspicion about scientific research and how research findings are used within society?

Clearly issues of class and race are paramount here, but also important are more local issues of how researchers explain what they are doing to and with research participants, and being open to discussion of how and why it matters. Within this, there may or may not be a shared understanding of these values.

The ways in which answers to these questions may be critical in psychological research is especially highlighted in studies of memory of trauma. The very notion of memory for trauma is itself a thorny issue. Even the definition of trauma within the psychological literature is problematic (see Brewin 2007, for a review). Some researchers rely on standardised diagnostic criteria that include intense fear, helplessness or horror. Other researchers have argued that trauma is in the eye of the beholder – it is the individual's appraisal of the event as traumatic that is critical (Lazarus and Folkman 1984). There is also controversy over whether traumatic memory is qualitatively different from more mundane memory, or whether trauma memory is on a continuum, following the same memory principles as other emotional memories (Kihlstrom 1995; McNally 2003; Sotgiu and Mormont 2008). Answers to these questions are beyond the scope of this chapter; here I focus on how research that recruits individuals who have experienced highly aversive and perhaps traumatic events might require the researcher to be especially cautious. In many of these studies, participants are recruited specifically because they have experienced a certain type of stressful event. As a researcher, it may be important to ask yourself the following questions:

- Does the participant know the reason they have been recruited? How might this change the interaction with the researcher?
- What might be the participants' motives for taking part in this research? For example, to share their story, to have their story heard and validated, to help the researcher learn more about trauma memory, to help others who have had similar experiences, and so on.
- Do these motivations map onto your goals? If not, how might this influence the research context?
- In addition, and perhaps most importantly, the participants have experienced a difficult event that has changed them in some way; the researcher

has not experienced this event, or perhaps any highly aversive event. How does the participant narrate their experience in a way that the researcher can understand?

These questions raise the ethical concerns of doing research with individuals who have experienced difficult and perhaps traumatic events. In particular, there is a widespread belief that asking individuals to relive their difficult experiences in a research context will elevate distress. Yet more careful considerations of participants' experiences of research suggest that most individuals actually benefit from participation (see Legerski and Bunnell 2010 and Newman and Kaloupek 2004, for reviews). Research participants report that their participation provided a safe space and an attentive listener for them to be able to reflect on their experiences in ways that ultimately helped them. However, there are individual differences, with a small minority of participants reporting increased distress, and level of distress and/or benefit depends to some extent on the type of event being recalled, the extent of individual trauma history, and methodology, with written responses creating less benefit overall than oral interviews. Thus researchers must be particularly vigilant in how they design studies examining difficult life experiences, and they must monitor individual participants and provide appropriate referrals when asked for or needed.

An example from my own research interviews with a group of women who had been severely sexually abused in childhood illustrates some of these problems (Fivush and Edwards 2004). As a white, middle-class, highly educated female psychologist, I recruited women into an interview study on childhood sexual abuse through contacts I had in a health clinic. All the women self-identified as abused in childhood, and knew that they were being asked to participate in a structured one-on-one interview about their experiences that would last about two hours. Most of the women who agreed to participate were middle-class, college-educated, white women, ranging in age from mid-twenties to mid-sixties. Even though I thought that I shared cultural world views with this group of women (gender, race, class, education), it became clear to me during the interviews that these women saw the situation very differently. In fact, what became clear is that they felt they had to take care of me – that they could not reveal details of their abuse as it would be too upsetting to me. For me, this realisation turned usual assumptions about power and authority on its head. These women were asserting their authority over their experiences and their power over the research project. I do not mean this in any negative sense; these women shared difficult details of their lives with me in the hope that their experiences would help others. Rather, I realised that assumptions about goals and tasks may be very different, and this may lead to participants providing certain kinds of narratives about their experiences and not others.

Thinking about the research context as a relationship embedded within a specific socio-cultural context changes assumptions about methodology and analysis in fundamental ways. First and foremost, it highlights that research participants are active creators of the research environment in which they are being assessed. It is not a matter of 'getting information' from them, but of constructing information together, understanding how the researcher and the participant each view the situation, what their individual and mutual goals are in this specific situation, and how they are able to work together to meet both the researcher's goals and the participant's goals. Thus researchers must be highly self-reflective about who their research participants are, how they were recruited and/or self-selected themselves to participate, and how the researchers and participants together understand the goals of this interaction. Rather than being an objective observer of participants, especially in narrative research, researchers must enter the subjective space and think about the narratives collected as richly co-constructed objects of analysis.

THE ANALYSIS STRATEGY: THICK OR THIN?

This perspective points to the need for deeply interpretive analyses of narratives provided in research contexts. Yet one of the major goals of scientific experimentation is to be able to generalise and predict across large groups of individuals. This allows us to develop large-scale interventions that benefit the greatest number of people possible. Here, I address this paradox using the expressive writing paradigm as an example (see Pennebaker and Chung 2007 and Frattaroli 2006, for reviews). In an expressive writing intervention, adults are asked to write about their deepest thoughts and feelings about an ongoing stressful event in their lives for three to five days in a row for about fifteen minutes a day. Those who engage in expressive writing are compared to both a writing control group, in which individuals are asked to write for the same period of time about daily activities and time-management, and to a non-writing control group, where individuals are simply tested on well-being at comparable time-points but do not engage in any structured intervening activity. All individuals are assessed on a battery of psychological and/or physical measures before beginning the writing intervention (baseline), and again several weeks or months after completing the intervention (follow-up). A great deal of research has now established that adults who are asked to engage in expressive writing about personal stressful events subsequently show higher levels of psychological and physical well-being than control groups. Individuals who engage in expressive writing show lower levels of depression and anxiety, higher levels of general well-being, visit the doctor less frequently, have higher grade point averages (when students are tested), are re-employed in higher numbers (when unemployed individuals are tested), show lower pain levels (when chronic pain patients are tested), and actually show higher immune system functioning at follow-up as compared to baseline, whereas there are no significant effects for writing or no-writing control groups. Expressive writing is a remarkably easy-to-implement intervention that has great benefits across large group comparisons. Should we therefore use expressive writing across all individuals to improve their well-being? Well, yes and no.

On the one hand, expressive writing is effective for most people most of the time. But when we start to delve deeper into this effect, the waters are muddied. As in all group comparisons, the effect is carried by some members of the group and not others. That is, there are many people who benefit from expressive writing, but there are others who either show no benefit, or who actually do worse following expressive writing. When we compare large groups of individuals to find effects between groups, this 'washes out' as error in the statistical analyses. There is some suggestion that males benefit more from expressive writing than females; there is also some suggestion that expressive writing may actually be detrimental for some groups, including young children and adolescents (Fivush et al. 2007), and perhaps for some individuals if they are pressured into expressive writing interventions too soon after a traumatic incident (Harvey et al. 2004). These findings suggest that a deeper understanding of expressive writing is warranted. And this deeper understanding requires a 'thicker' interpretation – an interpretation that goes beyond surface characteristics of narratives of large groups of people.

Several researchers have tried to ascertain the mechanisms underlying the expressive writing effects (see Pennebaker and Chung 2007, for a review); exactly what aspects of these narratives might account for increasing well-being? These analyses most often rely on a computerised word-count program – the Linguistic Inquiry and Word Count (LIWC) – developed by Pennebaker and Francis (1996). This program calculates the percentage of words used in the narratives that fall into predetermined categories, including pronouns (I, we, you, they, she, he), affect words (positive affect words including specific emotion words and general affect words such as 'pleasant' 'enjoy' and 'good' when it refers to a psychological feeling; and negative affect words such as 'difficult' and 'hard' when they refer to psychological states), and cognitive processing words (such as 'understand' and 'realise'). Higher use of cognitive processing words, moderate use of emotion and affect words, and higher use of third person pronouns is associated with higher levels of effectiveness for expressive writing interventions. One of the problems with this 'thin' analysis of the narratives is that the words are simply counted out of any context of meaning. 'I had a good time doing drugs but ultimately realised that I should stop' would be statistically equivalent to 'I had a good time doing drugs and realised I would never stop'. Similarly, 'I was upset at my mother and cried about it for days and could not stop thinking about it' is statistically equivalent to 'I was upset at my mother but we talked it over and cried about it together'. Thus, simple word counts cannot differentiate among loss of control, rumination, and brooding versus agentic control, cognitive restructuring and resolution. Across large groups of individuals these differences become statistical noise, but within individuals these are critical differences in how individuals are making meaning.

I want to be clear that I am simply using expressive writing paradigms as an example, and that I am not advocating either not using large controlled studies, or not using expressive writing interventions. Rather, my point is that we must combine methodological strategies, as each has advantages. More specifically, in-depth qualitative studies:

- allow close examination of individual differences and case studies
- provide rich interpretive data to develop better hypotheses for controlled experiments
- allow closer examination of contextualised and cultural differences.

In turn, large-scale experimental studies:

- provide statistical power to detect differences at the group level
- allow determination of causal connections.

Thus, I advocate that we conduct smaller, in-depth 'thick' studies of narrative that allow close investigation of the narrative being told, the individual doing the telling, and the context of the telling, and use this information to inform larger, more controlled studies that will allow us to make large-scale interventions that will help the most people possible. Smaller, in-depth studies of narratives that allow the investigator to work with the participants to understand the narrative telling and context are essential for theorising and refining a scientific understanding of narrative and memory. Both in-depth qualitative and large-scale quantitative studies are necessary, and each must speak to the other in an evolving dialectic that allows for scientific progress in understanding the phenomenon of interest. Examining narratives in depth, either through qualitative analyses, or through quantitative analyses that capture more holistic aspects of meaning-making, must be integrated with methods that provide more reductionist analysis of large numbers of narratives that allow for generalisability, replication and, ultimately, effective intervention (see McLean and Pasupathi 2010 for a collection of studies that do just this).

OBJECTIVITY, TRUTH AND MORAL POWER

Threaded throughout this discussion is the idea that narratives provide a window into how individuals are making sense of themselves and their worlds. Historically, research on memory focused on the issue of accuracy, defined as a match between researcher-provided stimuli and participant-provided responses. But as early as 1932, Bartlett argued that memory was not simply about an accurate record of the past; remembering was an 'effort after meaning'. Memory is about making sense of what has happened to us. This does not mean that accuracy does not matter, but rather changes the question to whose accuracy for what purpose? Within feminist theory, these questions have focused on the notion of objectivity (Bordo 1990; Code 1993). Again, arguing from standpoint theory, the question is whether any one person standing in any one place can be objective. Susan Bordo names this the 'view from nowhere' – the idea that any one person can be unbiased and see beyond their own subjective lens to whatever reality lies beneath. In contrast, objectivity can be better defined as the 'view from everywhere' – the integration of multiple voices. In terms of social, political and historical change, this means listening to those who have been oppressed and have not been allowed to tell their stories. Two examples of narrative research illustrate how researchers as attentive listeners can help individuals and groups claim moral authority. The first is research on survivors of sexual abuse. This has been a long-silenced form of trauma in most cultures, but with the rise of the second wave of the women's movement in the United States, the prevalence of sexual trauma became better understood (Enns et al. 1995). Individual stories of abuse and survival became woven into the fabric of cultural truth. Importantly, this does not simply change the cultural story; it changes individuals. Most individuals who participate in research studies that allow them to tell their stories subsequently report positive benefits as a result of study participation (Legerski and Bunnell 2010). Participants report that being asked, and especially being heard, helps them to reclaim their sense of self and to better cope with the aftermath of trauma. Simply being able to tell one's story, and having that story heard, allows one to once again become a member of the social world.

The second example comes from research by Chandler and Proulx (2008) on Aboriginal tribes in western Canada, where there is an astonishingly high level of teenage suicide. They discovered that among those tribes that retained and told their cultural-historical stories, the incidence of suicide was as low as in middle-class, Canadian samples; but among those tribes that had 'lost' their stories, where adolescents did not know any tribal history or myths, suicide rates were extremely elevated, suggesting that owning and sharing stories allows individuals to remain a part of a social group in ways that build resilience.

For narrative research, these examples indicate that allowing individuals to tell their stories without imposing the dominant narrative is critical to hearing how individuals are constructing their own truth and how they own their own stories. Listeners must be involved in this process; without listeners to hear and acknowledge, individual memory becomes unreal.

LAST WORDS

Psychological research on autobiographical memory sits at the nexus of objective experimentation and subjective meaning-making. Perhaps more than any other area of research in psychology, autobiographical memory research highlights the evolving tension between understanding the individual and the collective, and how each speaks to the other. Quantitative and qualitative research are both valuable and necessary if we hope to fully understand this deeply subjective yet collectively human process. Autobiographical memories are constructed within social cultural interactions, and, as researchers, we must always bear in mind that in the very moment of eliciting memory as an object of analysis, we are part of the process of transforming memory, both for the participants and for ourselves.

SUMMARY: KEY POINTS

- In this chapter I argue that autobiographical memory is a product of both individual and cultural construction.
- Quantitative and qualitative methods are complementary in the analysis of autobiographical memory, and so this chapter argues for an evolving dialectic between 'thick' and 'thin' methodologies.
- I explore the use of expressive writing as an example of a research method which can produce data that can be analysed both 'thickly' and 'thinly', and argue for the importance of combining these methodological strategies.
- I argue that narrative research must be sensitive to the ways in which individuals construct their own truths, and that the ways in which memories are elicited in the research process is involved in this construction, and so must always be taken into account.

FURTHER READING

For an early experimental exploration of autobiographical memory which begins to attend to the role of social and cultural contexts in the construction of memory, see Bartlett (1932). Jerome Bruner has written extensively on the narrative construction of reality from a psychological perspective, and has also attended specifically to the issue of autobiographical memory in this regard (Bruner 1991; 1995). More recently, Martin Conway of the Leeds Memory Group has written extensively on the interconnections between the self and memory (see for example Conway 2005). His work, along with others from the same research group, involves a range of methodological approaches to autobiographical memory. Of particular note is Conway's collaborative development of the self-memory system as an analytical framework for assessing autobiographical memory and its relationship to the self. Pennebaker and Chung (2007) provide a very helpful overview of expressive writing as a research method.

CHAPTER 2

Oral History and Remembering

Joanna Bornat

The invitation to contribute a chapter on oral history to this collection, with a focus on group and community memory, immediately presented me with a difficulty. Though the planning and outcomes of oral history projects will often speak of community and identity-specific groups, migrant, industrial, generational, gendered, ethnic or racialised, the oral historian's starting point is the individual recalling the past in dialogue with another person. Memory begins with individuals. In addition, oral history has more than one meaning in terms of academic endeavour; the memory work of oral history involves both method used and evidence produced. Along with this is the idea of memory having a purpose. Elicited in an oral history approach, memory is conceived as being agentic, both in terms of individual lives and in the practice of history making. Thus Thompson, the doyen of UK oral history, argues that oral history is 'not so much a specific list of titles in a section of historical bibliographies, as . . . an underlying change in the way in which history is written and learnt, in its questions and its judgements, and in its texture' (Thompson 2000: 83). His call, in the first edition of *The Voice of the Past*, was to those who shared his view that individual recall posed a challenge to the conventions of a historical practice which held the document, the printed word, as the sole and most safe authority. His challenge was as much political as epistemological, and the argument was persuasive to a post-sixties generation keen to redefine the past so that it might include those who previously had had no voice of their own in established accounts. Even if oral history had stood still, this would be an extensive range of activities and understandings to present; however, the picture is rendered more complex given oral history's change and evolution since the 1960s.

Oral historians are given to reflecting on their practice, pointing out what has changed and why (see for example Thomson 2006; Smith 2010; Ritchie 2011). Abrams, for example, points out how the 'international, multidisciplinary, multi-vocal, confident and mature oral history movement of the twenty-first century is a distant relative of the post-Second World War oral history field which struggled to find legitimacy within hidebound disciplinary traditions' (2010: 4). Nevertheless, it is still the power and authority of the individual voice, the witness to experience speaking in their own words, which continues to attract and engage academic researchers and community-based historians. Here, for example, is Diman Vasilev (pseudonym) answering a question about differences in the way he celebrates holidays today in Bulgaria, compared with when he was a child:

> Wait, wait – there is no room for comparison. In my memories as a young Pioneer there wasn't a holiday without a parade – be it 24th of May, 9th of September or 7th of November – and every time it was ... I don't know, I always enjoyed it. I liked when there were crowds, some waving flags, and others carrying posters. Somehow you feel part of the holiday, of something big, enthusiastic and you become affected. Now they criticise the parades. They say they were imposed forcefully on people. Get lost! It was a natural thing. I really found great pleasure in shouting 'Hooray', 'Glory', 'We live nice lives'. I did not interpret it politically I don't know why ...

Then, in answer to a question on intergenerational dialogue:

> I try to keep everyone true to their beliefs. We enter into church, light candles. I, for example, know that when you light a candle the flame goes up. It guides thoughts, it guides that which is not material, the flame goes up, somewhere there where the good ones are. That is why we will send them only good thoughts. Do you understand, this is neither pagan nor Christian. I have my own view on the issue. I know that we emit and this is it.[1]

What is inspirational in its authenticity to one investigator may be a confusion of challenging complexity to another. Diman's account might be treated straightforwardly as evidence of an unrepentant communist commitment, or as someone who has been liberated into religiosity. He could be describing lifelong feelings of humanistic connectedness, or he could be attempting to position himself as politically detached within post-communist public memory. Different interpretations are possible. However we analyse it, his remembering will have been affected by the occasion, the purpose, and his relationship with the person interviewing him.

In what follows, I will consider how such interpretations have become more typical in oral history by fleshing out the history of oral history, and in doing this draw on Thomson's notion of 'four paradigm transformations' (2006). Beginning with a brief account of origins, I go on to consider these changes using his categories: 'A people's history', 'post-positivism', the role of the interviewer, and digital memory.

A DEVELOPING PRACTICE

Abrams' depiction of oral history's early struggle to establish credentials within a hostile environment (2010) is accurate, but what her portrayal underplays is the multidisciplinary engagement which oral historians were initiating. In the UK, oral history's origins in an organised, self-defining declaration lies with a group of archivists, historians, broadcasters, dialectologists and folklorists who met in 1969 to 'bring together some of those scholars known . . . to be using the interview method in social and political history' (Oral History Society 1972: 1).[2] Some members of the group, notably George Ewart Evans (1956) and Brian Harrison (2012), had already been recording memories; others – Paul Thompson (1975) and Raphael Samuel (1975) – were soon to be writing up original and pioneering substantive and methodologically innovative research which would quickly enthuse and grow a movement of oral historians.

Mention of 'the interview method' and 'social and political history' establishes what were to be the defining characteristics of oral history in the UK and beyond: the interview and a focus on the conditions of everyday life. Even though the use of the interview as a tool of investigation was well established in social science by the beginning of the twentieth century, the particular way in which sociologists of the influential Chicago School used interviewing to generate a life history was what was to inspire those first and later oral historians (Thompson 2000). Working in conjunction with an historical perspective, the interview became more than just the extraction of information relating to specific topics; it became an object, an identifiable social relationship, with a shape, dynamic and totality emerging as an individual's life was told. From the first, oral history was multidisciplinary, drawing on theories and methods of sociologists and historians. In the UK, this distinctive characteristic came about largely because the historian Paul Thompson was writing and researching in the context of the sociology department at the University of Essex in the mid-1960s (Thompson and Bornat 1994). There he became familiar with the development of grounded theory as a solution to sampling from a population of survivors (Thompson 2000: 151) and at the same time was to draw inspiration from sociologists and ethnographers working with qualitative methodologies (Thompson 2000: 61–4).

PEOPLE'S HISTORY

The early US sociologists had been followed by others who were less certain of the reliability of qualitative data, teaching students to be wary of the interview's reliability because a 'standardized question' will not result in a 'standardized *meaning* of the question to the correspondent' (Maccoby and Maccoby 1954: 452; emphasis in original). Mainstream historians also doubted, and of course continue to doubt, the reliability of memory (Hobsbawm 2002), but oral historians were not so concerned. They felt they were tapping into an historical truth not available in documents. As George Ewart Evans explained in a brief account of his 'early experiences':

> the material I was getting from the old people was more accurate than the printed sources. And it was clear why this was so. To a man who had spent his life at a certain work or craft it was a point of honour to describe its details fully and without distortion; the work had become a part of him and to give a wrong description would have been an offence against his own person. (Evans 1972: 3)

The eagerness with which the first wave of UK oral historians sought and presented what they felt were authentic accounts of the past was coupled with their commitment to challenging what they saw as a history which lacked certain voices. Thus, oral history took on the commitment to right the wrongs of omission, snobbery and oppression. As Thompson puts it in the introduction to the first edition of his *Voice of the Past*, 'I believe that the richest possibilities for oral history lie within the development of a more socially conscious and democratic history'. However, he also points out that oral history could equally be part of a conservative agenda, though even then it would similarly have the effect of revealing to historians that 'their activity is inevitably pursued within a social context and with political implications' (Thompson 1978: x).

This commitment to a politically aware historical practice, one which sought to rebalance the dominant narratives of the past and change established ways of doing history, engendered a loyalty to interviewees which assumed veracity and the value of their evidence. Typical is Jill Liddington and Jill Norris's justification in the first edition of their study of the suffragists:

> Careful use of oral history and local records has helped to challenge the Pankhursts' version of the suffrage movement. It has helped to bring to life the forgotten suffragists and to show how their principles and tactics differed from those more celebrated national leaders . . . it has helped to challenge the view that women's suffrage was largely a middle-class concern. (Liddington and Norris 1978: 18)

They were not alone in their commitment. The History Workshop movement, from its beginnings in the late 1960s, could attract hundreds of people to annual events where 'history from below' was celebrated and debated (Smith 2010).

The impact and immediacy of voiced memories is an experience which all oral history interviewers will have experienced and which helps to explain why the pull of authenticity is so strong. My own experience, following up documentary-based research into West Riding textile trades unionism in the first two decades of the twentieth century with interviews with retired workers, was damascene in its effect (2004). Like others, I was inspired by the voices I had recorded, convinced that oral history as I then understood it would give me direct and unmediated access to the past.

POST-POSITIVISM

Oral historians' alleged unquestioning empiricism was criticised by the influential Popular Memory Group. Writing in the early 1980s, they argued that British oral history was lacking in theory and was demonstrating an epistemological naivety which embraced an uncritical and unmediated idea of the past (Popular Memory Group 2006). They argued that the 'social production of memory' developed in a struggle between 'dominant' and 'oppositional' representations and that the interaction between public expressions and individual interpretations and feelings about the past had been neglected during the formative years by English oral historians who were accused of adopting a rather un-political objectification of 'the past' (Popular Memory Group 2006: 84). In a rebuttal, Thompson argued that the Popular Memory Group was unaware of the influence of subjectivity in the writing of US and European oral historians such as Grele (1975) and Passerini (1979). However, he concedes of himself and other pioneers that: 'we focussed on the objective dimension at the start because we felt we had to show conventional historians and social scientists that our material was not totally invalidated by the vagaries of memory' (Thompson 1995: 28).

Thompson's references to developments in relation to awareness of the shaping and expression of memory highlighted the influence of European oral historians, in particular Luisa Passerini and Alessandro Portelli. Passerini's research into working-class life under fascism in the 1920s and 1930s had led her to raise uncomfortable issues relating to what she saw as a 'tendency to transform the writing of history into a form of populism . . . to replace certain of the essential tenets of scholarship with facile democratisation, and an open mind with demagogy' (1979: 84). What was called for, she concluded, was recognition of subjectivity in recall of the past:

a subjective reality which enables us to write history from a novel dimension undiscovered by traditional historiography. This will avoid its nature of piling up facts and its failure to make explicit the political nature of all historical writing, while also presenting in the concept of subjectivity a tool of analysis peculiarly appropriate to social history. (Passerini 1979: 86)

In her search for experiences of anti-fascist action she had been forced to recognise the significant contribution of silences and consensus around aspects of daily and private life, rather than the classic class-oriented manifestations of opposition within factory and work settings. In recognising the force and value of subjective expression and of omission, Luisa Passerini presented a challenge to oral historians which many have subsequently taken up.

An example is Thomson's work on the memories of Anzac survivors of the First World War with whom he explored living with experience which had at times conflicted with public accounts. From this he drew on the idea of 'composure', an internal strategy which enabled these combat veterans to tell their stories in ways that they felt comfortable with as the public story of soldiers' lives on the Western Front shifted around various forms of legend (Thomson 1994).

Thomson, and many other oral historians (see for example Bravo 1985; Summerfield 1998; Green 2004; Zukas 1993; Roper 2005; Allan 2005; Koleva 2006; Young 2007; Hamilton 2008; Nguyen 2008; Alexander 2009) have drawn on subjectivity when analysing their interviews and interview relationships, exploring ways in which memory is shaped and informed through cultural encounters, gender, ethnicity, national myths, emotional experiences and sensations generated through materiality and sensory experience. Nevertheless some, Green (2004) for example, are resistant to an over-determining role for public or collective memory, preferring to stress the role of agency and the tension between the private and the public in recall and remembering.

Oral historians have looked for ways to steer a course between positivist certainty on the one hand, and the uncertainties of over-interpreted subjectivity (Bornat 2008) on the other, while trying to preserve the status of memory as a reliable source of evidence about the past. They have been helped in this endeavour by the Italian cultural historian and oral historian, Alessandro Portelli. In an early essay titled, 'What makes oral history different?' he identifies the unique qualities of oral history as 'the orality of oral sources', pointing out how the sounds of language and speech convey meaning which can only be approximated in a transcript. He goes on to suggest that oral history, recalled memory, 'tells us less about *events* than about their *meaning*' and that 'the unique and precious element is the speaker's subjectivity'. He develops this point further to argue that because of this, 'oral sources' have 'a *different* credibility' that 'today's narrator is not the same person as took part in the distant events he or she is relating to'. It follows, therefore, that 'Oral sources are *not objective*'; they are '*artificial, variable and partial*' (Portelli 1981: 67, 100, 102–3, emphases in original).

While this might sound as though the oral historian is being condemned to endless relativism, Portelli forcefully identifies the conceptual and structural constants of class, culture, work, gender and race. The accounts he draws out in interviews interact with these broader determinants and, in the telling, demonstrate how they are both shaped by and also shape them. Here, for example, is Sudie Crusenberry in Harlan County, USA, talking about her life as a miner's wife and miner herself:

> Years ago, at one time, my husband's place fell in. He was working up in Coxton hollow in the mines, and his place fell in, so he came back to the house, and . . . You know, in them days, them little mines where them ponies worked, you either cleaned it up on your own, or you didn't have nowhere to work, no job. Well, we went down there on Sunday and geared the pony up, took some timbers in there. I went and helped him.
> Portelli: You went inside the mine?
> Crusenberry: Yeah. But . . . you know [there] were no motors, or trips, it was a pony mines. Yeah, I've been in. 'Cause, I tell you, didn't have nothing to eat. (Portelli 2011: 157)

Sudie Crusenberry offers a compelling account of the desperation of poverty and the basics of resistance. The modesty of her expression makes her words believable, as does the expressed physicality of the work she describes, not to mention Portelli's apparent incredulity. There are occasions, however, when private and public accounts conflict, as Portelli shows when he considers the stories which were circulated and which retold the circumstances leading to the shooting of civilians in Rome by German occupying forces in retaliation for partisan action. Where misinformation informs the public account, then oral history can play a part, not just to show how guilt comes to be attributed and victimhood constructed but also how, without opposing memories, myths live on as culturally and politically expressed certainties (Portelli 2003).

To recognise subjectivity is not only a question of listening for silences or accepting the complexity which emerges through layers of private and public memory. Remembered feelings and sensations present a materiality which have their own significance on hearing and in data analysis. Alexander draws on oral history and 'memory talk' to explore feelings about class and social justice expressed in accounts of childhood memories between the two World Wars in East End London. For her, these evoke the 'smell of poverty', the acuteness of sorrows and the physical experience of the spaces in which people lived, drawing out 'a dimension of the structure of feeling, of the history of the time' (Alexander 2009).

Sometimes the drama of events is recalled by the meanings imparted by an object. Bimal Bhowmick's family was part of the human traffic of the Partition of India during 1947. In his case he was aged seven, a member of a Hindu family suddenly fleeing from their Muslim neighbours:

> BB: Because it's not short distances, there were seventy miles, eighty miles to go in a canal and the people will be pulling the boat from both sides of the bank. They are Muslims as well. [laughing] Do you understand? And but they're locals, so some of them are loyal to us. So my father went to one of his friends . . . He was very kind and he said 'Yes I'll give you a boat but . . . You know you've got that His Master's Voice gramophone'. We used to have a gramophone, you know the dog and his voice in the olden days?
> *Interviewer: Yeah.*
> BB: You are too young to remember but . . .
> *Interviewer: I know the one.*
> BB: Yes. And it used to be the sort of a centre of entertainment in the evening, we used to play records, you know what I mean? And there will be mattress put on and all the Muslims will come, we'll go in the courtyard and the music plays and everybody will be nodding their head. He said 'If you give me that one I'll arrange a boat for you'. My father says 'Please take, no problem'. So he gave and, well it doesn't mean anything about him you know, but still he said he will arrange, though he wanted this little bloody thing, you know.[3]

The gramophone evokes the good times when his family were at the centre of village life, well-off members of the community with the means to entertain in a friendly, even harmonious way. It's a coveted object that will help to save their lives, but this means it also becomes denigrated when he recalls that for one of their neighbours it is equal in value to a family of two parents and five children – a 'bloody little thing'.

Oral history has come to play an increasingly significant role in the public sphere, as Thomson argues (2006), drawing on the example of Aboriginal accounts of the 'Stolen Generation' which, in Australia, have become part of national identity debates in law courts, literature and in supportive advocacy work. The truth and reconciliation movement similarly has foregrounded personal testimony and autobiography as a valid and reliable source wherever political change has sought some kind of consensual outcome. It has enabled victims to speak and be heard and for traumatic and brutalising experiences to be recognised. Such processes, whether formally organised or, as is more usual, being part of the political settlement reached, inevitably secure a majority statement which will leave out, marginalise or rebrand dissonant accounts.

The co-option of oral history, of memory, in the service of political change, or of consensus, has brought with it public and scholarly recognition, but with this also comes the possibility of the exploitation of certain stories as well as the silencing of self-expression and of accounts which may not fit a public narrative (Thonfeld 2011).

THE ROLE OF THE INTERVIEWER

The idea of the interview as a social relationship, Thomson's third paradigm transformation, has been integral to the development of oral history. The dynamics of that relationship have been understood in terms of differences of status, gender, ethnicity and class. Key texts advise on how to enhance the relationship, and to encourage interviewees to be forthcoming as they respond to questioning. All recognise what may be gained from approaches which are sensitive to people's preferences as to how and where to be interviewed. Some debate the pros and cons of being non-expert and also suggest that with appropriate preparation the interviewee will find the interview a positive experience which they will enjoy taking part in (Lummis 1987; Thompson 2000; Ritchie 2003; Yow 2005). Frisch's argument for a 'shared authority' with interviewer and interviewee working in partnership (1990) through to publication has inspired oral historians to achieve similarly democratic outcomes, though examples which present success are rare (see for example Sitzia and Thickett 2002; Thomson 2011).

That there might be more going on in the interview, that the intersubjectivity of the relationship might be working at a deeper and in a more mutually affecting way, was something which was to emerge with the influence of feminist oral historians.

Women's history had been a clearly identified focus for oral historians from the start in the UK (Bornat and Diamond 2007) and the Popular Memory Group was easier on feminist oral historians, describing their work as 'politically located, culturally sensitive projects around history and memory ... already (with) a strong past-present dialogue' (Popular Memory Group 2006: 82). The emergence of a more questioning epistemological stance among feminist oral historians was inevitable once the politics of feminism came up against the feelings and realities of older women migrants, war workers, mothers, domestic workers or farmers. Warnings from The Personal Narratives Group of the importance of recognising 'the narrators' own self-definitions ... in contrast to definitions imposed by interpreters of personal narratives ...

(and) . . . The importance of the political and institutional contexts of both the narrator and the interpreter' (Personal Narratives Group 1989: 12) were a reminder that interviewee and interviewer might have very different objectives in taking part and that assumptions as to gender solidarity might be misplaced. Other feminists recognised that the 'early, compensatory phase of women's history' was being followed by 'more sophisticated understandings' which recognised that 'negotiation and struggle' were at the heart of social interaction (quoted in Bornat and Diamond 2007: 26).

The deconstruction of the interview as a social relationship, into gendered, racial and cultural expressions and symbols, was argued in *Women's Words* (1991), a collection of essays edited by Sherna Berger Gluck and Daphne Patai. The contributors, most of whom were practised oral historians and ethnographers, reflected critically on issues such as the subjectivities of both interviewer and interviewee, power in an interview relationship where both parties are women, and ownership and control over the interview and its interpretation. Katherine Borland's chapter, revisiting an interview with her grandmother, has since been much cited. She details a clash of interpretations, concluding that, 'it bears repeating that important commonalities among women often mask equally important differences' (Gluck and Patai 1991: 72). Other contributors took a similar line, Judith Stacey wondering 'whether the appearance of greater respect for and equality with research subjects in the ethnographic approach masks a deeper, more dangerous form of exploitation' (Stacey 1991: 113). Daphne Patai confronted essentialist assumptions of shared standing among women with an attack on 'the fraud' of 'purported solidarity of female identity' which she saw as denying divisions of race, class and ethnicity' (Patai 1991: 144).

The Gluck and Patai collection resonated across oral history, beyond feminist circles. The issues raised weren't new; Maccoby and Maccoby had pointed out back in the 1950s that 'the *content* (their emphasis) of the communication . . . will be affected by the status relationships' (1954: 462).

In becoming aware of their influence on what and how memories may be evoked, oral historians have sought ways to include a check on their practice, to encourage sensitisation to their own feelings, preconceptions and even prejudices (Yow 1997). Turning oneself into the subject can sometimes be difficult. Revisiting an early interview that had always troubled me resulted in a reflection which enabled me to recognise the way my own cultural and ideological positioning had affected the interaction. I had deflected my interviewee's emotional expression in part because I could not see the relevance of the story she was telling, being moved as a child at a performance of the Messiah, to what I wanted her to talk about: her life as a young mill worker. Coming back to the interview after some time, I realised that her feelings were important in ways I had not recognised (Bornat 2010). I had also neglected to notice how, as McLleod and Thomson point out, 'emotional memories tend to be associated with moral judgements' and how this was affecting both my own and my interviewee's understanding of our encounter and my interpretation of it (McLeod and Thomson 2009).

There is one area where the role of the interviewer has tended to follow traditional lines. Community history has been a part of oral history project work since first beginnings in the UK at least. Linking to the work of radical adult educationalists and community development workers with projects in inner-city areas, rural settings and the erstwhile industrial heartlands, the recovery of a lost community life found expression in publications, exhibitions, theatre and inter-generational activities (Thompson and Corti 2008). The most commonly cited problems for community oral history are silences with respect to difference and diversity, tendencies to celebrate, and the management of conflicting memories. People may 'insist that others should remember as they do' (Hamilton 1994: 15), or a community member may feel unable to express what feels like a dissonant memory. Solutions advocated include recognizing when community members are adopting self-censorship, finding ways to incorporate different perspectives, increasing participation through the adoption of creative strategies such as the use of photographs, physical locations, drama and encouraging a critical perspective (Bornat 1992; Shopes 2006; Thomson 2006; Schweitzer 2007; Thompson and Corti 2008). However successful, what tends to be missing is the identity of the interviewer or group of interviewers who either position themselves as sharing the values or perspectives of the community in question, or render themselves invisible with regard to their own views, in an assumed neutrality or claimed membership. A contrasting strategy is to play up the instrumental role of community oral history and to take on an advocating or quasi-campaigning role so that the purpose is clearly eviden: for example revealing the hitherto hidden history of institutional life (Potts and Fido 1991), challenging assumptions about the migrant experience (Brown 2006), chronicling sexual diversity (Brighton Ourstory Project 1992) or extolling the history of public housing (Bornat et al. 2011). In such examples, the interviewer or facilitator is openly partisan in their role, and their subjectivity is clearly expressed, even if their biography, unlike those of the community participants, is rarely if ever revealed.

DIGITAL MEMORY

Thomson's fourth paradigm is the 'dizzying digital revolution in oral history' (2006: 68) and the changes he sees this bringing to the ways oral history is recorded, preserved, analysed and shared. He cites Frisch, who looks to a future when the transcript will be superseded by digital technologies which will make oral recordings accessible and searchable, thus rendering the transcript obsolete. Though he is sceptical as to the likely realisation of the transformations which Frisch predicts, he recognises that digital oral history is different in terms of its reach and methods and that it is already changing the ways people engage with remembering and in the presentation of memory (2006: 68–70). Certainly it is now the case that oral history data can be edited and displayed worldwide in formats which include additional sounds, images, and with all the advantages of online searching and links. However, what is perhaps most exciting is the possibility which online archiving presents for the reuse of oral history data. Going back to one's own or revisiting another project's data brings opportunities to reconceptualise earlier data sets, to ask new questions of archived data and to raise ethical questions which have a broad reach within oral history research generally. Reuse, or secondary analysis, brings the advantages of testing out ideas before embarking on a project, serendipitously searching earlier studies for evidence and, in the case of vulnerable people, avoiding the possible stress of further interviews (Bornat et al. 2012; Irwin and Winterton 2012).

Though digitisation is not essential, the recent growth in reuse studies has most definitely been boosted by computer-aided search and analysis and by online sharing of data. Reuse can lead to original and creative insights; it can also present challenges to oral history as a method (Elliot 2001; Bishop 2007). When memory becomes data detached from the original primary researcher and interviewee, its status changes, particularly if a secondary researcher introduces contextual, temporal and theoretical dimensions, generating new evidence, possibly questioning or revising what had previously been inferred or assumed (Hammersley 2010; Bornat et al. 2012).

While oral history has long been an international movement – with examples of memory work in a wide range of political systems and locales across the globe, celebrating difference and acknowledging the connectedness of memory through accounts of colonialism and memory for example – cross-national comparative work has rarely been attempted. Oral history's commitment to voice and self-expression has accepted the compromise which transcription introduces, but to add translation is to create another layer of distance from the original interview exchange. Cultural complexity, and attempts to balance generalisation against cultural relativism, add further deterrents. However, digitalisation with opportunities for cooperation in project development, immediate data sharing and joint analyses is proving helpful in tackling the difficulties, as recent examples from comparative oral history suggest (Coleman et al. 2012).

CONCLUSION

I have been taking an historical trip through developments in oral history in order to consider some changes which practitioners have initiated and responded to. Over the last four decades oral history has seen enormous changes in relation to recognition and practice. The term now enjoys public recognition and the method is clearly evidenced in academic research, community-based history and in film and television. The availability of national and local collections of archived interviews, the availability of digitisation and the implications of international work open up possibilities for new and original collection, interpretation and analysis. Oral history continues to raises issues relating to representation, subjectivity, interviewer role and context, yet any sense of resolution or conclusion would be unwelcome to a practice which, since it invites personal and public memory work through dialogue, necessarily engages in creating and reinterpreting what is meant by the past, how we live our lives in the present, and what we might expect from the future.

SUMMARY: KEY POINTS

- The chapter argues that by researching the past through memory, oral history changes the way that history is understood and the ways that historians work.
- Oral historians view the interview as a social relationship whose dynamics shape what is produced.
- In the UK, the origins of oral history lie in a commitment to ideas of a people's history challenging established historical narratives.
- Oral historians value and seek to include subjectivity and meaning evoked through remembering in their analysis.
- Being aware of one's own positioning in terms of, for example, gender, class, age or ethnicity, is a necessary aspect of oral historians' practice.
- The digital revolution increasing the accessibility and usability of oral history data presents opportunities as well as ethical challenges.

FURTHER READING

Publications which include an oral history approach have increased in number in recent years making a representative overview difficult. Interest in oral history crosses disciplinary boundaries, and while history underpins many studies, it's worth reviewing the literatures of sociology, geography, literature, cultural studies and migration. Key texts in oral history include

Paul Thompson's classic, *The Voice of the Past* (third edition, 2000), the comprehensive collection edited by Rob Perks and Alistair Thomson, *The Oral History Reader* (second edition, 2006), Valerie Yow, *Recording Oral History: A Guide for the Humanities and Social Sciences* (second edition, 2005) and Lynn Abrams, *Oral History Theory* (2010). Alessandro Portelli, inspirational to oral historians since the 1970s, explores issues such as meaning, dialogue, subjectivity, conflicting accounts and the contribution of cultural interpretation through exploration of political memory, Second World War events in Italy, and community memory (see for example 1991, 1997, 2003, 2011). Luisa Passerini's work on subjectivity and feminism is also influential (1987, 1998). Debates relating to oral history and public history, the emotions, language and interpretation, composing memory and the reuse of archived interviews, among other topics, are published in the two main oral history journals, *Oral History* and *Oral History Review*.

NOTES

1. Interviewed in Bulgarian for the Arts and Humanities Research Council (AHRC)/Economic and Social Research Council (ESRC)-funded project Marking Transitions and Meaning across the Life Course: Older People's Memories of Religious and Secular Ceremonies in Eastern and Western Europe, award No: AH/H008845/1. Part of Religion and Society Programme, 2010–11. Diman Vasilev was one of sixty people aged over seventy-five interviewed in three European countries – Bulgaria, Romania and the UK.
2. My focus on the UK is, in part, because this is the oral history that I know best, but also because UK and European oral historians took the lead in relation to theoretical reflection and problematisation of the method. Oral history had an earlier origin in the USA with Allan Nevins's first oral history interview in 1948. He went on to set up the Columbia University Oral History Research Office with a programme of interviews with leading US figures. Willa Baum, another US oral history pioneer, in an early review of developments, points out how the first wave of funded projects tended to focus more on prominent members of society in contrast with the focus on 'common folk' in Britain (Baum 1972: 15).3.

Professor Bimal Bhowmick, born 1947 in Bangladesh, interviewed for the ESRC-funded project, Overseas Trained Doctors and the Development of Geriatric Medicine, Res-062, 23-0514. Interview deposited at the British Library catalogue no. C1-356/01.

SECTION TWO

Qualities of Memory

CHAPTER 3

Experience and Memory

Steven D. Brown and Paula Reavey

For Sue Campbell

INTRODUCTION

The methodological contribution made by psychology to the diverse web of concerns that make up contemporary 'memory studies' is often considered to be quite singular. While sociologists, historians and media researchers find common cause around the use of textual methods for the 'thick description' of remembering and memorial practices, psychologists appear to be committed to experimental methods and the laboratory study of memory. Such methods have long been criticised on a variety of grounds, not least for their tendency towards reductionist and mechanist accounts of behaviour and their apparent lack of ecological validity. This may make it difficult to reconcile psychological research with cognate approaches in memory studies because of the unusual nature of both the data and the overall analytic mentality that psychologists express in their treatment of memory topics (i.e. driven by the need to calculate and model relations between variables).

It is not our aim in this chapter to resolve this 'family rift' in memory studies. Rather, we will try to trace the lineage of a particular tradition of psychological work that we will term 'social remembering'. While the social remembering tradition has departed from experimentation as its principal technique in favour of qualitative methods, it nevertheless maintains a strong link to some of the longstanding concerns that psychologists have developed around memory. These include issues such as the problem of continuity in identity, the relationship between memorial acts and their environment, and the expressive nature of remembering. We might sum this up with the proposition that central to a psychological approach to memory is the exploration of how remembering acts as the conditions of *reflective experience*.

William James famously placed a chapter on memory at the exact midway point of *The Principles of Psychology*, where it served as a bridge between a discussion of the continuity of experience within the 'stream of thought', and the perception of matters at hand in ongoing interaction. The problem, as James put it, was that although 'the stream of thought flows on' the majority 'of its segments fall into the bottomless abyss of oblivion' (James [1890] 1950: 643). It is therefore necessary to consider the recovery of these 'segments' through reflective acts – 'memory proper [is] *the knowledge of an event, or fact*, of which meantime we have not been thinking, *with the additional consciousness that we have thought or experienced it before*' (p. 648, original italics). For James, this meant that memory was the active reconstitution of some aspect of the past in the present for current purposes.

Memory sits then at the crossroads of two directions in which experience extends: one axis stretches back towards the past and forward to an anticipated future; the other axis mobilises memory to inform our current actions in relation to the changing world around us. James' fellow pragmatist, John Dewey, once offered the following helpful description of the directions in which experience extends: 'The two principles of continuity and interaction are not separated from each other. They intercept and unite. They are so to speak, the longitudinal and the lateral aspects of experience' (Dewey 1938: 44).

Our experiences of daily matters at hand are not disconnected from our ongoing sense of who and what we are over time. They 'intercept and unite' as though together they formed the coordinates in a cartography of possible experiences. Psychologists have consequently approached memory as central to this joint mapping of the dimensions of experience. However, the ways in which memory has been conceptualised in relation to experience have differed considerably. In what follows we will make these differing conceptions central to the contrasts we will draw between methodological approaches.

The chapter is organised in the following way. First we describe the emergence and development of discursive psychology in relation to studies of social remembering. Following this, we will highlight some of the meta-methodological difficulties encountered in the 'discursive turn', and show how these were addressed in the work of David Middleton and colleagues. Finally, we will discuss how our own work seeks to elaborate these concerns by developing a different kind of relationship between theory and method.

COLLECTIVE REMEMBERING AND DISCURSIVE PSYCHOLOGY

The volume on *Collective Remembering* edited by David Middleton and Derek Edwards in 1990 represented a firm break with experimental psychology. Although Middleton and Edwards' background was in social and developmental psychology, they took issue with what they saw as the limited and limiting concern with the individual that dominated the psychology of memory as a whole. Key to their argument was the idea that psychological processes have social foundations – personal memories are located in a broader collective framework. This argument had some pedigree outside the discipline. Maurice Halbwachs ([1925] 1992) famously developed the notion of 'collective frameworks' to describe the formative role of context in shaping individual memory. But what was dramatically different about the work brought together by Middleton and Edwards was the systematic way in which they showed how persons participate in social mnemonic practices through skilful displays of 'public mentation'. The psychological is not a private realm that is shaped by social context and then expressed through individual behaviour. What we typically call 'memory' is instead the social-communicative act of remembering and forgetting with others in the course of some activity. The contrast with experimental psychology is then as follows:

> In experimental designs, meaning and context are defined as variables, factors whose effects on the accuracy of recall are manipulable. In the study of discursive remembering, significance and context are intrinsic to the activity, constitutive of it and constituted by it, rather than causally influential upon some other thing called 'memory'. (Middleton and Edwards 1990: 42)

Psychological experiments are designed to explore the causal effects of varying *independent variables* (i.e. those controlled by the experimenter, such as the information provided by participants, or aspects of the environment in which it is presented) upon *dependent variables* (i.e. a measurable response made by the participant, such as the accuracy of their subsequent recollections). The logic of experimentation forces a conceptual separation between these variables such that 'memory' is treated as independent of, yet influenced by, the contexts in which remembering happens. Middleton and Edwards here argue against that separation, claiming that what it means to remember something on a given occasion is utterly intrinsic to the nature of the act itself. Memory is never independent of the context where it is enacted; rather, those contexts form an indivisible part of the phenomenon that psychologists study. Remembering is then a social accomplishment performed as a joint activity with others, on particular occasions in specific contexts.

While it is possible to conceive of experimental designs that do not force such conceptual separation detailed above, Middleton and Edwards turned instead towards qualitative methods to develop their approach. They gathered 'naturalistic data', where the researcher observes and tape-records an activity occurring in its usual context (such as parents and children interacting together) without participating. The following example comes Edwards and Middleton's (1988) study of conversations around family photographs. Here, a young boy, Paul, and his mother are looking through photographs of family holidays:

Example 1 (from Edwards and Middleton 1988)
Mother: it must have been a sunny day in that photograph (.) mustn't it?
Paul: yeh (.) oh let's (.) see see that comes (.) bigger
Mother: mm (. . .) where were you then? (.) can you remember?
Paul: there and there's Rebecca look at (.) her ugh ((laughs))
Mother: she's pulling a funny face (.) isn't she?
Paul: yeh (.) she thinks it it's so mm let's see let's see what that boy don let's see if there's any (.) agh (.) it's big (.) do you like (.)
Mother: you didn't like that bouncing castle did you? (.) do you remember?
Paul: yeh
Mother: it kept falling over (.) you couldn't keep your balance
Paul: no ((laughs quietly))
Mother: do you like them now?
Paul: yeh
Mother: *do* you?

In this extract we see how remembering operates as a shared activity. Paul and his mother are working together, assisted by the use of the photographs, to establish an account of a past event (in this case, a particular family day out). The mother points to particular features of the photographs, such as the light or the facial expressions of family members, as evidence in support of a particular narrative. In this respect she is actively tutoring Paul on how to make inferences about the past. Each inference sets up a kind of puzzle that is offered to Paul – 'she's pulling a funny face . . . ?', 'you didn't like that bouncing castle did you?' He is then interactionally appointed to complete the inference by filling out the experiential details, even if in somewhat minimal terms – 'she thinks it it's so', 'yeh'. This involves making attributions about what he and other family members (such as his sister Rebecca) were thinking or feeling at the time. These kinds of 'meta-cognitive' descriptions are not reports of a past or present cognitive state, but rather discursive formulations that enable a narrative reconstruction of the past to be agreed upon. Moreover, Paul's mother invites him to construct a continuity between their joint reminisced past and his current experiences – 'you didn't like that bouncing castle . . . ?' > 'do you like them now?' In this way, we see that continuity is not a psychological given, but rather a claim about the relationship between past and present that is actively accomplished (and also contested) in this kind of conversational remembering.

Middleton and Edward's approach to qualitative data was informed by an emerging turn towards discourse analysis (DA) in psychology. Jonathan Potter and Margaret Wetherell had proposed that the social psychological study of attitudes and attributions could be revolutionised through discourse analysis as the study of interactionally occasioned and rhetorically organised claims about self and others. Their jointly authored *Discourse and Social Psychology* had an enormous methodological impact on the discipline since it finally offered a viable empirical strategy in which the conceptual and philosophical alternative to experimental psychology could be pushed forward (see Brown and Locke 2008). Potter and Wetherell's work on attitudes, and Middleton and Edward's work on memory, was brought together under the umbrella discursive psychology (see Edwards and Potter 1992a). This revised approach was highly influenced by conversation analysis (CA) (see Edwards 1997). As a consequence, there was an explicit rejection of formal theorisation in favour of close readings of transcripts of audio recordings. Following this approach, Edwards and Potter (1992a) argued that if a cognitive process such as memory is studied in the 'real world' settings within which it is occasioned, the central focus needs to be on the conversational pragmatics through which the psychological act is accomplished. In the case of memory, they took issue with the way experimental psychologists make the assumption that it is possible to clearly establish the truth or veridicality of a given recollection, in such a way that claims can be made about the accuracy or distortions present in testimony. But establishing 'what happened' is precisely what a great deal of social interaction around memory is seeking to accomplish. For example, Ulrich Neisser's (1981) famous study of the testimony given by John Dean to the Watergate hearings does step outside the laboratory to explore a real world instance of recollection, but Neisser relies on the idea that it is ultimately possible to establish the truth of Dean's recollections. By contrast, Edwards and Potter (1992b) propose that what is analytically interesting here is to look at how the participants in the Watergate hearings (including Dean) fit their claims about what happened into the evolving conversational contingencies of the hearings.

Discursive psychology, as developed by Edwards and Potter, is noteworthy because it insists on the considerable interactional skills of ordinary people.

From an early age, we are all capable of using discursive and rhetorical resources to accomplish an enormous range of social acts. For Edwards and Potter, psychology ought to be principally concerned with the social development and enactment of these abilities. Psychology loses its way when it appeals to a concept of 'mind' (and private 'cognition') as an explanation of action without having first grasped the situated, contextual nature of activities such as remembering. However, the call to dispense with the central organising concepts in modern psychology (e.g. mind as the cognitive engine which drives action) was not entirely welcomed with open arms by the community of experimental psychologists. In a series of vituperative responses to an invited article (Edwards et al. 1992) in *The Psychologist*, a parade of senior scholars took issue with what they saw as an approach lacking in both theoretical coherency and empirical (i.e. experimental) rigour, displaying an obsession with language, an ignorance of established doxa in experimental studies of memory, and a distasteful predilection for philosophical relativism. While these comments are probably best seen as occasioned responses to the somewhat pugnacious argumentative context set by Edwards et al.'s (1992) target article, they do raise one immensely significant concern: Is there not some aspect of memory that is not captured by the study of discourse? Is all of memory 'occasioned' by the contexts in which it is enacted? Do we not have some sense of continuity that exceeds these conversational contexts? Or, put slightly differently, does discursive psychology push too far towards Dewey's interactional dimension? To address these questions it seems necessary to overturn the moratorium on 'theory' imposed by the approach.

THE SOCIAL PSYCHOLOGY OF EXPERIENCE

David Middleton's work in the 1990s followed a different trajectory to discursive psychology. Influenced by work in socio-cultural psychology (see Valsiner and Rosa 2007), Middleton became increasingly concerned with the problem of how individuals cede their memorial concerns to a notion of collectivity (see Middleton 1997a, 1997b, 2002). That is to say, how we invoke the idea of a group, organisation or nation to underline that the meaning and importance of what we are remembering is 'bigger' than us alone – it is a concern that either is or ought to be shared by many others. Middleton characterised this as an 'interdependency' between personal and collective experiences that was shaped through recollection. Understanding how this interdependency was produced and managed would, in effect, require a return to Dewey's continuity dimension.

Middleton and Brown's *The Social Psychology of Experience* proposed reworking notions of continuity by engaging simultaneously with the work of

Henri Bergson and Maurice Halbwachs. Typically these thinkers are treated as opposed, but Middleton and Brown (2005) claimed that if the relationship between the individual and the collective is posed in temporal terms, there is a remarkably productive relationship between the two, such that Halbwachs can be seen as detailing the processes through which the multiple, overlapping temporal trajectories – 'durations' – posited by Bergson as the basis of social and organic life are held together. The notion of duration differs considerably from the way that time and continuity is usually thought of in psychology. Bergson argues that the time we live is not social or 'clock time', neatly divided into measurable instants, but rather an ongoing indivisible flow, which we experience as expanding and dilating according to our needs and concerns. Moreover, we are continuously turning around on our experiences and seeing new patterns and temporal relationships, such that the past is never really 'over' but is instead continuously active in transforming the present. Finally, duration is not singular; our lives and those of others consist of multiple durations that resonate and intersect with one another. Halbwachs' concepts of localisation, projection and implacement serve as good descriptions of how these relations between durations are managed in social settings.

While clearly departing from the discourse and conversation analytic proscription on theorising, the empirical studies described by Middleton and Brown nevertheless used recognisable D and CA techniques to inductively read naturalistic and interview transcribed data, along with visual materials. The point of difference with discursive psychology was the attempt to use theoretically derived concepts to 'amplify' or further articulate inductively derived analytic observations into broader descriptions of settings and processes. Take the following example, which derives originally from Buchanan and Middleton, 1995. This data was taken from a recording of a reminiscence group held at a hospital, where elderly people were asked to discuss their favourite 'tipples' (i.e. alcoholic drinks). The main speaker here, Sue, is in her seventies, and while she does not particularly enjoy drinking alcohol, makes this contribution to the ongoing conversation:

Example 2 (from Buchanan and Middleton 1995)
Sue: I mean I've got nothing against drink (.) if people enjoy drink I- I think they're entitled to it (.) but erm (.) it's not for me (.) apart from er (.) lemonade and (.) shandy (.) I don't mind that ((another conversation intrudes for some seconds at this point, until Sue continues))
Sue: I remember when er (.) my father was alive (.) he used to like a bottle of stout (.) used [to (. . .) bottle about like this (.) and (and)

Rose:	[mm (.) *stout* oh yes (.) stout
Sue:	(and) er (.) where we lived er (.) we had a (.) erm (.) a (.) firegrate with erm [(.) *hobs* I think they called them (. . .) hobs (.) and er (.)
Female?:	[ehh [
Meg?:	[yeah that's (yeah) [
Ted:	[ah yeah [
Female?:	[(. . .)
Sue:	(and) dad used to (.) drink it out the bottle (.) and er (.) he used to stand it on the hob (.) an- and he used to say it was [*beau*tiful (and)
Ted:	[warming
Sue:	(and) (.) and er ((laugh)) a- you'll think (. . .) and er (.) I used to go to church in those days (.) and erm (.) the parson (.) we had a parson that used to visit (.) and er (.) I said to me dad (.) the parson- (.) I said that the parsons coming (.) [(and)
Ted:	[is that why he kept it on the hob
Sue:	(and) I said that you won't drink your stout while he's here will you (.) ooh my [(and)
Ted:	[((laugh))
Sue:	(and) dad was disgusted he said I *will* (.) drink me stout (.) he said you ought to be ashamed of yourself (.) and ther[e it stood on the hob y'know (and)
Male?:	[(. . .)
Sue:	(and) and in walked the parson with his (.) dog collar on I didn't [know what to do (.) and ((cough)) to make (and)
Rose?:	[((laugh))
Sue:	(and) matters worse this erm (.) *stou:t* was (.) chchchch ((imitates noise of stout bubbling)) you could hear it (.) bubblinglike (and)
	((general laughter))
Sue:	(and) (.) yeah and er (.) me father said to him er (.) ooh and er (.) this parsons name was a Mr Jackson he was a very very nice man (.) and m- me father said er (.) I don't (.) I don't think going to church is doing my daughter much good (.) he said er (.) she asked me (.) not to have my bottle of stout (.) cos you were coming (.) and Mr Jackson said well I've never heard such a thing in me life he said (.) I like one meself occasionally (.) I never felt so bad after tha::t ((laughing tone)) [
	((general laughter))

The problem here for Sue is how to participate in a conversation about drinking while professing her dislike of alcohol. She is in the difficult situation of having to account for her views in a way that avoids the appearance of 'taking the moral high ground'. Middleton and Brown draw on Sack's (1992) notion of 'entitlements' to argue that Sue shows how and why she is entitled to her view, rather than simply stating it, through the account she gives of an episode from her younger days. She uses a great deal of 'reported speech' (i.e. performing the voices of Sue-in-the-past, her father, the parson) to set up a contrast between the 'moralising voice' of Sue-in-the-past against 'legitimate pleasures' claimed by her father and the parson, which recruits the other speakers in the interaction into the narrative, as seen by the multiple overlapping contributions and laughter. Sue thereby demonstrates her entitlements and simultaneously ironises them, such that she is able to successfully accomplish a position of 'non-judgemental abstinence' and still participate in the reminiscence activity.

But there is a further aspect of the account that is interesting. Middleton and Brown point to the careful description of the setting where the recollected event occurred, the positioning of the people present and the objects with which they interact. The physical environment is offered up here in such a way that the listeners are invited to vicariously experience its contours – as Ted, for example, does when he latches onto Sue's turn with a description of the 'warming' taste of the stout. Sue's narrative literally 'incorporates' the listeners, directing their gaze back and forth across the room, asking them to hear and savour the 'chchchch' of the bubbling bottle and to enjoy the spectacle of the increasingly desperate Sue-in-the-past caught between her obstreperous father and the imminent visit of the parson. That is to say, they are asked to 'imaginatively place themselves in a localised set of personal relationships, to vicariously experience what it must be to move through that physical environment' (Middleton and Brown 2005: 124). To properly engage with this act of recollection we need to see it as not just a rhetorically organised stretch of conversation, but as the actualisation of the past in such a way that it affords a 'potentially habitable world' in which the participants can place and locate themselves – establishing a form of membership – for the time taken by the telling of the narrative.

Middleton and Brown's (2005) work appeared at the time when a number of critical psychologists were attempting to reclaim the notion of 'experience' (see also Bradley 2005; Stephenson and Papadopoulos 2006). The phrase is usually associated with humanistic psychology, with its central image of a bounded, self-contained psychological subject. However, following the efforts to 'de-subjectify' the psychological initiated in the work of Foucault and Deleuze, among others (see Brown and Stenner 2009), it is possible to treat experience as emergent from and shared across persons and the material world with which they interact. Our experiences are not then entirely 'ours', but are interdependent with others and with things (Reavey 2010).

Remembering is the means by which we turn around on interdependencies in our temporally structured experience (i.e. overlapping durations). And while remembering happens partly through talk, analysis cannot be limited to a strict focus on conversational interaction because of the importance of material mediation through artefacts and settings, along with our embodied participation in the worlds (or 'zones of personal relations') that are made actual through recollection.

The philosopher Sue Campbell (2009) offers a fascinating alternative reading of the example in Extract 3. She observes that the participants in the reminiscence group most likely share a common 'cultural imaginary' since:

> there is no confusion about the nature of the place and objects that anchor the relations of Sue's scenario – they all seem to know what hobs are – and Ted knows that the norms of the environment make the stout his for the tasting. We might also suspect that Sue's interlocutors are normatively happy in her world. They do laugh at her embarrassment rather than objecting to the patriarchal norms that have determined it. (Campbell 2009: 223)

It is this shared cultural imaginary which makes the participants 'at ease' in the habitable world produced in the recollection. But the same processes of embodied engagement may be at work in the performance of inhospitable worlds where conflict and contestation are opened up. We may bodily relate through collective recollection to worlds that we do not like and in which we do not feel at all at ease. This may be deliberately so, since as Campbell observes 'the very intent of drawing someone into the past may be to encourage the contesting rather than the affirmation of values' (Campbell 2009: 223). Far greater attention needs to be given to the nature of both the setting and the activity through which recollection is performed than Middleton and Brown are prepared to allow. It really matters whether the world that is being performed through memory is one in which we can live and whose values we share or, conversely, is one which is difficult, distressing and conflictual.

VITAL MEMORIES

In this penultimate section, we will describe our own recent work, which we see as in the tradition of and building upon the work we have discussed above. In this work, we have used a variety of empirical approaches, including mixed media methods, memory work and interviews. To return, for a final time, to

Dewey's cartography of experience, we see our work as tacking back from the concern with continuity (which we, of course, share) to a re-enagement with the problem of interaction. This term comes freighted with some problematic meanings. As Campbell (2009) shows in relation to Middleton and Brown's work, what is at stake in recollection is not just how we act in relation to others, but rather how we jointly and bodily *participate* in the making and unmaking of recollected worlds. This can take the form of a complex affective involvement along with very difficult identifications with the sorts of persons we consider ourselves to be, have been, or aspire or fear to become.

Over the past few years, we have worked across a series of studies with groups of participants who have 'trouble' with some aspect of their past or that of others they care for. These include adult survivors of child sexual abuse (Reavey 1998; Reavey and Brown 2006, 2009), parents conducting life story work with their adopted children (Brookfield et al. 2008; Brown et al. 2013), people affected by the 2005 London Bombings (Allen and Brown 2011), elderly users of a reminiscence museum (Bendien et al. 2010), and forensic mental health service users in medium-secure settings (Brown et al. 2013). While the settings and activities differ considerably across these studies, one common feature is that recollection in each case is fraught with difficulties, both in terms of what is being recollected and its significance for ongoing identification with self and others. We have proposed the term 'vital memories' as shorthand for the simultaneously *problematic* and *essential* character of these kinds of recollections (Brown and Reavey 2013). It is sometimes convenient to imagine that since the past is reconstructed in social remembering, there must in principle be an endless creativity to the ways in which past experiences can be mobilised and made relevant in the present. Yet the sorts of experiences that the people in these studies are invoking are difficult to manage, often threatening and destabilising, while at the same time felt to be utterly necessary to one's sense of self.

This does not mean that we are going back to a reified notion of a core self or bounded subjectivity. While we think it is analytically and politically important to affirm that persons do indeed have a reflexive sense of self-continuity that is reiterated across individual interactional episodes, this felt continuity has no particular substance. It is not a psychological 'thing' or measurable property, but our ongoing participation in the overlapping durations that make up our lives. While it clarifies matters methodologically to concern oneself – as discursive psychologists do – only with what is 'readable' in the particular narrow slice of recorded interaction selected for analysis, it is highly disingenuous to suppose that a reflexive concern for the place of what is happening right now in a broader sense of one's life is not at play to some degree in any interaction, whether or not it can be read off talk-in-interaction through D and CA means.

Consider the following extract, taken from a study (Reavey 1998) where adult women discuss the meaning and significance that their experiences of child sexual abuse have for them in the present:

Example 3 (from Reavey 1998)

Participant: It was my brother, we I would think that when he started, it was, er curiosity, but I think, erm . . . one thing I tried convincing myself of, that that he was naïve and he didn't know what he was doing was wrong, but he used to lock the door to to, we didn't have key locks, he used to take the handle and take out the bar.
[later in the interview]
Participant: I'd say the main problem there is is, the guilt for enjoying what he did, and that can really tear me up sometimes, and I think that's been, big problem, actually specifically before I realised the feeling of confusion, and why should feel about enjoying this. I do feel guilty about writing it down, cos it makes it solid, it makes it er, it's evidence and it's just . . . like I say, it makes it, it makes it real, which of course it was, but some of me wonders how much of it as real . . . but there's a big part of you that wants to be believe he didn't know what he was doing, but I don't think I can convince myself of that, like I say, going to the extent of locking the door . . . by the time he got to fifteen, he must have known, he must have done . . . I think so . . . but it would have been nice if he didn't.
Interviewer: Would it make a difference?
Participant: Yeah because of the way I feel about him, because . . . because if it was basic curiosity, if if, and, rather than actually knowing that it was wrong . . . he must have known how it would affect me.

In this extract, a woman in her late twenties discusses an episode of sexual abuse perpetrated by her elder brother when they were both children. The first thing to note about this extract is that it demonstrates the extent to which particular kinds of difficult recollected episodes endure across lives, having an ongoing significance and relevance for a range of relationships and activities. Rather than say that the past is being invoked in the present to some end, it would be better to say here that addressing this particular aspect of the past is felt to be an inevitable feature of dealing with questions of who one is now. Recounting this particular episode involves considerable dilemmas. The form taken by the recollection – in this instance, committed to an audio recording in a research interview – matters. For example, the woman describes how, on other occasions, 'writing it down' produces guilt because it 'makes it solid, it makes it evidence'. The dilemma surrounds the future consequences of having placed the recollection in a particular form, of having 'settled' the past as having a particular set of meanings. These are not necessarily formal (i.e. legal) consequences, but rather what it means for this woman to have established what her brother now is to her as a result of what he knowingly did in the past ('Would it make a difference?' 'Yeah because of the way I feel about him').

The dilemma of establishing whether or not the brother-as-child acted intentionally is an example of what Middleton (2002) calls the interdependency of the intentional and the incidental. Ceding either intentional or incidental attributes to a past action can be a central part of what is accomplished in social remembering. But in this extract, we see a pull in the other direction. The woman emphasises ambiguity about the episode. Pleasure is mixed with distress, which gives rise to 'confusion' and 'guilt for enjoying what he did'. The recollection is highly affectively charged, it carries forward a range of embodied experiences – feelings and sensations – that this woman struggles to frame in a definite way. Note, however, the role played by the door and the lock. The woman describes how her brother would remove the central bar from the door handle to ensure that the room was locked. The materiality of this mechanism has considerable consequences for 'settling' the matter of whether or not the brother acted intentionally (see Reavey and Brown 2009). We would say that the door and the handle are here participants in the recollected episode. The door distributes and marks out particular kinds of relationships between brother and sister (as deliberate perpetrator of sexual abuse and victim locked in a room against her will). It makes visible and thinkable a complex moral order in which the working up of choice is spatially distributed (Reavey 2010). Space, thus, participates also in the making of subjective agency. In doing so it is the means by which the past is settled in a particular way (albeit perhaps provisionally), and emotional matters and future consequences are actualised ('it makes it real').

The material and affective dimensions of recollection are pivotal to our analysis of vital memories. This is why we have often built in visual elements to our data collection, which we would argue bring the material setting and affective participation into view (Reavey 2011). We think that the central question for social remembering is how we ought best to collectively relate to and work with others with whom our memories and pasts are interdependent. In all of our studies, we begin analysis by applying D and CA tools to the empirical material, rather than starting with theory. This grounding of analysis in concrete, everyday settings – in 'what happened' as Sacks puts it – has greatly informed our work. But we feel that concepts and theoretical resources are ethically (as well as analytically) necessary to give a just account of the 'memory problems' faced and managed by our participants. We propose that theory 'amplifies' and 'performs' the inductive analysis of data. It elaborates and transforms what is readable in the empirical material in such a way that we – as analysts, as readers – can relate to the broader lives and settings in which these memory problems are inextricably embedded. This raises the obvious danger of both a certain nominalism in the choice of theoretical resources, or of 'cherry picking' material that conveniently fits with one's pre-established theoretical frame. To avoid this, we offer the following four points of guidance:

1. At any point in the development of the conceptual or theoretical amplification of the data, we must be able as readers to return to a bare account of 'what happens' prior to amplification. This requires presenting sufficient amounts of data in an appropriate form (e.g. transcription).
2. The analysis must always begin in an inductive fashion. The choice of concept or theories needs to be explicitly guided by the features of the material that are identified through inductive means – i.e. 'what's in the data?'
3. Theory is there in the analysis to allow the analyst and the reader to deductively arrive at what plausibly feels like the conditions of the particular experiences being described. In other words, theory makes the concrete practice of recollection into a 'habitable world' for the analyst and reader.
4. The amplification of the empirical material should, in principle, always be explicable within the lifeworld of the participant. This involves an acknowledgement of 'what the participant is already doing' in relation to memory making. If participants already use mixed media and objects, then further consideration is needed of how to write this into the research process. Furthermore, although technical terms may be used, the account they afford should be one that can be recognised by participants as workable and plausible.

SUMMARY: KEY POINTS

- In this chapter we have described how and why social psychologists adopted discourse analysis as a means to study remembering from the perspective of experience.
- We showed, using examples, how close analysis of transcript data can identify how persons jointly construct the past as a situated interactional accomplishment, rather than a cognitive operation.
- We argued that discursive psychology offers a stronger account of interaction than it does of continuity.
- We described how Middleton and Brown's work attempted to analyse the joint production of 'habitable worlds'.

- We discussed the ways in which our own recent work adds a concern with materiality, place and affect to the social remembering tradition.
- Finally, we offered some guidelines for combining theoretical elaboration with an inductive approach to analysis.

FURTHER READING

The three books we have discussed in the chapter – Middleton and Edwards (1990); Middleton and Brown (2005) and Brown and Reavey (2013) – cover the main ground. The classic study of Chancellor Lawson's memory by Edwards and Potter (1992b) gives a good introduction to discursive psychology, which could be followed by the book-length account (Edwards and Potter 1992a). Middleton's (2002) paper on succession and change shows how discursive psychology can be developed by drawing on socio-cultural psychology. Allen and Brown's (2011) analysis of remembering the 2005 London Bombings shows the relevance of conceptualising affect, while Reavey's (2011) discussion of remembering child sexual abuse points to the importance of space and place.

CHAPTER 4

Between Official and Vernacular Memory

Sabina Mihelj

Qualitative interviewing is one of the most common methods of data collection in the social sciences, and its relative weaknesses and strengths have generated a wealth of literature. Researchers from across several disciplines can turn to specialist books designed to provide advice on appropriate interviewing techniques, and interviewing is discussed in virtually any methodological handbook (e.g. Banister et al. 1994; Gubrium and Holstein 2001; Wengraf 2001; Silverman 2006; Bernard 2011). The study of memory often relies on interview data as well, yet, all too often, the methodological and epistemological challenges brought by it are left unaddressed. Interviews tend to be treated as transparent windows onto recollections of the past, as if these were a stable element of an individual's psyche, permanently stored in one's brain and retrieved on demand. With the exception of some of the work stemming from the methodological tradition of biographical narratives (e.g. Bertaux and Kohli 1984; Rosenthal 2004; Miller 2000) the impact of the interviewing context and techniques are given only scant consideration. Curiously, such a naïve approach to interviews can easily coexist with an acute awareness of the shifting, context-bound nature of memory, as if the research process would be somehow miraculously exempt from the vagaries of memory work in everyday life.

The choice of interviewing poses a range of important questions for memory scholars. First, are interviews always the best choice, or might it be better to consider alternative methods of data collection, such as naturally occurring conversations or large-scale surveys? Second, what aspects or types of memory can interviews help reveal? And finally, how should memory scholars conduct interviews and how should we analyse interview data? Answers to these questions will depend on the specific research problem we are faced with. Are we interested in the nature of official memories, fostered by governments, educational systems and political elites? Or are we rather seeking to understand how these official memories relate to what John Bodnar (1992: 13–14) calls vernacular memory, namely the diverse and changing forms of memory 'derived from first-hand experience in small-scale communities'? Does the research focus on national or transnational memories, or perhaps on the relationship between memory and gender and memory and class? Are we dealing with memory formation in a society that has recently undergone a major political, economic and cultural transformation, or in a society that has remained relatively stable for decades?

This chapter examines a range of dilemmas facing the researcher when seeking to use interviews for the purpose of analysing vernacular memory, and, in particular, when seeking to unravel the nature of vernacular remembering and its relationship with official, national-level memories in a post-socialist context. Much as with the broader literature on memory, existing research on post-socialist memory often gravitates towards macro-cultural memories, inscribed in official documents, elite debates, national commemorations, museums, heritage sites and official apologies, without paying much attention to their reception and appropriation among the general population (e.g. Kopeček 2008; Sarkisova and Apor 2008; Tileagă 2008; most of the contributions to Todorova 2010 and Todorova and Gille 2010). Alongside this body of work, however, a smaller but nonetheless notable range of studies emerged that move beyond the realm of the official and the elite and examine the microprocesses of memory formation at vernacular level and in everyday life (e.g. Skultans 1998; Wanner 1998; Berdahl 1999; Ballinger 2003; Mark 2010). In all of this work, interviews feature as one of the key methods of data collection.

The first part of the chapter discusses the strengths and weaknesses of interviewing and its suitability for the purpose of researching the dynamics of public memory at vernacular level. Interviewing may well be among the most commonly chosen methods in existing research on the topic, but is it necessarily the most appropriate one? Rather than rehearsing the usual arguments about qualitative interviews and survey questionnaires, the chapter examines the debate surrounding another type of qualitative data – namely, naturally occurring conversations – and its relative advantages and disadvantages compared to interviewing. Even when interviews are the best choice, it is important to acknowledge their interactional nature and recognise that the accounts of the past they generate are not representative of recollections arising in the context of everyday life. How should we design the questions and approach interview materials to gain the best insight into the nature of vernacular memories, and minimise the potential drawbacks of interviewing?

The solution suggested here involves treating interview recollections of the past as products of a double-layered conversation: on the one hand, the actual exchanges between the interviewer and the interviewee; and on the other hand, the broader 'conversation' with alternative ways of talking about the past circulating in a specific political, social and historical context. To demonstrate how this approach might work in practice, the second part of the chapter considers examples drawn from interview materials collected in the Slovenian town of Nova Gorica, situated at the Italo-Slovenian border – and hence at the former border between the capitalist West and the socialist East. The concluding section considers the ethical implications of the proposed approach and reflects on what it offers to our understanding of national and public memory more generally.

INTERVIEW AS CONVERSATION

Qualitative interviewing has its obvious attractions. From early on, its proponents have contrasted it favourably with survey questionnaires, and praised it for its flexibility. Especially from the 1960s onwards, qualitative interviewing was seen as a research resource able to elicit accounts that eschew researcher's expectations and reveal authentic emotions and attitudes, as well as a means of establishing a more equal relationship between the interviewer and the interviewee (Platt 2001). From this point of view, interviewing appears as an ideal instrument for investigating the nuances of vernacular memory, and a welcome alternative to large-scale surveys often used in memory research.

More recently, however, the notion of interviews as privileged windows onto reality began to be questioned. Instead, a growing body of work began to examine interviews in their own right, treating them as social or communicative occasions during which individuals actively construct different versions of reality (Holstein and Gubrium 1995; Silverman 2006: 118–19, 127–33). These versions of reality vary depending on the respective social positions and stakes of each individual involved in interaction, the phrasing of questions, the available cultural conventions for addressing particular topics, as well as the broader political and social environment. For instance, the same interviewee would most likely provide a different account of the same past if asked to do so by her or his grandchild, or if interviewed by a journalist in front of television cameras, or if interviewed by the same interviewer a decade earlier.

For some, this means that interviews cannot be used as a means of accessing objects external to themselves – be they conceived as emotions, attitudes, historical facts or everyday conversations – and should be seen as 'data only about a particular research conversation that occurred at a particular time and place' (Wengraf 2001: 1). This is the point often made by conversation analysts, who argue that interview materials cannot be treated as representative of social interaction, and that one should instead seek to record and analyse naturally occurring conversations, or at the very least acknowledge the specific interactional nature of interviews and analyse them by drawing on conversation analytical methods (Potter and Hepburn 2005; Wooffitt and Widdicombe 2006).

The study of conversational remembering by means of naturally occurring interaction has much to offer. Studies in this tradition have shown, for instance, that conversational remembering and forgetting is not solely a reflection of an inner cognitive state – i.e. the simple fact of knowing or not knowing – but can also be used instrumentally to avoid teasing or scapegoating, or to achieve other ends (e.g. Drew 1989; Edwards and Potter 1992b). The application of such methods in the context of research on national vernacular memories could help address a range of interesting questions. Under what interactional circumstances, for instance, might people choose to avoid engaging in a discussion of particularly controversial national historical figures or events, and why? How would family members or friends of different political leanings manage the discussion of the national past over a common meal? Would a museum exhibit or an official celebration designed to promote a new reading of national history manage to challenge alternative readings? How, if at all, would the new narrative be picked up in conversations among people visiting the exhibition or observing the celebration? These are all pertinent questions, and point to the potential of drawing on naturally occurring interactions in this branch of memory research.

This is not to say, however, that interviewing should be abandoned. In some cases, it may simply be unfeasible or impossible to gain access to such material. For instance, obtaining access to relevant conversations in private settings may prove too cumbersome or time-consuming, and result in a wealth of material that does not touch on relevant aspects of memory at all. Moreover, recordings of interactions in institutional or public settings such as museums or schools will inevitably provide access only to a limited segment of a population – children, history buffs, or tourists – and therefore impose limits on the kinds of research questions we can ask. In short, choosing naturally occurring data often requires relinquishing a substantial amount of control over the research process and accepting a more inductive, data-led approach to investigation. Not everyone will be willing to adopt such an approach, and the scope of vernacular memory research would become severely limited if interviews were abandoned.

Instead, we can conduct and analyse interviews with an awareness of their interactional nature. This does not mean that we need to accept the rather extreme view of interviews as data that cannot provide any insight into external reality. As some conversation analysts argue, the interactional context works in tandem with cognition, and it is possible to show how cognitive states become visible in interaction (e.g. Shaw and Kitzinger 2007). By the same token, one can argue that conversational memory is shaped in part by the particular cultural conventions of remembering and the broader social and political context, and cannot be explained fully by looking exclusively at the micro-dynamics of conversation. This is true also of interview conversations. Every interview account arises out of a process of 'co-construction' (Gubrium and Koro-Ljungberg 2005; see also Wetherell 2003); as interviewers, we inevitably influence the interviewees with our questions, yet at the same time, their answers are also guided by the wider historical and cultural context that is independent from the interactional situation. This wider context includes publicly expressed views and arguments on particular issues of controversy. Each attitude to the past expressed in the interview can thus be understood as an argument, as a stance taken in a matter of public controversy, vis-à-vis other possible attitudes to the same past (see Billig 1987).

Approached in this way, recollections of past events generated in interviews can be analysed as products of conversations that occur on two levels simultaneously. On the one hand, every interview account of the past is a product of actual exchanges between the interviewer and the interviewee; on the other hand, it also embodies a set of positions taken in response to the different ways of talking about the past circulating in the broader political, social and historical context. The awareness of this double-layered conversation can be usefully embedded both in the design of the interview questions and in the process of analysis. For instance, the interview protocol could involve a strategic deployment of semantically loaded, controversial terms and expressions for past events and processes. National memories are replete with such terms; an event perceived as a grand 'national victory' in one historical context may later be seen as a senseless 'massacre', and a story of national 'liberation' and 'progress' can be turned into a narrative of 'humiliation' and 'national decline'. Any strategic deployment of such terms, however, requires close familiarity with the particular narratives, cultural conventions and the historical and political context within which interviewing takes place. In this sense, interviewing techniques and methods of analysis, however meticulously designed, are of little help unless accompanied by traditional methods of scholarship, which involve wide reading across a plethora of sources and rely on the ability to draw connections between seemingly unrelated events and processes (see Billig 1988).

The following section demonstrates how such an approach may work in practice, by focusing on examples involving the term 'Iron Curtain', drawn from research conducted in the border town of Nova Gorica. It starts with a brief overview of the history of the Italo-Yugoslav (today Italo-Slovenian) border and the discourses surrounding it, proceeds by discussing the interviewing techniques and concludes with an illustrative analysis of two interview excerpts.

REMEMBERING THE 'IRON CURTAIN'

The launching of 'Iron Curtain' as a label for the border stretching 'from Stettin in the Baltic to Trieste in the Adriatic' is typically credited to Winston Churchill and his speech in Fulton, Missouri in 1946, although the term has a considerably longer history and originally referred to a device used in theatre (Wright 2007). As a metaphor, the term acquired a myriad of meanings that kept changing throughout the Cold War and were shaped as much by political interests from above as by local players from below (Sheffer 2011). To this day, it remains part of everyday vocabulary and has an afterlife of its own independent of the walls, border check-points and barbed wires that used to divide the European continent.

The use of the 'Iron Curtain' as a label referring to the Italo-Yugoslav border, however, can be disputed, at least as far as the period after 1948 is concerned. In the early post-war years, the conditions of life at the border were indeed rather grim. The shape of the new border was established only gradually and after protracted negotiations that saw the local dispute between Italy and Yugoslavia become increasingly enmeshed in the global confrontation between the capitalist West and the communist East (Sluga 2001). The newly erected wires, walls and border posts disrupted long-established circuits of work and trade, and severed ties between communities. The familiar neighbouring villages, towns and cities, along with family members, fiancées, friends and property, suddenly became part of a foreign, politically hostile country. The border separating Nova Gorica from its older sibling, the Italian town of Gorizia, is a case in point. Following the agreement reached in 1947 and sealed with the signing of the Paris Peace Treaty, the town of Gorizia was torn in two; most of the town was annexed to Italy, while its eastern suburbs and the railway station – the part of the city that would soon be transformed into Nova Gorica – became part of Yugoslavia. Obtaining permission to cross the border into Italy could easily take several months, with the applicant being asked to supply additional documents or even visit the office in Ljubljana to explain why the visit to Italy was necessary (Mihelj forthcoming).

After Tito's split with Stalin in 1948, however, things began to change. Yugoslavia gradually abandoned its original political, economic and cultural policies, modelled on the Soviet Union, and instituted a series of reforms anchored in the notion of 'direct self-management' – an idealistic vision of a society in which all public affairs are run directly by workers and in which all property, including factories, is 'socially owned'. By means of self-management, went the argument, Yugoslav society would steer away from the dangers of excessive bureaucratisation that allegedly plagued the Soviet Union, as well as from the corrupting effects of unbridled economic liberalism supposedly rife in the West, and thereby move towards a more advanced stage of socialism (Rusinow 1977: 47–58). An integral part of these changes was the gradual opening towards the West, and the relaxation of the border regime.

The first signal of changes to come was the signing of the first Udine Agreement in 1949, which opened the doors for limited trade relations with Italy, as well as bringing in an arrangement for those local inhabitants whose land remained on the other side of the new border (Sambri 1970). The 1954 dismemberment of the Free Territory of Trieste – the final patch of the disputed border territory – was another milestone, which brought enough stability for the two countries to introduce further changes to the border regime. Most important from the point of view of everyday life were the special border passes, which could be obtained by all inhabitants residing up to ten kilometres from the border, and initially allowed up to four border crossings per month (Šušmelj 2005). The volume of border transits increased rapidly; by 1958 the total number of transits by Yugoslav holders of special border passes reached 1,431,348 (Sambri 1970: 74, 86). The abolition of the visa regime between the two countries in 1965 prompted another notable increase in transits. Yugoslavs grew increasingly accustomed to shopping trips to Trieste, while Italian tourists flocked to Yugoslav restaurants and seaside resorts.

These changes were accompanied by major shifts in public discourse. Instead of being seen as an 'Iron Curtain', the border that separated Yugoslavia from its capitalist neighbours was increasingly referred to as 'the world's most open border'. In line with the notion of Yugoslavia's privileged position vis-à-vis the rest of the communist-ruled Eastern Europe, it also became common to compare the relative openness of the Italo-Yugoslav border with the more impermeable borders in the Soviet block. The following excerpt from a reportage published in the daily *Novi list* in 1971 provides a telling example of the new border discourse:

> For many of our people, used to what are today the most open borders between the two systems – namely our borders with Italy and Austria – crossing the state border is no longer an extraordinary experience. In contrast, for citizens of many other states, who are still closed off from the world, it represents a huge excitement and an unattainable dream. (*Novi list*, 18 September 1971, p. 4)

The label 'Iron Curtain' returned to public discourse after 1991 and became particularly popular at the point of Slovenia's accession to the EU in 2004, and again in 2007, when the country became part of the Schengen area. At that point, the border with Italy was transformed into an internal EU border and the former border check-points were gradually dismantled. Due to its peculiar history, Nova Gorica became one of the main points of public attention, and media reports in national newspapers and broadcast news were replete with references to 'our small Berlin' and reports about the final disappearance of the 'Iron Curtain' (Širok 2009: 49–58). However, national discourse on the matter was not entirely homogeneous. On both occasions, reports and interviews occasionally acknowledged the peculiarity of the Yugoslav political system, the relative openness of Yugoslavia's western borders, and differences between Berlin and Nova Gorica (e.g. Žerdin 2004; Hladnik-Milharčič 2007). When the then Prime Minister Janez Janša suggested that Slovenia was situated 'behind' the Iron Curtain, members of the opposition and historians objected and argued that such a statement is historically inaccurate and manipulative (RTV Slovenija 2008).

These divergent representations of the border formed part of a broader mnemonic landscape consisting of competing memories of the socialist past. On the one hand, the socialist era was associated with notions of 'brotherhood and unity' among Yugoslav nations and with 'socialism with a human face'; on the other hand, Yugoslavia was seen as a 'dictatorial regime' and 'the prison of nations' (Velikonja 2008: 14). Together with the historically formed layers of meaning and terms attached to the border, these contemporary discourses constituted the specific culture of memory the residents of Nova Gorica were likely to be accustomed with at the time of interviewing. Given this historical and political context, it was feasible to expect that some of the interviewees may object to the use of the term 'Iron Curtain' as an adequate description of their experience with the border, or avoid the term altogether and instead use alternative expressions. To put it differently, their narratives of life at the border should be seen as arguments developed in response to other possible ways of talking about and remembering life at the Italo-Yugoslav border, and the socialist past more generally.

The interview protocol was developed with this specific historical, argumentative and ideological context in mind. Interviewers were told to avoid using potentially controversial terms and metaphors such as 'Iron Curtain', 'totalitarianism' or 'capitalism' and instead instructed to start the conversation with a question aimed at soliciting a narrative about life at the border: 'You have been living here, next to the state border, since [year]. We are interested in the way this immediate proximity has shaped the life of people. How was this in your case? Can you give a short description of your life at the border?' The interviewers were expected to avoid directing or interrupting the narrative, and ask further questions only once the participant appeared to have exhausted his or her life story. The subsequent questions differed depending on whether or not the participant used the term 'Iron Curtain' (or other controversial terms) spontaneously as part of her or his life story. If the term was used, the participant was invited to elaborate further on its meaning and applicability to the past and present. If the term wasn't used, she or he was asked about the familiarity with the term, about its applicability to the

Italo-Yugoslav border, and about its contemporary relevance. If the term was used in the initial narrative, the interviewer oriented to that, probed further into the participant's understanding of the term, and proceeded with questions about its contemporary relevance. The narratives generated by such questioning were thus shaped by the particular course of the conversation, grounded in researcher's interests, but also provide an insight into how participants drew upon the different historically and socially situated ways of talking about the border, and upon diverse ways of remembering socialism.

In the remaining paragraphs, we shall briefly consider two excerpts from two different interviews. The first excerpt is taken from an interview with a local inhabitant who avoided using the term 'Iron Curtain' in his initial biographical narrative and also rejected its applicability when asked about it directly:

Excerpt 1
1 Interviewer: Do you perhaps remember whether you used any
2 particular term for this border here?
3 BG: A particular term? I think I didn't.
4 Interviewer: I mean, did you call it just border, or?
5 BG: No, I really don't know. 'I'm going to Gorica.'
6 Interviewer: I see.
7 BG: To old Gorica. I didn't say that I'm going to Italy. To old
8 Gorica.
9 Interviewer: Earlier you spoke about the fall of the system.
10 BG: Yes, system, yes.
11 Interviewer: Erm, and I'm interested what the term 'Iron Curtain'
12 means to you.
13 BG: Well, I said this already earlier, this is, this is, they were saying,
14 as if it was a thing, an Iron Curtain, and there was a ghost on the
15 other side. That everyone is evil, everyone is corrupted on the other
16 side, but it wasn't like this, was it?
17 Interviewer: Mhm.
18 BG: The Berlin Wall, maybe it really was like this, because there
19 one was, there, there was an enormous difference, wasn't it?
20 Germany and Eastern Germany. There there was Russia, while here
21 there wasn't such a difference. People were always saying, they had,
22 had, had jobs in Italy years ago. And it was much cheaper then, as
23 we could only go down there once a month. We could go more
24 often, but once a month you could bring goods of a certain value up,
25 right? And also, we found a way back then, didn't we? So, if it was
26 necessary, somebody else went instead of me, who didn't need,
27 right? So that it was all right, wasn't it?

28 Interviewer: And/
29 BG: There really was no Iron Curtain.
30 Interviewer: Mhm. And do these terms, for instance Iron Curtain,
31 seem a matter of the past, or also of the present?
32 BG: I think, for me there wasn't one even then, right?
33 Interviewer: Mhm.
34 BG: Uhm, now, I don't know, if there was an Iron Curtain, maybe
35 there was an Iron Curtain for someone from a systemic point of
36 view, I don't know, a way of life, but. Except, except certain, now, I
37 don't know, I didn't have any experience. History says that they did
38 also at this border, if there was something wrong, there was the
39 Yugoslav army, the border guards, who were engaging in some
40 repression at some segments of the border, right? But apart from
41 that, there was no Iron Curtain, I think.
(Interview with Branko Gosar,[1] b. 1961, 30 June 2008)

To support his stance, the interviewee draws on a number of strategies of authentication or legitimation, all of which can be linked to the historical and argumentative context outlined earlier. To start with, he contrasts the Italo-Yugoslav border regime with the Berlin Wall and the border separating Eastern and Western Germany, and suggests that the term Iron Curtain may be applicable there (lines 18–22). To lend credence to his view, he resorts to the widely used strategy of using personal experience (Tunsting et al. 2002, Tileaga 2008) and mentions his ability to cross the border and buy goods in Italy (lines 22–5). Rather than emphasizing the limitations imposed on cross-border movement during socialism, he dwells on the locals' ability to circumvent the rules or bend them to their advantage (lines 25–7). Born in the 1960s, this interviewee grew up accustomed to regular border crossings, and in that sense, his account is grounded in part in his own practical encounters with the border. These encounters, however, gain meaning only in relation to the contrast drawn with East Germany – a strategy that originates in the border discourse outlined earlier, established in the 1970s, and which typically comprised notions of openness, freedom of movement, normality, and the perception of Yugoslavia's western border as 'the world's most open border'.

As the rest of the excerpt shows, the interviewee also acknowledges other possible positions and perceptions of the Italo-Yugoslav border, by mentioning that 'maybe there was an Iron Curtain for someone from a systemic point of view' (lines 35–6) as well as by referring to 'history', which 'says that they did also at this border, if there was something wrong, there was the Yugoslav army, the border guards, who were engaging in some repression at some segments of the border' (lines 37–40). Nonetheless, he defends his own stance by yet again resorting to personal experience, and noting that he did not personally experience anything that could support such alternative views (line 36–7). His account is thus shaped by the historically rooted discourse originating from the socialist period, but also arises from a conversation with competing narratives of more recent origins.

The second excerpt provides a very different recollection of life at the border. In this case, the interviewee did not hesitate to use term 'Iron Curtain' in his earlier narrative, and continued to use it when prompted by the interviewee:

Excerpt 2
1 Interviewer: Well, you called this border 'Iron Curtain' and this
2 label comes from the Cold War period. You, I mean also all the
3 inhabitants of this area, actually lived next-door or opposite to
4 different social order. Do you think this had an impact on you?
5 VB: As I mentioned already earlier, at the beginning. I was
6 probably jumping ahead a bit. There was a certain influence …
7 Yes, being motionless. As I mentioned. Border, the army,
8 proving your identity, this can't be. If you want to move freely,
9 this can't be, or if you want to communicate, this can't be.
10 Already the fact that you had to show a document at the border
11 and that you had to prove with this document that you haven't
12 used your quota in the previous month, these concessions, which
13 you could bring a kilo of coffee or anything else, was a kind of
14 obstacle. And then this feeling, that you can never go across
15 freely, even if that border was only twenty metres away, and
16 even when you came to the other side it was still. You had the
17 border pass in your pocket; you weren't an inhabitant of the
18 Gorizia region on this side. It was a particular feeling, which
19 always arose in you when you crossed the border and then when
20 you came back. 'What do you have, why this much, why not',
21 'you already used this, take this back' and so on. These were …
22 Unpleasant feelings.
23 Interviewer: Earlier it was very interesting, you mentioned river,
24 or rather a river with crocodiles and the Army as a barrier you
25 mentioned now also the Iron Curtain, the border passes, and we
26 also talked a bit about these differences, capitalism on the one
27 side and Yugoslavia, a socialist republic, on the other side. Do
28 these expressions, these labels seem to you a matter of the past or
29 do they still have their meaning today, their relevance?
30 VB: No, if I look at it in this way, they are a thing of the past.
31 That's how it seems to me, the first impression. Because it really
32 was. It was represented in this way and also executed in this

33 way. This was unfortunately the system that was alive then
34 and you can't ignore it. You can keep persuading yourself that
35 it wasn't like this, but it was. If you went across the border, for
36 instance, and didn't have anything with you, it was already
37 suspicious. They would check you. If you had something,
38 then it wasn't right either, because you had something.
[*Laughs.*]
39 Interviewer: Nothing was good.
40 VB: Nothing was good. Well, I mean, I don't talk only about
41 negative things, because it wasn't all black. After all, we lived,
42 we lived, in Gorizia they lived, and in Trieste they lived. The
43 border was only a factor between, which both tried to use to
44 their advantage, on both sides, and all of this was happening at
45 the border.
             (Interview with Vlado Brajkovič, b. 1960, 30 June 2008)

As in the previous excerpt, we encounter the use of personal experience for the purpose of authentication, and again, the focus is on personal experiences of crossing the border. It is important to note that this interviewee belongs to the same generation as the one encountered earlier, and his account relates to the same historical period and to the same border procedures and rules, which involved the use of special border passes and limitations on the number of visits and value of goods bought in Italy. However, the interviewer's take on these experiences is rather different from the one encountered in Excerpt 1. Instead of focusing on the locals' ability to circumvent rules and enjoy the (albeit limited) opportunities for crossing the border, he associates these experiences with 'being motionless' (line 7), obstacles to free movement (lines 8–9), lack of freedom (lines 14–16) and 'unpleasant feelings' (line 22). Further on, he also insists that '[y]ou can keep persuading yourself that it wasn't like this, but it was' (line 34–5), thereby implicitly acknowledging – and dismissing – the alternative stance, which disputes the relevance of the term Iron Curtain for the local experience of the border. In short, the two excerpts demonstrate how the same historical realities can serve as the basis of markedly different vernacular memories.

Note, however, how the interviewee instantly modifies his attitude in response to the interviewer's comment towards the end of the excerpt. Instead of sticking to the neutral 'mhm' as the interviewer in the previous excerpt did, this interviewer responds to the rather negative account of life at the border by commenting: 'Nothing was good' (line 40). This prompts the interviewee to qualify his earlier description by saying that 'it wasn't all black' (line 41) and even mentioning that inhabitants on both sides tried to use the border to their own advantage (lines 44–5). With this turn, his narrative of the border comes remarkably close to the more positive account seen in Excerpt 1. This is a telling example of the argumentative and context-bound nature of memory, and shows how attitudes and recollections of the past generated in interviews can be influenced by the course of the interview conversation.

SOME ANALYTICAL AND ETHICAL IMPLICATIONS

Already these two brief excerpts demonstrate the plural and dynamic nature of vernacular memory, and the full range of interviews conducted in Nova Gorica reveals a much wider range of possible ways of engaging with the socialist past. It is tempting to suggest that this plurality and flexibility sets vernacular memories apart from the rigidity and uniformity of official, nation-level representations of the past, and see the two layers of public memory in dichotomous terms. From this perspective, the two contrasting recollections of life at the Italo-Yugoslav border could be interpreted as embodiments of two divergent vernacular ways of remembering the border and life under socialism – one that accepts the official, largely negative representations of the socialist past, and agrees with the perception of the Italo-Yugoslav border as an 'Iron Curtain', and the other that proposes an 'alternative', more positive perspective, and emphasises Yugoslavia's openness to the West.

Such a dichotomous reading of the nature of vernacular memory and its relationship with official memory emerges also in Daphne Berdhal's (1999) study of memory and identity in the former East German border village of Kella, as well as in John Bodnar's (1992) classic discussion of American public memory. According to Bodnar, official cultural expressions lack complexity and ambiguity, and originate in the concerns of cultural authorities who 'share a common interest in social unity, the continuity of existing institutions, and loyalty to the status quo' (ibid.: 13). In contrast, vernacular culture 'represents an array of specialised interests', which are 'diverse' and 'changing' and 'can even clash with one another'. The very existence of vernacular culture, argues Bodnar, 'threatens the sacred and timeless nature of official expressions' (ibid.: 14). In a similar vein, Berdhal (1999: 206–25) shows how the local acts of remembering and forgetting in Kella departed from the blanket discrediting of the socialist past imposed at national level, and refused to remember the former East–West German border solely in terms of suffering.

Yet, as other studies have shown, vernacular memories are not necessarily opposed to official ones. Rather, there are several possible ways for vernacular and official memories to interact – sometimes they are openly opposed, in other instances they might mirror each other (Corney 1998; Rowe et al. 2002). Likewise, it would be misleading to think of official memory as uniform and vernacular memory as plural. Rather than agreeing on one single official version of the past, political elites often disagree on which past events are worth remembering, what they mean, and how they should be commemorated (Olick 1998; Forest et al. 2004). Post-socialist elites are a case in point; the dominant tendency may well point in the direction of damning the communist past, yet this does not mean that negative representations are the only ones available in the public domain. As demonstrated earlier, the national public realm in Slovenia was indeed dominated by references to the 'fall of the Iron Curtain', yet at the same time, several politicians and intellectuals also contested the use of the term and its applicability to Yugoslavia's western borders. To put it differently, Bodnar is correct in stating that public memory is 'an argument about the interpretation of reality' (1992: 14), but this is an argument that takes place at both vernacular and public levels, both in everyday conversations and in large-scale public exchanges about the past. The suggested methodological approach to interviewing provides us with a means of exploring this double conversation.

Apart from its analytical gains, this approach to interviewing also has ethical implications. Memories of socialism remain deeply contested and as researchers we can find it difficult to divest ourselves of our own political convictions, ideological preferences and, indeed, memories. It is not surprising that much of the research on post-socialist memory is normative in nature, designed as an intervention with direct political and cultural consequences rather than as a reflexive practice aimed primarily at understanding. For instance, the collection of oral testimonies in post-socialist Central and Eastern Europe is often aimed at giving voice to particular kinds of memories – those reflecting expriences and facts that remained marginalised or suppressed – and ultimately at teaching post-socialist citizens to remember the communist past in appropriate ways (Mark 2010: xxi–xxiv). No scholarly endeavour can extricate itself entirely from the political contests over its object of research; already the very choice of a controversial research topic entails a form of political statement, at the very least in the sense of affirming the status of the chosen topic as a problem worth scholarly treatment. It is also true that, in some circumstances, a normative approach is necessary and appropriate. Nonetheless, it is importat to navigate through the research process in a reflexive manner and endeavour to separate understanding from judgement. Approaching interview materials in the way suggested here enables us to do so, by forcing us to look closely at how our own assumptions are embedded in the choice, wording and arrangement of questions, and by digging into the layers of both historically constituted and contemporary arguments about the past in the particular context we are examining.

SUMMARY: KEY POINTS

- The first part of the chapter discussed the strengths and weaknesses of qualitative interviewing and its suitability for the purpose of researching the dynamics of public memory at a vernacular level.
- The debate surrounding another type of qualitative data – namely, naturally occurring conversations – was examined, along with its relative advantages and disadvantages compared to interviewing.
- Even when interviews are the best choice, it is important to acknowledge their interactional nature. Interview recollections of the past should be treated as products of a double-layered conversation: on the one hand, the actual exchanges between the interviewer and the interviewee; and on the other hand, the broader 'conversation' with alternative ways of talking about the past circulating in a specific political, social and historical context.
- To demonstrate how this approach might work in practice, the second part of the chapter considered examples drawn from interview materials collected in the Slovenian town of Nova Gorica, situated at the Italo-Slovenian border.
- The concluding section considers the ethical implications of the proposed approach and reflects on what it offers to our understanding of national and public memory more generally.

FURTHER READING

For the original formulation of the distinction between vernacular and official memory see, John Bodnar's *Remaking America: Public Memory, Commemoration, and Patriotism in the Twentieth Century* (1992). A critical account of interviewing from a conversation analytical perspective is provided by Jonathan Potter and Alexa Hepburn in an article published in *Qualitative Research in Psychology* (2005), while Kathryn Roulston's article, published in *Qualitative Research* (2006), offers a useful review of ethnometodological and conversation analytic studies of interview data. For a recent interview-based study of post-socialist memory, see James Mark's *The Unfinished Revolution: Making Sense of the Communist Past in East-Central Europe* (2010).

ACKNOWLEDGEMENTS

The interview materials presented in this chapter were collected in the framework of the project *Border Communities: Microstudies of Everyday Life, Politics and Memory in European Societies from 1945 to the Present*, based at the Ludwig Boltzmann Institute for European History and Public Spheres, Vienna, Austria. Thanks to Cristian Tileagă and Jovan Byford for their comments on an earlier version of this chapter.

NOTE

1. All names used are pseudonyms.

SECTION THREE

Media and Memory

CHAPTER 5

Televised Remembering

Ann Gray

In his introduction to the edited collection, *Television Histories: Shaping Collective Memory in the Media Age,* Gary R. Edgerton tells us his 'first and most basic assumption is that television is the principal means by which most people learn about history today' (Edgerton 2001: 1). For this reason Edgerton frames his book with the concept of 'television as historian' to the extent that it is through fictional and non-fictional portrayals of the past that millions of viewers form ideas about historical figures and events. Television, then, plays an important role in representing the past for its viewers, and in doing so is a major agent in the production of national and social memory; thus, developing methods for investigating and analysing this phenomenon is an important activity for those interested in the significance of memory in contemporary societies. Furthermore, in the period since 1995, televisions factual output has shown evidence of a 'history boom'. As Erin Bell and I have discussed elsewhere, history on television takes many forms and crosses a range of programme genres (Gray and Bell 2013), but I will focus in this chapter on examples of those programme genres and hybrid genres that seek to commemorate what are considered to be important events in a nation's past. In general, these include programmes that coincide with and celebrate the anniversaries of such events, and which can be understood as 'historical event' television. Broadcasters themselves often refer to them as 'landmark' programmes that have high production values and, depending on the significance of the anniversary, include seasons of programmes across the schedules. In addition, and by contrast, broadcasters use the 'hook' of anniversaries to produce material which otherwise would not have made it through the commissioning process and onto the screen.

Television has undergone significant change in the last decade, largely due to the development of digital technologies resulting in the emergence of a multi-channel environment. This has led to the fragmentation of audiences, exerting pressures of competition on terrestrial broadcasters and networks, noted especially in the UK and US. However, while audience share for terrestrial channels has certainly decreased since the days of limited channel availability, there is evidence that terrestrial broadcasters, particularly in the UK, can still command significant viewing figures, especially for 'historical event' television.

Scholars have noted the increased interest in the past and have variously attributed this to, for example, the millennium, with its associated feelings of looking back and assessing where 'we' are as well as where 'we' are going, actual political changes in, for example, Europe and, in the UK, the move towards devolution. Many have noted that these developments also raise questions of identity at national and personal levels, answers to which are often sought through investigations of the past. Pierre Nora, for example, expresses these developments as evidence of an upsurge in memory in what he calls 'the age of commemoration' which he argues is in part due to the acceleration of history in that the characteristic of the modern world has shifted from continuity and permanence to change (Nora 2002). This results in a swiftly retreating past. Nora suggests that this leads to a desire, even a necessity, to 'stockpile' the past and endows a 'duty to remember' on nations and individuals.

Andreas Huyssen has also noted this history and associated memory boom and especially the role of the media in enabling the reproduction and representation of the past: 'The past has become part of the present in ways simply unimaginable in earlier centuries' (Huyssen 2003: 1). Huyssen draws our attention to the voracious nature of forms of representation in trawling the past for evocative and powerful content which, in the age of multiple channels and platforms, has become a valuable commodity. Huyssen also notes changes in the function of history in producing historical memory in that the boundary between past and present is much more malleable than before. For Huyssen, representation of the past 'used to mark the relation of a community or a nation to its past', whereas now, many versions of the past and many known or, until recently, unknown stories and events of the past reach the airwaves and circulate across public discourse in a much less fixed and stable way. These developments present challenges to national broadcasters in their choices of what versions of the past should be presented, how commemoration should be visualised, and which conventions and codes of television programming serve best to achieve this. For the memory studies researcher questions are raised, such as how do these programmes with their high production values, heavily marketed and supported by materials across platforms, construct public memory for their audiences. In addition, what is being remembered ([in terms of] periods, subjects, topics and events), and how ([in terms of] programme styles, formats and modes of address) are therefore important questions to ask of these genres of programmes. Further, does the commemoration of events through television stabilise the past in relation to the nation, or are there ways in which the past narratives are troubled and disturbed? This could be seen, for example, in the telling of hitherto unknown stories, giving voice to actors and agents who provide different or challenging accounts, or in presenting versions of the past from a number of perspectives. In the case of commemoration of war, this would include accounts from behind 'enemy' lines so that the story is not told only from 'our' (national) perspective.

However, it is important to be wary of treating these texts as free-floating cultural artefacts and to consider them rather as products of a major component of the creative industries. They are produced, made and crafted within organisations, whether they are large broadcasting institutions or small independent production companies. These organisations are shaped by regulation, professional codes and conventions that are developed, maintained and sustained in the main through working practice. Consideration of these dimensions of the creative production of any specific television output is critical to our understanding of the nature and characteristics of the programme itself. For example, its marketing, promotion and positioning in the schedules, its significance in terms of public and critical reception, and its importance to the reputation of the broadcasting institutions and production companies themselves. These products then have industrial, cultural and political salience in that they are a highly significant part of broadcasting output, as well as providing a notable contribution to the circulation of public knowledge about the past. We can formulate these organisations as complex organisms of 'memory making' and, as we have seen from other essays in this collection, the memories constructed are social, national and personal. Questions then emerge about how the layers of memory are constructed at institutional, professional and textual levels. In addition to paying attention to the industries and their products, we must also be mindful of how television is consumed. Apart from exceptional circumstances, this is still likely to be in a domestic setting and as part of and alongside the routines of everyday life. Our viewing habits and patterns over a lifetime provide us with memories of growing up with particular and often loved (or loathed) programmes and personalities, but also of watching 'significant' events with our family. This provides what Bourdon refers to as the 'two major frames of memory', the nation and the family that, I would argue, through television overlap and coalesce in powerful ways (Bourdon 2003). Thus the representations of a nation's past on screen can best be thought of as a palimpsest, a memoryscape that is layered through its production, its style and aesthetic, and its reception. Drawing on methods developed within media studies, this requires a multi-layered set of research strategies, and I propose that there are a number of levels of analysis through which we can pose the key research question of what mnemonic signifiers are included in each programme and why and, further, how might they engage the viewer. The layers, although intricately connected, can be best understood for analytical purposes as 'sites of investigation' and those I will categorise as: institutional; professional; textual; reception. The activities within each site mediate, shape and construct national, family and personal memories through the cultural artefact. None of the sites is neutral, and in framing our exploration of them it is helpful to think of each site as having its own 'logics', a set of imperatives, which to a greater or lesser degree influence its practice and outcomes. As Zelizer reminds us the process of shaping collective memory is not linear or necessarily rational 'but dynamic and contingent' (Zelizer 1995: 221).

Examples of the 'logics' or 'imperatives' that provide the frameworks for each 'site' are:

Institutional: organisational structures; responsibility and accountability to regulators, for example, for programme standards; commercial imperatives to, for example, shareholders and advertisers; consideration of publics, audiences and markets; financial and economic constraints.
Professional: professional codes; social relations; custom and practice (memory); genres and programme types; target audience and professional perceptions of audience.
Textual: genre, sub-genre and hybrid; formats; techniques and conventions; narrative, character and style; music, lighting, camera techniques; presenters, actors, narrators; mnemonics: archive footage, still images, documents, architecture, witnesses.
Reception: social audience, bringing to the viewing engagement: existing knowledge, based on textual or lived experience; memory banks; identity; viewing memories.

In order to flesh out the proposed 'sites' I have selected two examples as 'case studies' in which I outline the key characteristics of each in order to tease out the 'mechanisms' of memory construction. They represent different kinds of commemorative programming and television output and, at points, I introduce some findings of my recent research into history on television.[1] The first is the 'landmark' documentary *D-Day 6.6.1944* (BBC 1, 6 June 2004);[2] the second is *Empire's Children* (Channel 4, 2007), broadcast as part of the sixtieth anniversary of the independence of India and Pakistan. I will then turn to a discussion of the particular methods best suited to explorations of the different sites.

CASE STUDY 1: *D-DAY 6.6.1944* (BBC 1, 6 JUNE 2004)

This was a high-profile historical event programme that was the centerpiece of the BBC's commemoration of the sixtieth anniversary of the allied landings in France in 1944.[3] It ran for two hours from 8pm on 6 June 2004 and employed innovative techniques of drama documentary. James Chapman suggests that this programme and others in the commemorative season, *Dunkirk* and *Blitz*, broke new ground in aesthetic modes of television history programming in their combination of dramatic reconstruction, archive, testimony and computer generated imagery (CGI) which were produced in cinematic mode with high-production values (Chapman 2007). Taking this programme as an exemplar of the production of national memory, I will now address each site of investigation.

Institutional Imperatives – the BBC

As an institution funded by the licence fee established by the prevailing government the BBC must steer a careful course to ensure its continued presence by demonstrating its value as the public service broadcaster. The BBC has obligations to the nation and its sense of national identity through commemoration or 'memorialisation' that places a high level of responsibility on the commissioners and producers for such programmes. Therefore institutional reputations ride on the successful, or otherwise, coverage of such national events. The public, the press and other interested parties have strong, often conflicting, views about what are appropriate forms of representation of such significant events. The BBC Charter is renewed every ten years, and the 2004 memorial season coincided with a difficult period for the BBC when the results of Lord Hutton's enquiry into the death of Dr David Kelly concluded that there had been serious defects in the Corporation's processes and procedures (Hutton 2004). This led to the resignations in January 2004 of the Director General and Chairman of the Board of Governors. The then Culture Secretary, Tessa Jowell, was quoted as saying that 'the Hutton Report would be taken into account in the 2006 review of the BBC's Charter'. Although caution must be exercised when making direct links to institutional vicissitudes and programming strategy, it is nevertheless useful background within which to locate the commissioning of high-profile quality event television that indubitably fulfils the public service remit. In addition to this, as James Bennett has pointed out, a striking feature of the commemorative programming in this season was its 360° delivery across different platforms accessed through iTV. This included *The People's War* website, of relevance to the suite of programmes in the commemorative season, which invited viewers to put their experiences on the site exhorting that, 'Your memories are part of our history', and specific applications linked to *D-Day* providing, for example, the contextualisation of the events of D-Day in 'real time' and the 'back story' of the characters appearing in the programme. In an interview with James Bennett, Mark Goodchild (BBC Senior Executive Interactive Producer), clearly states the institutional role as memory agent:

> D-Day was ultimate public service. On the television level, we were addressing the nation . . . At the iTV level, we were dealing with the personal and emotional level . . . The Internet was . . . sort of an archiving process. Here it was about capturing the stories for the future, building collective knowledge. (Bennett 2008: 289)

Bennett suggests that the audience demographic for these programmes would coincide with those least digitally familiar, i.e. older and within living memory of the war, or of a generation whose parents lived through the war. Audiences could access digital spaces through the more familiar television fare, and the persuasive and potentially powerful content of the programmes would encourage this 'target' audience to engage in 'digital Britain'.

Finance and Funding

For a large project such as *D-Day 6.6.1944* co-production funding was of critical importance and had consequences for its scope. *D-Day 6.6.1944* was a co-production between BBC, Dangerous Films, the Discovery Channel, ProSieben (Germany), France Deux and TelFrance. This form of financing reflects wider industry patterns and, as Doris Baltruschat notes, such co-productions are likely to be 'popular genres, often simulating Hollywood productions, such as . . . shows that contain hybrid elements drawn from a variety of genre' (Baltruschat 2002). This emphasis on the popular is important in order to attract the largest possible audiences, and the national base of the co-funders will also be reflected in the content, casting and locations of the filming. This was critical in this case as the narrative was not cast from one nation's perspective, but encompassed the forces of British, German, French and the United States.[4] For example, the US audiences were appealed to by reference to the memoirs of General Eisenhower and the US-based *Time Life* photographer Robert Capa who 'covered' the landings on Omaha beach. Both characters appear in the dramatisation and, along with a previously 'unknown' soldier, provide a US perspective. However, in addition to the US audience appeal, 'Eisenhower' furnished information about the Allied Forces strategy, and 'Capa' the eyewitness 'recording' and visual documentation of the landings, thus providing the broader military and strategic context of the event and, by implication, some of the 'raw' evidence upon which subsequent media memories have been based.

Professional Imperatives

Doing history on television differs to greater or lesser degrees from the written form adopted by historians. Most obviously this involves images, but television has its own programme logics that are brought to bear on the production of all television, including programmes about the past.

Professional Codes

Television producers insist that the basis for 'good television' is a combination of striking visuals, strong narrative and compelling characters. This rubric is applied to history programming. These views are driven by assumptions about the audience and the need for television to engage viewers immediately and to maintain their interest. Television must strive for viewer attention against many diversions within the domestic setting, not to mention the competition from other channels should programmes fail to make an immediate impact. The narrative must therefore be capable of keeping the audience and offer up tension as well as pleasure, and the desire to see what happens next. These are aspects of viewer engagement that are more usually associated with fictional genres. Television has evolved its own dominant modes of address, and one of these which is powerful and effective on the small screen is that of the 'talking head' which, in history programming terms, is represented either by 'experts' on the period or events or, and more significantly for our purposes here, the eye-witness account of those events. Witness testimony from those who lived through events and who experienced them 'first hand' is a powerful, pervasive and affective form of television. These elements must be clearly shown in the beginning of the realisation of a history programme. Nowhere is this more important than at the commissioning stage.

Commissioning

The first hurdle in the production of any television programme is to obtain the commission. How do major programmes, such as the one under consideration here, come to be commissioned? The commissioning editors of history programmes on terrestrial and satellite channels are key agents in mediating the production of memory, and as such are also the gatekeepers of memory. Many producers I spoke to during my research into history programmes on television described commissioning as a 'mysterious' process, often quite informal, and largely driven by the needs of the broadcasters which can be related to the kinds of institutional needs referred to above, or to the need to attract a specific audience or expand existing audiences.[5] For *D-Day*, the BBC commissioned Dangerous Films, a company founded that year, as their first production. Given that this was to be a high-profile, big budget two-hour programme, forming the centrepiece of the sixtieth anniversary season and broadcast at prime-time on the actual anniversary, this would appear to be a high-risk commission. However, Richard Dale, who was the Director and Executive Producer [of Dangerous Films] had, since his graduation from Cambridge University, worked for 16 years at the BBC where he had researched science documentaries and then, in his words, been given a big opportunity to direct the 'landmark' seven-part series *The Human Body* (BBC1 1998) presented by Sir Robert Winston. This was enormously successful, and Dale then took the opportunity to move into drama, creating and producing the first series of *Teachers* for Channel 4. He then decided to return to documentary and had ambitions to produce something on a large scale for the BBC. He told me in an interview:

> I thought I had a new set of skills to bring to it with drama, with drama director's skills and I had big ambitions so I decided that we could do it by using many of the same people at the BBC who were leaving and the BBC was changing. (Interview 12 March 2009)

Dale set up Dangerous Films with former BBC colleagues, Tim Goodchild and Peter Parnham. Thus the BBC co-produced *D-Day* with Dale's new company. This is an example of the working relationships and reputations that are a critical part of the commissioning process. When interviewed, Dale noted the desire of the BBC to reach a wide audience with this programme and described his vision about the different modes of history.

> I chose to make it with drama, with interviews and with archive as a collage, not attempting to make it clear at any point what was what – of course the audience is very astute they know exactly what's what – but attempt to kind of reconcile these different points of view and different frames of reference that happen in big events that people from different sides come to it with precisely the same motivations and yet are diametrically opposed. (Interview 12 March 2009)

Textual Imperatives

For *D-Day*, Dale's 'collage of different looks and feels' was achieved by shooting on different cameras, and CGI was used to great effect in the re-enactment of the Omaha landing, filmed on Saunton Sands in the UK. James Chapman describes the combination of these elements as a radical use of testimony, reconstruction and archive in which each mode 'bleeds' into the other without breaks or explanations in order to maintain the powerful and cinematic effect of the television production.

The use of archive footage is common in history programmes dealing with modern history. The archive film is itself, of course, a product of its time, and cannot be regarded as 'raw' documentation of what actually happened. Michael Chanan reminds us of the importance of asking questions of the archive, such as where does it come from, and for whom and by whom was it produced. Chanan further usefully states that 'the historical documentary [which] in order to be made must become a work of memory which renders its excavation public' (Chanan 2007). In *D-Day*, Dale played fast and loose with the use of archive, subordinating its 'authenticity' and source to the demands of the seamless narrative. This is anathema to historians and does raise ethical questions about the use of given footage, its framing, and the status accorded it within the text. However, James Chapman agrees with Dale when he suggests that, although no actual distinction is made between actual footage and reconstruction, 'the differences between actuality and reconstruction are quite obvious to all but the most untrained eye' (2007: 22). This is in part helped by the fact that the archive film is in black and white and the reconstruction in colour. To seek a further explanation for this amalgamation of actuality and reconstruction we could follow Mjøs in noting the 'blockbuster logic within factual television' of much co-produced material, which echoes Baltruschat's points above (Mjøs 2011: 186). Dale justifies his aesthetic decisions by resorting to the notion that for audiences of history 'a television programme is not the last word but the first word and should . . . inspire the viewer to explore further' (Interview 12 March 2009).

The testimonies are gathered from eyewitnesses of British, US, German and French soldiers and, in the French case, a civilian, who are also portrayed by actors in the reconstruction scenes. Their testimony includes relatively long silences, and a number of participants reflect movingly on their memories of the day and their sense of loss of comrades. Dale told me:

> I wanted you to see these people and to feel that they are pouring their heart out to you as if you are the only person in the world . . . can you imagine where they are in their heads to be able to ignore the filming process? So for me that was a part of what I was trying to say about their lived experience. (Interview 12 March 2009)

These layers of witnessing and reflection add depth as well as different perspectives on the event. The combination of documentary and fictional strategies produces a strong mixture of 'reality' and desire, emotion and affect, combining to produce powerful constructions of memory. These strategies are arguably peculiar to television. Indeed, the aesthetic freedom of the television film to combine all of these elements should be acknowledged. This is especially the case in the use of eyewitness and other forms of testimony in combination with reconstruction and archive film. The eyewitness and other accounts are also combined with the still image, while past and present perspectives are woven together. In this way the viewer is drawn in to the memories recounted by the veterans, 'seeing' them as they must have been at the time. The images and the often harrowing and hesitant accounts of the witnesses offer powerful forms of identification and empathy for the viewer – perhaps achieving Dale's aims of giving a sense of what it must have been like to have been there.

In addition to the 'unknown' soldiers, airmen and navy involved in the event, powerful figures from the administrations are also characters within the reconstruction. In this way the more 'public' narrative, and certainly the strategies and decisions behind the 'events', are presented, encouraging the audience to reflect on how these things, along with blunders, errors and deadly risks, come into being.

Reception Imperatives

While audience research has, at times, been a dominant feature of television studies, it is notoriously difficult to gather data of sufficient depth and quality which has the potential to answer questions about meaning in general and, by extension, the role of memory in the viewing process. However, some studies have contributed to our knowledge and understanding of the place of television in everyday life by attending to the actual programmes viewed (for example, Morley 1986; Gillespie 1995; Mankekar 1999), while others have worked with oral testimony which recalls memories of television itself (O'Sullivan 1991). I will therefore briefly indicate some ways of approaching research into this part of the circulation of memory.

As Roger Smither observes, 'history documentaries based around oral testimony often resonate in the memories of a large part of the audience, and with the family tradition of most of the rest of it . . . history on screen reacts with the workings of memory and tradition within the watching audience' (Smither 2004: 61). This is a useful starting point from which we can draw on more conceptual work within memory studies as a basis for further research. Scholars have referred to the media as constructing 'secondary memory', or what Pierre Nora describes as prosthesis-memory. Alison Landsberg, in her work on cinema, takes up this notion and has developed the idea of 'prosthetic memory' whereby mnemonic cultural artefacts such as film, museums and, we could add, television programmes, can 'create shared social frameworks for people who inhabit, literally and figuratively, different social spaces, practices, and beliefs' (Landsberg 2004: 8). While accepting this, we could, in relation to more nationally focused representations, look to generational links to the past which, along with television viewing, has been part of familial or community knowledge. This knowledge of the past, and the desire to find links to it, intensifies with age and generational progression. As John Crace, writing in *The Guardian* on documentaries about the Second World War said: 'the further away it all gets, the more personal it increasingly becomes'. The loss of parents – the generation who fought and lived through the war which shaped their lives, and therefore indirectly our lives, 'keeps us close' (Crace 2012). Similarly, Michael Chanan found himself searching for a sight of his maternal grandparents, whose appearance he knows only from family photographs, while watching 16mm archive footage of the Warsaw Ghetto at an academic conference and seeing those images in a way she [the speaker] has not allowed for. His reaction is, as he describes it, 'both interrogative and emotional', and this confirms for him that 'a reading of the images depends on the position of the viewer', not just in physical terms, but 'the viewer's disposition ... external knowledges and personal memories' (2007: 267).

While these observations are anecdotal, for me they carry a certain power in relating a deep experience which is hard to pin down to more conventional understandings of the meanings we take from cultural artefacts. Listening to and watching the witnesses of the D-Day Landings gives viewers an insight into what it must have been like to be there, but also what it must be like to have lived with those memories. An exploration of the interplay of memory, imagination and desire triggered by such programmes would be an important addition to our knowledge of the construction of memory, but should not be embarked upon lightly. Such an exploration, with actual viewers, requires extreme sensitivity, understanding and respect abiding by a strong ethical code of practice, to which we will return.

CASE STUDY 2: *EMPIRE'S CHILDREN*

For the sixtieth anniversary of the independence of India and Pakistan, Channel 4 offered *Empire's Children*, produced by Wall to Wall, transmission of which began in the month before the anniversary. In a similar vein to Wall to Wall's hugely successful celebrity genealogy series on BBC 1, *Who do you think you are? (WDYTYA?)*, it followed a number of celebrities on their journeys across parts of the former British Empire, and by inference back in time, in order to discover more about their family history and, more broadly, British identity. Using the quest narrative form apparent in *WDYTYA?* the series went beyond India and Pakistan and used the anniversary to consider questions of the British imperial legacy.

Institutional Imperatives: Channel 4

Part of Channel 4's original remit at its launch in 1982 was to produce innovative programming, and although the channel has gone through changes since its inception it retains that ethos, as Ralph Lee, Commissioner of Factual Programmes explained during an interview with regard to history programmes:

> At C4 we are obsessed with originality. It is kind of one of our absolute credos – we are only going to survive if we are going to surprise people. Some people misinterpret C4 and think the BBC does the big subjects and C4 does the small subjects. I think that's rather wrong-headed. We shouldn't just consider ourselves shining a light on the dark little corners of history – we should be doing big history but from different points of view. (Interview 26 March 2009)

Lee had spoken admiringly about *Who Do You Think You Are?* and its ability to capture large audiences, and then talked to me specifically about *Empire's Children*

> Doing a series like Empire's Children was to try to make people think differently about both Empire and the end of Empire and modern multi-cultural Britain and identity today and try to use an idiom that may surprise them – through biographies of people whose personal family stories were tied up in Empire and its dismantlement – doing it that way and that's a very big mainstream subject but I was trying to encourage them to think about it differently. (Interview 26 March 2009)

Thus, Channel 4 took a well-established format from BBC1, giving it the Channel 4 ethos and making a contribution to the sixtieth anniversary.

Professional Imperatives

The format of the genealogy programme has provided broadcasters with a tried and tested format that has been disseminated worldwide. By drawing upon an already popular hobby, Alex Graham, Wall to Wall's Chief Executive Officer, successfully merged existing public interest in family history with insights into celebrity lives. The increasing importance of celebrities to television networks has been noted (Bennett and Holmes 2010) and history programming has certainly not been immune to this pressure. Programmes such as *Who Do You Think You Are?* and *Empire's Children* have further expanded the interest in, and popularity of, television personalities ranging from, for example, news readers, comedians, actors, television and radio presenters, chat show hosts and chefs. Amy Holdsworth notes how the series represents memory and memory work, particularly through the use of family photographs, as well as searching through the public archive for one's antecedents (Holdsworth 2010). The particular power of this format, according to Holdsworth, is its reliance on 'memory' as what she describes as a 'softening' of history. Although it combines elements of social and cultural history through the use of archives and other forms of explanation, there is a blurring of the documentary and personal narrative – a process which Holdsworth describes as 'domestication'.

Textual Imperatives

Within the *WDYTYA?* format there are occasions when uncomfortable or 'risky' stories are unearthed in the process of genealogical research. The celebrity is taken back to places associated with their family in search, as it were, for their roots. In the main, however, what is discovered can be surprising and also moving.

Perhaps because of the more focused topic, the controversial aspects of British imperial history were drawn out in several episodes of *Empire's Children*. For example, comedian Jenny Eclair sought to find out more about her childhood in Malaysia, and her father's role in the oppression of Chinese communist 'bandits' in the 1940s and 1950s.[6] In the programme, Eclair is confronted by an ethnic Chinese man whose father had been executed by the British for his communist activities. The two descendents had completely different received (family, and in Eclair's case, national) memories of the past, and the programme format shaped and revealed this confrontation at a national, familial and personal level. In this example we can see the emergence of a memory that has been suppressed or silenced in the past family history and the uncomfortable encounter with a different version of the past. This challenges the certainty of memory and the role played by Eclair's father in the Empire, which Eclair found hard to accept. This, and other episodes in the series, relied on the narrative of a journey in search of the 'truth' that is 'revealed' in the climax of the episode. The 'reveal' is a familiar trope of popular factual television and is reflected within this history genre.

Reception

The *Who Do You Think You Are?* format on BBC1, the corporation's main channel, attracts a regular four to six million viewers per episode, and while audience figures alone do not provide sufficient evidence of engagement with programmes, we can tentatively conclude that the format has contributed to the expansion of interest in genealogy, belonging and 'search for identity'. This is evidenced in the further expansion of online genealogical research sites, the successful BBC magazine *Who Do You Think You Are?* and, from the producer's point of view, the recommissioning of a tenth series. In addition to exploring this further within the social and cultural context of genealogical practices, another approach might be to ask what viewers take from individual episodes. For example, this could be framed within a dichotomy of the 'personal narrative' of the celebrity and the 'public narrative(s)' of the historical context included, along with the actual process of researching a family tree.

CONCLUSION: THE CIRCUIT OF TELEVISED MEMORY

I have argued in this chapter for the importance of adopting a holistic approach to the analysis of televisual memory construction. Each site of investigation requires its own specific set of methods, the combinations of which will, of course, depend on what the overriding research question is and what kind of research data is required. In addition, ethical dimensions of the proposed research should be considered before approaching any fieldwork. Inviting groups or individuals to engage in any kind of 'memory work' calls for scrupulous sensitivity on the part of the researcher. This is obviously important in relation to engagement with the audiences for these programmes, but also in any encounters with professionals in exploring their working practices. As in all forms of social research we must take responsibility for our actions and methods and approach our subjects of study as participants in our research and not as 'objects' to be investigated, being open about the aims of research and honoring requests for confidentiality.

Sources of data – institutional

This part of the analysis produces the broader context within which programmes are commissioned, made and consumed. The regulatory frameworks of broadcasting institutions, their sources of income and the internal structures of the organisations provide invaluable insights into the frameworks and key actors responsible for decision making, ensuring programme quality and delivering programmes that have salience for their intended audiences. It is important to consider this information not simply as the backdrop against which the action takes place, but rather as the important constitutive context of the production of memory. Sources for the gathering of this data are: government policy documents; regulatory reports, e.g. from Ofcom;[7] press reports; BBC public statements. Economic structures of the BBC and other broadcasters should be explored, including co-production partnerships and practices. Secondary sources on media structures, economics and global connections should also be consulted.

Sources of data – professional

Studies of production have, until recently, been largely absent from media studies. Two exceptions are Georgina Born and John T. Caldwell who carried out ethnographic research into television and film industries respectively, and this mode of production study, although time-consuming and expensive, is certainly one method which could be adopted (Born 2004; Caldwell 2008). However, other more manageable methods of exploring these professional values include close reading of 'trade' publications – that is, reading for implicit assumptions – naturalised approaches, and views about what makes 'successful television'. Another strategy, and one also adopted by Caldwell, is to attend, if possible, professional media gatherings such as the annual History Producers'[8] conference, or documentary festivals, for example the one held annually in Sheffield[9] which brings together documentary producers and scholars. With an ethnographic eye these social professional events reveal much about the professional ethos, practice and ways of working within this part of the television industry. One of the most productive methods for this purpose is the one-to-one interview with media professionals and one that, if you are clear about your aims, commissioners, producers and researchers are often happy to provide. As is the case with all interviews conducted for the purposes of social research, the researcher needs to be aware of the limitations, as well as the advantages, of such a method. Sources of professional data may include interviews with media professionals, the analysis of trade journals, e.g. *Broadcast, Televisual*, broadcasters' websites, and professional events.

Sources of Data – the Text

The part of the circuit of the television process which has received the most attention from scholars is that of the text, examples of which have been analysed through different frameworks – for example, content analysis, structuralism, semiotics, discourse analysis and, although less commonly, psychoanalysis. Reading texts for the construction of memory requires the analyst to consider those elements which evoke memory in the potential viewer along with those memories which are expressed through, for example, eyewitness accounts of events. The visual components of the text: archive, images, landscape, architecture, and so on, combine, as they do in the *D-Day* example discussed above, to create layers of memory through their skilful interweaving in the overall narrative. I would again invite you to consider the unique characteristics of television in its ability to juxtapose so many visual and aural codes, crossing and combining modes of documentary and narrative fiction. Key areas of textual construction are aesthetic codes, tropes, authority and legitimacy, and 'authoring'.

Sources of Data – Reception

Perhaps the key questions for the exploration of television viewers and memory are: How do different generic modes engage audiences in terms of empathy, emotion and affect?; How are identities and belonging invited through the text?, and; How are aspects of memory mobilised? Useful strategies would involve setting up screening/viewing with selected groups to explore reception of specific styles and aesthetics of programmes, and the use of television in identity reinforcement and memory building through empathy and other strategies. Groups could be drawn from different types of audiences to explore the impact of variables such as region, age, class, gender and ethnicity. Helen Wood has carried out important work into how viewers engage with such styles of programming, such as the talk show and reality television (Wood 2009; Skeggs and Wood 2012). She has called her method 'text-in-action', and by recording viewers watching and aligning their responses with broadcast transcripts she can identify significant moments of emotion and affect triggered by the studio discussions or filmed encounters. This strategy would be particularly useful for our purposes here. Follow-up conversational interviews with individuals from the screening groups could then be conducted and, in view of the potentially sensitive subject matter, the researcher should also respond to requests for further discussions from individuals or groups involved.

As referred to above, broadcasters increasingly involve the use of support website material and offer viewers the opportunity to participate in 'remembering' past events by sending in their memories and stories. In addition to these 'official' broadcaster websites there are diverse sources of responses to programming on other internet sites that invite viewers' and wider communities' thoughts on broadcast material. Paying due regard to issues of access and confidentiality, this material could be analysed in relation to identity and memory. Examples of diverse sources include: Blacknet Village, a UK-based African Caribbean social networking site; digitalspy.co.uk – a TV discussion forum; and international forums linked to particular historical events, e.g. the Great War forum and online reviews.

The fourfold framework I propose presents interesting challenges in the combination of data analysis. Each site of investigation involves the analysis of 'texts' which are generated from a range of sources: observation, 'focus group' discussions, online chat, interviews, television programmes, journalism, government reports, to name but a few. I have argued elsewhere for the usefulness of discourse analysis for such multi-sited studies (Gray 2003). Employing this method is to identify 'discursive regimes' produced through particular contexts, e.g. by broadcasters and producers, the construction of television texts and user talk.

I hope to have demonstrated through the above case studies the rich potential offered by such television programming in exploring the sites of construction, (re)presentation and reception of memory at the levels of the national, familial and personal. Though it will not always be possible to attend to all the layers of memory construction to which this chapter has referred, an awareness of the limitations of separating out each site for specific consideration will be important. Each focus necessarily excludes important contexts, whether of production, text or reception, and those studies that, at the very least, relate one site to another will offer great potential in mobilising rich and varied data through which to analyse 'televised remembering'.

SUMMARY: KEY POINTS

- In examining the role of television in constructing national, familial and personal memory it is important to conceive of the television process as a circuit of production, distribution and consumption.
- Each point in the circuit can demonstrate the dynamic production of memory and, as such, can be the focus of analysis.
- However, those studies which enable the examination of ways in which the activities involved in each site relate to each other will move towards a deeper understanding of these important 'memory sites'.

FURTHER READING

Although television represents aspects of personal and familial memory on screen as public memory, Bell (2011) considers UK history programming for the ways in which it offers resources for individuals to reflect on their individual past and present identities while also relating them to a wider public context. Two useful edited collections on television, memory and history are Edgerton and Rollins (2001), and Bell and Gray (2010), while Gray and Bell (2013) explore the different television genres of British history programming over the last two decades, tracking their commissioning, production, marketing and distribution. Rather more broadly, Jerome de Groot (2009) examines how society consumes history through popular culture, ranging from computer games to heritage sites, daytime TV to internet genealogy.

NOTES

1. This research was undertaken as part of the AHRC-funded Televising History 1995–2010 project (2006–10) conducted at the University of Lincoln.
2. Available on DVD. BBC DVD1431.
3. This period included anniversaries of the beginning of the conflict (1939), the Battle of Britain and Dunkirk (1940), the Blitz (1940–1), D-Day (1944), the liberation of Auschwitz and other camps, VE Day and VJ Day (1945). All were marked through history programming.
4. It is notable that another programme in the 2004 series, *Dunkirk*, was internally funded by the BBC and, as Chapman suggests, was the programme which most conformed to the existing narrative and myths surrounding the event.
5. See Gray (2010) for a further discussion of this process.
6. For an overview of episodes see: www.channel4.com/programmes/empires-children/episode-guide/series-1
7. Ofcom is the independent regulator and competition authority for the UK communications industries www.ofcom.org.uk/
8. http://www.historymakers2011.com/
9. http://sheffdocfest.com/

CHAPTER 6

Vernacular Remembering

Michael Pickering and Emily Keightley

REEL MEMORIES

The previous chapter dealt with methods for researching and analysing television's construction of memory through programming designed to commemorate a specific, historically significant event, or delineate the family history of famous people in relation to a broader historical canvas. As was shown, memory as resource and re-enactment in these programmes becomes operative through various combinations of personal and public memory, and while they are nationally broadcast, their reception is local and particular. It is to the local and particular that we now turn in a more concerted fashion. We continue to focus on visual media, but move from memory construction in its most widely shared forms, where the audiences are scattered and multifarious, to such construction in its most proximate and personally significant forms, where the audience is concentrated and familiar. The shift is from diverse locations to focused gatherings where mediated acts of remembering have value primarily to familiar, known individuals. In referring to these small-group acts of remembering as vernacular, we develop a different methodological focus to that of Chapter 9, but one that is complementary to television remembering, not diametrically opposite to it.

Vernacular remembering is at once personal and shared, immediate to self as well as being intersubjectively negotiated and inherited from others across the generations. It draws upon situated and mediated experience, with first- and second-hand forms of remembering acting reciprocally to shape and inform each other within particular social and cultural contexts.[1] It is remarkably varied, and accordingly there are many different aspects of it that need to be studied. Since this chapter is designed as a companion piece to the previous one, we shall attend initially to the personalised, amateur uses of media technologies in creating images – both moving and still – that act as subsequent vehicles of memory. The use of such technologies is long-established, extending back to the widespread adoption of visual recording machines such as the hand-held Kodak camera and later the cine camera, both of which were used as ways of capturing such events as family holidays or celebrations. Despite this longevity, turning scholarly attention to these personalised uses of visual technologies of remembering has been slow and gradual, not least because it has had to counter the blanket assumption that home-made photos and recordings are inherently trivial in social, cultural and political terms when compared with mainstream visual media. It has also had to steer around the prejudice that has cast such images and recordings as the abject aesthetic 'other' of professional media production. This evaluation stems from the imposition of inappropriate criteria and the adoption of inapplicable perspectives. Acts of recording-as-remembering can of course be looked at in various different ways, but wherever possible, they have first and foremost to be attended to in the light of what their interpretative agents intend. When this is done, amateur uses of recording and viewing technologies begin to reveal the purposes, aims, values and conventions which underpin them. These are often quite at odds with professional standards and formally artistic objectives, and because of this they need to be understood within the cultural grain of their mundane deployment.

In looking at their deployment as vehicles of vernacular memory, we want to consider the methods and methodological issues specifically associated with researching how visual media have been used in practices of remembering. We begin with home-made cine and video recording because, although these have been examined a good deal less than amateur photography, there has nevertheless been some interesting work on them by anthropologists and historians as well as media scholars. Despite the anthropological input, the major lacuna in such work has been the failure to develop any extended fieldwork. Patricia Zimmerman's *Reel Families* (1995) offers a social history of amateur filmmaking in the United States from the 1890s to the 1960s, drawing on a range of sources such as specialist magazines and documentation from manufacturers, but she does not deliver an oral history of family participation in amateur film. There is no evidence from participants of the importance of such film in creating and preserving a record of the past. This can be seen as facilitating (or at least as presenting no obstacles to) the development of her argument that amateur film-making during the twentieth century was gradually privatised and rendered trivial, unable to engage in social or political issues and confined by the early post-war period to the idealisation of the nuclear bourgeois family. There is a further methodological problem here in the consequent reliance on archival sources, for these are not necessarily representative of family filmmaking and one cannot simply infer from a film in a historical archive what value it may or may not have had to those who made it and (re)viewed it. This is, for example, a limitation with what is otherwise an interesting discussion of how childhood experience, place and memory interact in the work of two amateur film-makers, Charles Chislett and Ralph Brookes, whose work has been preserved in two film archives in the north of England (Nicolson 2001).

James Moran is critical of Zimmerman for basing her argument on an outdated 'ideology of familialism local to the sentimental model of the nuclear family' (2002: 35), but despite championing amateur video-making as an 'authentic, active mode of media production for representing everyday life', his own study offers no empirical data on how shifts in family structures and interactional orderings of familial life may have affected the uses of home movies or home videos, especially as vehicles of remembering (2002: 35, 59). Authenticity is claimed, but not explored, precisely because of Moran's unexplained reluctance 'to discuss any actual examples of home-mode video or of the people who make it' (Buckingham et al. 2011: 20). We would agree that home-mode video can 'provide a material articulation of generational continuity over time', and 'a narrative format for communicating family legends and personal stories', but we need to go beyond such claims and show, in people's own words, the various different ways in which vernacular remembering actually operates in establishing such continuities, and transmitting family stories, whether this is via video or some other personalised use of communications technology (Moran 2002: 60–1).

The term 'home-mode' was coined by Richard Chalfen (1987) in a widely referenced work on domestic uses of photography and film-making. The book remains one of the most rewarding studies of such uses. It focuses on middle-class families in the USA during the 1960s and 1970s and inevitably relates to the home-mode technologies of the time. A key purpose in the book is to contrast the making and viewing of home movies with the instructions and guidance provided in 'how to do it' manuals, and a key finding is that in celebrating rites of passage and landmark events the emphasis is on memories of good times, preferred views of past occurrences, and designated pleasurable viewing on subsequent occasions. Such selectivity is central to the practice of making and viewing home movies and videos, and so part and parcel of the pleasures of family remembering that are associated with them. These are far from trivial for those involved, and cannot simply be dismissed as reproducing the ideological construct of the family, bourgeois or otherwise. Chalfen identifies a number of characteristics, themes and cultural functions associated with and arising from these home-mode artefacts. Among them is their value in stimulating and ordering 'memories of people, events, and places', as well as helping in the mnemonic retention of significant details. In a husband-and-wife interview, the husband stated that with home movies 'you do create a much fuller scene, much fuller memory than you can from prints, or the written word for that matter'. In another such interview, the wife said on behalf of them both that the main reason they made home movies was for the sake of their children, providing them with a record and a resource 'so that they can look back and understand a little more about themselves' (Chalfen 1987: 137–9).

As these quotations attest, Chalfen did engage in qualitative interviewing, though the use of this material is rather limited compared with his use of secondary sources of various kinds. The number of collections of home-mode imagery he consulted was impressively large – approximately two hundred belonging to white, middle-class Americans living in the north-eastern United States – but it is not clear what range of qualitative, face-to-face interviews was conducted as opposed to the questionnaire survey he includes as an appendix. Interview data of this kind is only occasionally cited. This leads to a serious impediment. It lies in Chalfen's primary focus on 'the pictorial representation of people in a symbolically formed community rather than a real life community of living, in-person people'. He claims that such representation provides us with the perspective necessary 'for asking how these two types of communities are related to one another' (ibid.: 11), but it evinces a methodological problem rather than a virtue, for while such representation certainly shows how everyday life has been transformed into particular claims, statements and interpretations concerning individuals, families and communities, we cannot be satisfied with our own claims, statements and interpretations of what such representation signifies. The problem lies in Chalfen's assumption that people 'see themselves in everyday life the way he interprets their appearance in snapshots and home movies'. His formalist approach 'cannot adequately account for or explain the broader range of family dynamics and ideologies of home that escape the lens of a Polaroid or Brownie camera' (Moran 2002: 37). There is, in other words, a leap of analytical faith in both the assumption and the approach, for what remains largely absent is evidence of what people bring to the images of themselves and others. What is the relationship between how home-mode images are constructed and how they are used in the common coinage of everyday remembering? In order to address this question at all thoroughly, we need to ask 'living, in-person people', who preserve and cherish their self-made or inherited images, what in their own claims, statements and interpretations these images mean, how they are used and why they are valued. The meanings, viewing practices and qualities invested in such images cannot simply be 'read off' from the pictorial content alone.

This is a tendency that commonly occurs as a result of the lack of ethnographic fieldwork. Somewhat paradoxically as well, Chalfen considers snapshot photography and home movies as if they are more or less coextensive, so running together their formal features of signification even though these are his main initiating point of analysis. This would have been offset by extensive interviewing on precisely how home-mode users differentiated between self-originating still and moving images. One of the most recent studies of amateur video-making overcomes the methodological limitations and weaknesses we have identified so far because of a concern to gather evidence from amateur users themselves of how recording media are put into practice in their everyday lives. Conducted over a three-year period, *Camcorder Cultures: Media Technology and Everyday Creativity* examines the popular uses of video production technology. The book emerging from this project focuses on the private world of domestic life with an emphasis on the content of what is recorded in home-mode video rather than on its aesthetic characteristics, such content holding out the prospect at a later date of helping to facilitate or maintain the memory of particular people or places.[2] Twelve households were recruited and given a video camcorder to use over a fifteen-month period. The uses to which this technology was put were discussed with members of these households, who were also asked to keep diaries providing details of such uses. The results illustrate the diversity of vernacular forms of recording and remembering which we noted at the start of the chapter. They range from the usual birthday parties and holiday footage to the less expected video diary and documentary, with some forms being more private and some more public than previous studies have shown. Video-taping becomes an integral part of the processes of shared remembering and reflecting on the passing of time. It also holds out the promise of re-experiencing feelings and emotions associated with past experiences, so providing 'a sense of security and continuity amid the ongoing experience of change and loss' (Buckingham et al. 2011: 96). The book highlights the various experiential themes running across the participating households, and attends to the ways in which video-making became absorbed into the structure and texture of everyday domestic life. It is a major advance on previous work because of its avowed ethnographic intent.

FAMILY ALBUMS

The most important personalised use of communications media as a mode of vernacular remembering, and historically the most extended, is that relating to photography, both in family albums and in household display. This stands in stark contradiction to the critical disdain it has met with. Such disdain is broader than that which has sometimes been directed at home movies and videos. In addition, amateur photography hasn't attained the same reference for authenticity sometimes accorded to home movies and videos (an 'authenticity' encapsulated in the 'candid camera' attribution). The disdain may seem rather peculiar in that, while the cultural practices and material products of both are obviously different and shouldn't simply be run together, we can, in the interrelated terms of recording and remembering, see video-making as a cultural extension of the practice of compiling a family album. Despite this overlap between them, the family album has been much more the focus of cast-wide-aside criticism, on both ideological and aesthetic grounds. In terms of content it has been said to produce or pander to a sentimentalist or romanticised view of the nuclear family which trails various oppressive gender, class and racial implications in its wake, while in terms of form it has been said to be highly conventional and predictable – 'all family albums are alike', according to Susan Stewart (1996: 49). The allegation is that they have neither the potential to be stylistically innovative nor the power to make us see the world anew, as the photographic work of Brassaï or Brandt may do.

Such critique has in some ways been entirely valid, but it has perpetuated the sweeping dismissal of the family album. It is also at times analytically and methodological flawed. Following a similar wrong step in the work on home movies, it is analytically flawed in either taking the aesthetic templates used to judge professional and art photography and applying them to vernacular photography at an entirely formal level, or in exercising some blend or other of visual semiotics and textual/discourse analysis in order to expose and demystify the ideological work the image is said to perform. This is not to say that photographs are innocent of such ideological work, for of course they are not. The point is that this sort of approach to visual analysis is innocent of any voice apart from that of the discerning social and cultural analyst. Methodologically it is one-sided, with its analytical acumen and critical prowess untested by reference to what the makers and viewers of vernacular photographs say about what they do. Recognising that this is a limitation we need to move beyond does not entail rejection of the analysis of visual images in themselves. The importance of such analysis is self-evident, for photo-images do not simply speak for themselves, even though their power often lies in the elision of their form by the indexical insistence of their referents. Clearly, how they operate as visual discourse either on their own or in their domestic assemblages requires careful treatment. But the danger is always that of inferring the social meaning and significance of an image without conferring with those who took it, treasure it, and return to it along particular pathways of remembering. With vernacular photographs in particular this danger looms large, for unlike news photos or famous images of stars and celebrities, which are reproduced and received in a wide range of social and cultural contexts, they are usually specific to their makers and viewers. They are also always embedded in cultural practices that relate to such situated processes as managing identities across time, or celebrating certain intimate relationships within time. These practices and processes are not only specific to particular social groups and material locations, but also to definite historical periods across which they change, along with the configurations of social groups and material locations, and the ways in which they are culturally known and understood. It is because of this that family albums are alike neither in time nor over it.

Gradually, there is increasing acknowledgement that image analysis needs to be supplemented and complemented by other methodological and analytical approaches. For convenience sake here we want to identify three methods that have been taken in the analytical study of family albums, and in doing so we are differentiating them from the methods used in more directly historical work on photo albums, as for example that conducted by Marianne Hirsch (1997/2012), Patrizia di Bello (2007), Martha Langford (2008) and Elizabeth Siegel (2010).[3] The first method is to take an album of your own family and review its contents through some analytical procedure that reads it against the grain of its conventional associations. The feminist critiques developed by Jo Spence (1991), Valerie Walkerdine (1991), Deborah Chambers (2003) and Annette Kuhn (2002) are examples of this approach. This has the advantage of being able to relate autobiographical memory and experiential knowledge to specific images while proceeding on the principle that just 'as there is more than one way of making photographs, so there is more than one way of making use of them' (Kuhn 2002: 24). At the same time it is limited to one person's particular interpretation of these images offered with the post-hoc benefit of a quite different way of seeing than that into which the authors were first socialised within their families. The whole purpose of the analysis hinges around the alternative perspective this provides, which is fine, but it is entirely reliant upon it.

A second methodological approach is required when there is no autobiographical memory to draw upon, either from the maker or the inheritor of an album who is herself represented within it. Photo albums imply a narrative, are constructed with that narrative in mind, and are accompanied in shared viewings by the spoken enlargement of it. Looking through the subjective ensemble of photographs that an album brings together always requires this imaginative re-engagement with the narrativisation of memory that extends beyond the looking but is vividly informed by the images that are thematically structured and arranged. In the absence of an album maker or possessor, Andrew Walker and Rosalind Kimball Moulton suggest an analytical technique which involves an inductive reconstruction of the narrative that would have accompanied its viewing as a thematic whole. The implicit narrative will vary according to the type of album involved, but the method is based on imagining 'the structure of the narrative which would reasonably accompany it', binding together its cast of characters and their interrelationships across certain key themes, such as family continuity and unity. Walker and Moulton acknowledge that the reconstructed narrative will not necessarily be an exact fit with the actual narrative that the album-maker would have told – how could it be? – but they hold that the analyst can nevertheless, with due care and attention, come 'close enough to the latent original to provide an interpretative framework for assigning meaning to any particular photograph in the album' (1989: 175–7).

Another, perhaps more reliable way of tackling the problem of an absent narrator is to interview other people about the content of a photo album, asking them in detail what they – as opposed to the analyst herself – make of this content. An example of this is provided by Martha Langford who, building on her earlier historical work, took an album that was not part of her original archival study group – a snapshot album of the interwar period, compiled by a young woman and lodged in the same archive – and interviewed five women who could be regarded as subsequent descendants of the remembrance environments in which the album would once have figured. In doing this she took into account such key variables as age and generation, family structure and social status, and in discussing the album with these women, Langford felt the interviews moved towards conversations 'in which the women automatically affiliated themselves with the compiler, answering my questions in that person's stead' (Langford 2006: 230). As a process of visual hermeneutics, the method involves a collectively produced assessment of the album, and has the benefit of enabling a comparative analysis of various different perspectives on the same material. It also to some extent recreates the shared narrative context – or what Langford calls the oral-photographic framework – in which the album would once have been situated, though of course it can only do that at several removes. Both this and the reconstructive method are complementary, and can be used alongside each other, yet both raise some difficult questions about cross-temporal perception and understanding, and how to negotiate the differences between first-hand experiential engagement and second-hand empathetic engagement.

In the end, the most reliable way of revealing an album's construction of a story about a person's life or set of relationships is to interview their compilers and users. This is our third method for investigating how albums are put together and how they relate to remembering practices in everyday life. Interviewing, whenever it is possible, can happily sit alongside some form of visual textual analysis. An example of this is Deborah Chambers' autobiographical exploration of her own family photos from the 1950s, when she herself was a child, combined with ten oral history interviews with women who compiled family albums when they were in their twenties during the same decade (Chambers 2003). This enabled a comparative evaluation of albums resulting from both interpretative perspectives, so highlighting both similarities and variations in their meanings and functions. More recently, scholarly work on family albums and their place in vernacular remembering has concentrated more directly on semi-structured qualitative interviewing on a larger scale. In her study of family photography, for instance, Gillian Rose (2010) conducted twenty-eight one-off interviews with middle-class women in two towns in the south-east of England, all of whom had young children and were either working part time or at home with their children full time. Rose justifies her exclusive gender focus on the grounds that family photography is largely the preserve of women, but in our own research on family photography we have found considerable variation on this. Her study is one of the most valuable pieces of research on such photography to date, but variations on women's role in family photography – perhaps especially deriving from the shift from analogue to digital cameras – suggests the need for a broader sample.[4] Enlarging our informant base in this way has been central to a research project on home-mode media and remembering practices which we have conducted at Loughborough University. In the remainder of this chapter we want to outline what this involved and the various methods we used, including a new method which is especially suited to studying vernacular remembering.[5]

TECHNOLOGIES OF REMEMBERING

The project focuses on the use of cultural technologies by individuals and small groups, not only in processes of remembering but also in constructing their life-narratives and narratives about themselves in their relationships with each other. Among other things, we are concerned with the complex, multi-layered ways in which remembering is socially experienced, practiced and performed across different social categories. In the pilot interviews we conducted for the project the most cited technologies of remembering were photography and recorded music, in both analogue and digital forms, so in the many interviews we have conducted, these two media have been central to our questioning strategy. This has the virtue of enabling us to attend to visual and sonic media as vehicles of memory alongside each other, and to compare the already personalised embedding of camera technology in everyday practices of remembering with the transformation of mass-mediated music into cultural objects of personal and interpersonal remembering that often have a deep affective resonance in people's lives.

Subsequently we have found that a similar interlocking group of studies into personal and family photography has been conducted in North America, likewise involving an extensive range of semi-structured interviews, though mainly among young middle-class Americans. As with our own study, the researchers visited participants in their homes (at least whenever possible) and asked them about specific images in their collections: 'what they were about, why they were taken and what was done with them, and why' (van House 2011: 127). This shows that the 'relative lack of ethnographically informed research on people's actual, daily practices of photography' is slowly being overcome, but with our own project it seemed important to combine such research with a similar investigative focus on the relationship between music and remembering (ibid.: 125).[6] This is important because remembering practices are not connected to a single quotidian cultural technology, but to several, and these operate in different ways. Methodologically the virtue of comparing and contrasting photography and recorded music as vehicles or catalysts of memory depends on their obvious differences, the most basic being their relation to distinct senses of perception, yet at the same time our investigative focus on memory provides an illuminating means of bringing them together and overcoming the strong tendency to study them in distinct fields of enquiry.[7] If the two technologies mark past events and periods in people's lives and help reanimate them in their memories in alternative ways, their roles in remembering are not at odds because of these differences. What our study has shown is that, often enough, they cross-refer and are used interchangeably as creative resources of vernacular remembering.

Our methodological orientation in the project is best characterised as a life story approach, with a specific focus on how cultural technologies of remembering figure as component parts of self-narrativisation. Such an approach involves two relatively discrete stages in the research process. Firstly, there is the generation and the collection of appropriate data, using a variety of tools and techniques. We conducted interviews with over a hundred people, mainly through face-to-face semi-structured interviews, but these were not all one to one. We tried to introduce certain variations of approach in order to foster different possible outcomes: so for example, sometimes two of us interviewed one person, so expanding the perspectives involved in our questioning, and sometimes one of us conducted interviews with families about the shared negotiations of memory and memory artefacts, or discussed the relationship between memory and the personalised use of media technologies with members of community groups. Our recruitment of participants involved snowball sampling from local contacts, circulating a call for participants through community networks, writing and distributing a leaflet about the project, and approaching community groups of one kind or another, with a premium being put on achieving a balanced composition across gender and generation, and including participants from various ethnic and social class backgrounds.

We decided to use a combination of qualitative methods primarily so that we could draw on their different strengths to gather a rich set of data about experience, media use and remembering. The various methods were linked by their use of the same questioning strategy. Among other things, this covered participants' past and current uses of media in relation to remembering, including how they stored, displayed, looked at/listened to, and shared these media. Our various methods were linked as well through photo and audio elicitation techniques for facilitating the exploration of remembering practices and drawing out people's accounts and assessments of their mnemonic uses of different media. This was particularly successful in working from photographs in family albums as it showed both the value of single images in maintaining the quality of people's memories and the importance of selection, organisation, structure and sequencing in the arrangement of images illustrating a life story or episodes within a life story. Working with memory-objects as an elicitation technique is appropriate for both visual images and recorded music, but recorded music does not of course have the same formal mnemonic properties as photographs. Photographs are often arranged in albums or displayed in the home in ways which do not apply semiotically to music. Musical sources of memory are not self-constructed in the same way as photographs. This is what we hoped to find at the outset of the project. There is virtue in these contrasts precisely because they show visual and sonic media operating as mnemonic vehicles in quite divergent ways.

Secondly, the analysis of data follows from the process of transcription. With such a large data set, it was useful to begin analysis with the software package 'Nvivo' in order to identify themes, commonalities and divergences across and between interviews and discussions.[8] We then built on this by taking a more detailed and fine-grained approach to analysing how particular samples of material illustrate the ways in which the everyday media of photography and phonography are used in giving expression to people's individual and social relationships with the past and with the passing of time. For example, informants may reflect on the sense that those captured in a photograph or brought to mind by a song from the past are thereby associated with a time that is quite gone by and will never be lived again. There is of course considerable variation on what is deduced from this and how it makes people feel about the incessant movement of events into the past, but discovering in detail all that is involved in the relation between lived experience and temporal recession is exactly what research of this kind is designed to uncover. How personal photography, for example, aids in understanding and coming to terms with this relation in the ways its assemblages construct patterns and mark progress through the days and years of people's lives is central to what studying the mediations of vernacular memory is all about. The remembering function involved in making videos or taking photos helps tie together the distinct tenses of 'this is being recorded', 'this was recorded' and 'this will be viewed'. It gives rise to a series of dialectical shifts, across the relations of past, present and future, between home-mode participation and viewing, personal and shared experience, temporal projection and retrospective narration, and the re-feeling and restructuring of past events and episodes.[9]

THE SELF-INTERVIEW

Attempting to gather and accumulate data which reveals such shifts is not always successful and may encounter various obstacles. One of these may be the extent to which informants are able or willing to think reflexively about their own remembering practices and their relation to everyday media. Another may be the difficulty of bringing certain memories clearly back to mind or piecing them together in ways which cohere as responses to interview questions. Remembering certain events or times in your life is not like opening a window and looking into a sunlit garden where everything seems whole and complete. It is a reconstructive process in which we put the past back together again from the fragments that remain, and as we do this we find that memory is full of shadows and lacunae as well as areas of brightness and prominence. There are times when reassembling past events or periods cannot be done instantly; we need to think carefully about particular details or sequences; we need to project ourselves back imaginatively to a period in our lives we may not have considered for a long while. This creates a predicament for memory research. It reveals certain limitations and drawbacks in qualitative interviewing when normally we have been amply rewarded by its reciprocal to-and-fro exploration of people's experience and reflections on that experience.

Our response to this predicament has been to devise a new method for use in memory studies. It is related to qualitative interviewing but does not involve face-to-face dialogue in the manner conventional to such interviewing. With such dialogue the general expectation is a continual interflow of talk – of questions and responses, of talking and listening, with the interviewer doing most of the listening. This expectation would be disrupted by long hesitation, by not responding more or less immediately to a query. Interviews hate silence, at least silence that is anything more than a considered pause. Such is the weight of the expectation that continuity of dialogue will be maintained that any silence lasting longer than even a minute would begin to seem like a prolonged withdrawal from speech. There is, then, a severe restriction in conventional qualitative interviewing on stopping to think, to take time out for a while to engage in the process of reconstruction or reflection that we have found to be sometimes so necessary either in remembering or in stepping aside and considering how one remembers, along with the social practices and cultural technologies that are integral to this. It is in order to overcome this restriction that we have developed the new method of the self-interview.

This may sound like a contradiction in terms when we note that, by definition, the interview means seeing each other in person at a meeting of two or more people for the sake of what will ensue between them when they confer. That would of course be the case if we left informants entirely to their own devices and with no brief at all as to how they should proceed. The method instead depends on the sense of an absent interviewer, with informants speaking into a digital voice recorder in response to a detailed guide-sheet that covers pretty much the same area of questioning as a more conventional interview. Informants have told us that as well as having the sense of an interviewer in mind because of this written guidance, they also have the sense that in the longer term they are speaking to the interviewer rather than to themselves. The virtue of the interviewer being physically absent from the scene of the recording is that this allows the informant to be entirely in control of the recording process. It also removes at a stroke the prohibition on pausing that is characteristic of a conventional qualitative interview. As a result, a space is created in which informants can stop and think, can pause the recording while they go through certain photographs or listen to a song or piece of music. They are able to choose the appropriate moment when they talk about how certain images or sounds are interwoven with their acts and practices of remembering. This has helped considerably in facilitating the reconstructive and reflective processes to which we have referred. An image or song might evoke a particular person or scene, but often there is also a bigger story behind that person or scene, and it may take some time to go back over this and all it involved. The self-interview provides the opportunity for this. But its advantages go beyond this for reasons which again make it seem particularly well suited to researching vernacular remembering and its relations with everyday media. Sometimes remembering can be fraught with emotion, as for instance when you turn the page in an album and find a photograph of your sister who died tragically in a car accident, or hear a song again that instantly brings to mind your first serious love affair. These memories may carry with them a powerful wave of feeling, whether of grief or intense regret. It is not easy to then jump straight into talk about how your remembering has operated in relation to the image or song which generated such feeling. That is precisely when an informant might need to press the 'pause' button and turn away from the process at hand.

Having an informant break into tears was another reason we decided to devise the self-interview. Although that person recovered and was able to continue with the interview, it felt like his privacy had been breached; our physical presence seemed intrusive, especially in the face of his repeated apologies for crying. He would have been spared any embarrassment if he had opted to do a self-interview, which he did subsequently agree to do following our rather fragmented first encounter with him. It is of course difficult to know in advance how an informant may be affected by their participation, so it has proved useful to have the option of a self-interview as an alternative to face-to-face interviews. Informants themselves have spoken of the greater scope and latitude afforded them by the self-interview. Setting down their account at their own pace, and with the opportunity for breaks, made for a more satisfying experience in thinking of how they remember via images and sounds. The self-interview does not suit everyone, and some people felt uncomfortable or even inhibited at the prospect of talking by themselves into a voice recorder. The advantage for us is the wider choice of mode of participation that we are able to offer our informants and the greater breadth of viewpoints on remembering practices that follows from this. And when it works well in allowing participants in our research the opportunity to tailor the time and space of recording in ways that suit them best, the self-interview has yielded some fascinating descriptions of ways of remembering in everyday life.

We end with an example that illustrates the quality of participation a self-interview is able to produce. It is a short extract from a self-interview by Helen, a white British woman in her late-forties, who is talking about the relationship between recorded music and memory.

> Another piece of music which I love and which has all sorts of associations is Butterworth's 'Banks of Green Willow'. Now I listened to that again this morning to rehearse this trigger and it was a different recording from the one I knew and that got in the way so it didn't trigger it except for the general associations which I have with Butterworth which reminds me so much of my childhood, my parents' love of the Worcestershire and Herefordshire countryside and how as a family we'd go out in the car on nice weekends and picnic. So all those associations, erm, but the specific association that is particularly important for Butterworth that is pinpointed by the recording I know is that I discovered this particular piece not directly through – from my parents, but by myself in buying a recording for them. It was my first term at university and I was desperately homesick and I bought this partly because I thought it would be a good Christmas present for them, that they would like it, although at the time they didn't have a record player but also because for me it sort of summoned up my memories of home. So I have this quite specific memory of sitting on the floor in my room in my flat where I had the little Dansette record player on the floor beside me playing this and having this mix of emotions and association with Christmas because it was a Christmas present and yet there were also the memories of summer trips as a child to Wenlock Edge or all those places associated with Butterworth and his music.

The extract shows how recorded music – in this case both a specific recording of a specific piece of music, different recordings of the same piece of music, and others beyond it by the same composer – can set various clusters of remembering in motion around each other. Helen speaks of how listening to George Butterworth's 'The Banks of Green Willow' triggers all sorts of emotional associations in her memory with her childhood, her parents, and certain rural landscapes and events in the countryside. Along with this the recollections generated through these associations flow back and forth across time, linking together for her different periods of her life – childhood, youth, middle age – and different seasons and places, some shared with her mother and father, some lived through alone, when she was yearning intensely to be back home. The extract shows not only how music can act as a mnemonic catalyst but also how it resonates across densely layered banks of memory whose relation with each other shifts according to when certain recollections occur and as one moves through a life in its loosely defined, yet successive stages.

SUMMARY: KEY POINTS

- We began the chapter by discussing home-mode visual media and their role in practices of remembering, moving from home movies and videos to the family album.
- We espoused an approach which attempts to see such practices most of all from the point of view of their participants and interpretative agents.
- We noted the lack of ethnographic fieldwork in the investigation of vernacular remembering and pointed to the need to make good this lack in future work.
- We discussed the value of looking at different technologies of remembering alongside each other, so bringing us closer to the ways they intermix in everyday life.
- Finally, we compared the conventional qualitative interview with the self-interview as a new method that is especially well suited to studying vernacular remembering, but may well prove a useful research technique in studying other topics in the human and social sciences.

FURTHER READING

One of the most interesting recent studies of the relationship between personalised media and autobiographical memory is José van Dijck (2007). She discusses mediated memories in relation to such forms of recollection as diaries and blogs, recorded music, home movies and digital photos. Marianne Hirsch (1997/2012) offers a wide-ranging and rewarding study of photographs as the primary means of self-representation in the family, one purpose of which is its integrative function (Bourdieu 1996: 19–35), while Gillian Rose provides the best recent example of an ethnographic approach to family photos as objects of vernacular remembering, seeing them as always embedded in practices that are part of broader structures of social relations. Langford (2008), Batchen (2004), di Bello (2007) and Siegel (2010) are all historical studies of photo albums that are definitely to be recommended. Spence and Holland (1991) also remains a valuable collection. Photography and recorded music are discussed alongside each other as mnemonic devices in Keightley and Pickering

(2006) and Pickering and Keightley (2008). For more on the self-interview, see Keightley et al. (2012) and Allett et al. (2011). Finally, for extensive treatment of the creative dimension of remembering that informs our whole approach to memory and vernacular uses of media, see Keightley and Pickering (2012).

NOTES

1. Vernacular remembering includes what José van Dijck calls 'personal cultural memory', but extends beyond this within particular social and cultural milieux that are the immediate and local material settings in which people live their everyday lives. Personal memory is of necessity cultural as well as social, whereas vernacular remembering is distinct from official or state remembering.
2. Buckingham et al. (2011). The research project was based at the Institute of Education in London and funded by the AHRC. Another book to emerge from the project (Buckingham and Willett 2009) is an account of dedicated and sustained uses of camcorder technology by serious enthusiasts, rather than its more intermittent and occasional vernacular uses.
3. These are highly rewarding studies that require separate discussion in terms of their analytical approaches and the historiographical issues they raise.
4. This is Chalfen's view, in his otherwise appreciative review: 'Rose's methodology that did not allow for interviews with fathers may represent a lost opportunity' (see *Visual Studies*, 2011, 26 (2): 176–8).
5. The project, *Media of Remembering*, has been funded by The Leverhulme Trust over the period 2010–13.
6. See van House (2011) for the various publications arising from these US studies; also van House (2009) for more details of the methods of data collection that were used.
7. For more on this, see Keightley and Pickering (2006) and Pickering and Keightley (2008). Where work on mediated memories does draw on empirical sources, these are often secondary rather than primary. For example, José van Dijck is one of the few people who have recently investigated the cultural relations of music and memory, but she has done so through 'a readily available online set of narrative responses generated through a national radio event: the Dutch Top 2000 . . . an extensive database of comments and stories, opening an intriguing window into how recorded music serves as a vehicle for memory' (2007: 78–9).
8. For a handy guide to using Nvivo, see Deacon et al. (1999/2007): 343–55.
9. For more on all that is entailed in this, see Keightley and Pickering (2012).

SECTION FOUR

Locations of Memory

CHAPTER 7

Memoryscapes and Multi-Sited Methods

Paul Basu

As David Lowenthal has observed, 'the locus of memory lies more readily in place than in time' (1997: 180). From Halbwachs' foundational work on the 'spatial frameworks' of collective memory ([1925] 1941), through Yates' explorations of the architectural 'arts of memory' in the middle ages (1966), to Nora's highly influential project charting the *'lieux de mémoire'* of the French nation (1984–92), the relationship between 'mental spaces' of memory and the 'material milieu that surrounds us' has been a dominant theme in memory studies (Connerton 1989: 37; Schama 1995). Indeed, *après* Nora, the concept of the site of memory has become *the* dominant metaphor for exploring cultural memory. However, despite its wide influence, the notion of *lieux de mémoire* has also been criticised as being 'one of the most inchoate and under theorized concepts of cultural memory studies' (Erll 2010: 1). And yet, its apparent limitlessness – its ability, for example, to encompass material and immaterial 'sites' as diverse as *La Marseillaise*, the tricolore, Lascaux and Joan of Arc – provides its very strength. Perhaps, as Peter Carrier suggests, Nora's contribution is, above all, a *methodological* one (2000: 37): a framework for exploring the cultural construction of collective identities through the tangible sites at which shared historical consciousness is inculcated ... and contested.

Whereas the nation is foregrounded in Nora's and many other studies of public memory and commemoration (e.g. Gillis 1994; Koshar 1998; Olick 2003), there are, of course, other 'social frameworks' which both shape historical consciousness and are shaped by it. Halbwachs, for example, discusses the intersecting communities of language, family, religion and social class that provide some of the specific group contexts through which individuals remember or recreate the past (Halbwachs 1925; Coser 1992: 22). Such social frameworks influence both what is remembered and how it is remembered, binding group members together in a shared 'community of memory' and contributing to an individual's sense of belonging to the group. While there are numerous debates regarding the boundaries between public and private forms of remembering, I favour the term 'cultural memory', since, as Erll argues, it 'allows for an inclusion of a broad spectrum of phenomena . . . ranging from individual acts of remembering in a social context to group memory . . . to national memory with its "invented traditions"' and beyond to accommodate transnational and diasporic contexts (2010: 2; see Basu 2007a for an investigation of the latter). These are neither discrete phenomena, nor necessarily continuous or consistent. Pursuing the spatial metaphor, we might conceive of this varied mnemonic terrain as a 'landscape of memory' – or, better, a 'cultural memoryscape'.

CULTURAL MEMORYSCAPES AND MULTI-SITED METHODS

Cultural memoryscapes accommodate not only different sites and social frameworks of memory, but also what Radstone and Hodgkin term different 'regimes of memory' (2003). Rather than a dichotomised world of authentic *'milieux de mémoire'* and self-consciously commemorative *'lieux de mémoire'* (Nora 1989), the memoryscape is comprised of a multiplicity of different forms of remembering: those that are intentional and communicable through language, narrative or material form, as well as those which are unintentional and 'inherently non-narrative', such as embodied forms of memory (Erll 2010: 2). These different forms are not necessarily temporally or spatially distant, but interact with one another, cohering into new creolised forms, or accumulating at specific sites to form palimpsest-like accretions (Basu 2007b). The idea of the memoryscape also invokes Arjun Appadurai's characterisation of the shifting, perspectival and disjunctive dimensions of contemporary global dynamics (1990). Rather than inhabiting neatly bounded communities of memory (as invoked above), in which all citizens share in a common imagining of the nation's past, for example, individuals actually negotiate a plurality of allegiances and identifications (national, ethnic, linguistic, religious, etc.), which transgress group boundaries and are not necessarily isomorphic. Appadurai describes such entities as 'ethnoscapes', 'mediascapes', 'ideoscapes', and so on, using the common '-scape' suffix to indicate that 'these are not objectively given relations which look the same from every angle of vision, but rather that they are deeply perspectival constructs, inflected by the historical, linguistic and political situatedness of different sorts of actors' (including nation-states, diasporic communities, sub-national groupings, villages, families, etc.) (Appadurai 1990: 7). To these -scapes, we might add the memoryscape, an inhabited 'medium *for*' and 'outcome *of*' conscious and unconscious mnemonic practices (Tilley 1994: 23), and another important dimension of 'the multiple worlds . . . constituted by the historically situated imaginings of persons and groups spread around the globe' (Appadurai 1990: 7).

The location of the 'Sierra Leonean' memoryscape with which I shall be concerned in this chapter, is not, therefore, only to be found by searching for authentically 'indigenous' memory practices and oral traditions among rural communities in the country's interior (e.g. Ferme 2001; Shaw 2002), nor even by identifying hybridised sites of memory and commemoration within the borders of the modern Sierra Leonean nation-state. Rather, this memoryscape also extends to the cultural imaginings and practices of second generation diasporic communities in Washington DC (D'Alisera 2004), to Pentecostal church congregations in South London, to collections of Sierra Leonean objects dispersed in museums throughout Europe and North America (Basu 2011), and, for that matter, to the CO 267 series of colonial records held in the UK's National Archives at Kew. The objective in surveying such an array of sites – what marks this as an exercise in memory studies rather than historical research, for example – is not so much to facilitate the triangulation of data to arrive at a closer approximation of 'historical truth', but rather to investigate how people both shape and are shaped by this landscape of memory, how they inhabit it and transform it, how they negotiate its consistencies and inconsistencies, and what this tells us of the nature of historical and mnemonic consciousness in particular socio-cultural contexts.

These, at least, are some of the objectives of my ongoing research concerning the Sierra Leonean memoryscape, and it is this work that I should like to draw upon here to consider some of the methodological dimensions of exploring such a fragmented and dispersed mnemonic milieu. This has been a long-term research project in which I have engaged with sites as diverse as specific species of trees, historical personalities, sites of resistance against colonialism, sites of diasporic return, masquerade traditions, ancestral relics, as well as regimes of memory introduced in the colonial and postcolonial era such as Sierra Leone's National Museum, its Monuments and Relics Commission, and National Dance Troupe. Since this chapter is primarily intended as a methodological contribution, I shall not attempt to provide a detailed account of such sites (see, however, Basu 2007b, 2008, 2011, 2012, 2013). Rather, I restrict myself to a couple of case examples, which are intended partly to illustrate the differing material qualities of different sites of memory (archival traces, deserted settlement remains, ancestral objects), partly to emphasise some of the relational dimensions of my approach (how such sites relate with one another, for example, or how they relate to oral traditions), and partly to introduce some of the ways in which the pasts remembered at such sites are 'active' in the present (for example, explaining a town's failure to 'develop', or establishing the legitimacy of a lineage's claim to chiefly status).

Before turning to these case examples I should state that my disciplinary orientation is primarily that of an anthropologist, and given the dispersed and mobile character of the sites and practices that make up the cultural memoryscape, the methodological framework I employ is largely grounded in recent debates concerning the development of 'multi-sited' approaches to ethnographic fieldwork (Marcus 1995; Amit 2000; Coleman and von Hellermann 2011). Since many of the social groups and practices that contemporary anthropologists investigate are often 'no longer tightly territorialized, spatially bounded, historically unselfconscious, or culturally homogenous' (Appadurai 1991: 191), the classic ethnographic method of long-term 'participant-observation' in a single field site has become increasingly inadequate and researchers have had to develop more agile and adaptive methods of tracing the 'circulations of cultural meanings, objects and identities in diffuse time-space' (Marcus 1995: 95).

In his well-known essay, 'Ethnography in/of the World System', George Marcus proposes a framework for multi-locational research which acknowledges that the posited objects of study may themselves be emergent and discontinuous, and this shifts the researcher's role to that of discerning the 'logics of relationship, translation, and association' between these mobile and multiply-situated objects (ibid.: 102). Marcus summarises this approach as follows:

> Multi-sited research is designed around chains, paths, threads, conjunctions, or juxtapositions of locations in which the ethnographer establishes some form of literal, physical presence, with an explicit, posited logic of association or connection among sites that in fact defines the argument of the ethnography. (ibid.: 105)

Such an approach can be effectively employed to investigate the associations and connections between the distributed sites of memory (whether embodied practices, oral histories, monuments, commemorative rituals, archival traces, etc.) that make up the cultural memoryscape and with which the researcher can physically engage. The task then becomes one of 'following' a particular 'memory', which may itself follow the migrations of people, or things, or narratives, or aesthetic motifs, or predispositions, or forms of record keeping, for example (ibid.: 106–10). In order to discern these logics of association, one might say that the researcher is called to follow the mnemonic trace from site to site, acknowledging that each site may require quite different sets of research skills. I shall return to this point in due course. In the meanwhile, rather than pursuing this in the abstract, it is perhaps more helpful to examine examples of these paths, threads, and juxtapositions in a specific context. And so, let us turn to the Sierra Leonean memoryscape.

ARCHIVES, LANDSCAPES, ORAL TRADITIONS — REMEMBERING COLONIAL VIOLENCE

Governor HAY to LORD KNUTSFORD, January 5, 1889
(Telegraphic)
Mackiah's Town Fanima taken and burnt down 2nd January, in 1 hour 20 minutes; 668 captives have been recovered, principally those taken from Sulymah. Official list of casualties, three constables wounded; native contingent, two killed in action, 10 wounded.
Could not ascertain enemy's loss, as town was burnt down. Mackiah's capital, Largo, taken 3rd January, without resistance. Mackiah said to have escaped to Manoh on the way to Nyagwah. Active operations will close. I leave for Jehomah 6th January.

LORD KNUTSFORD to Governor HAY, January 9, 1889
(Telegraphic)
Referring to your telegram of 5th January, it gives me much pleasure to congratulate you on your very successful military operations.

In the 1880s, prior to the declaration of the Sierra Leone Protectorate, as the British were extending their interests in the region, there was a great deal of unrest in the hinterland of Sierra Leone. With little apparent awareness of how their own activities were destabilising the region, the British perceived the local inhabitants to be a 'wild savage people, continually at war amongst themselves' (Abraham 1978: 4). The British method of expansion in the area was to form treaties with 'friendly' local rulers, and to protect the interests of these rulers against the incursions of others who resisted the entreaties of the British crown. This process went hand in hand with the development of British economic interests in the region and with a 'civilizing mission', which sought above all to stamp out local slavery practices. Local elites were often reliant on slave labour to maintain their status, and slave raiding was widespread throughout the region.

The above quoted exchange of telegrams between Sir James Shaw Hay, who served three terms as Governor of Sierra Leone between 1886 and 1891, and Lord Knutsford, Secretary of State for the Colonies between 1887 and 1892, recalls one of the many British military interventions in these so-called 'tribal wars'. These slips of paper are to be found among the several hundred volumes of Colonial Office correspondence concerning Sierra Leone held by the UK's National Archives, and their text was also reproduced in a Parliamentary report of 1889 concerning the 'disturbances in the native territories adjacent to Sierra Leone' (House of Commons 1889: 52). Unusually, on this occasion, the military expedition, which was led by Captain Robert Copland Crawford, was

Figure 7.1 Remembering the destruction of Largo. The archival photograph as site of memory. Photograph by Captain H. B. Mackay, Royal Engineers, 1889. The National Archives CO 1069/89.

accompanied by a photographer (actually Captain H. B. Mackay of the Royal Engineers, who, according to Fyfe (1963: 481) 'came along for fun'), and so, in addition to the written correspondence and reports, there is also a surviving visual record of the events. Figure 7.1, for example, shows the charred remains of Largo photographed just two days after the town was 'taken'. The extent of the devastation is shocking.

The destruction of the towns of Fanima and Largo was provoked by the aggressive actions of a mercenary named Mackiah, described by the Sierra Leonean historian C. Magbaily Fyle as 'the terror of Mende country in the second half of the nineteenth century' (1981: 78). Mackiah was a notorious warrior and, from his headquarters at Largo, he and his followers attacked towns and villages throughout the Gallinas region (in what is now southeastern Sierra Leone), capturing slaves and plundering the lands of chiefs who were on friendly terms with the British. Snubbing the colonialists' invitations to make a treaty, it was generally agreed among the British that 'pacification of the country' would only be achieved by the 'removal of Mackiah' (CO 879/27/2). In 1887 Mackiah had attacked the British trading post at Sulymah and, in late 1888, hostilities intensified again when he captured the friendly towns of Jehomah and Bandajuma. While there was little appetite at the Colonial Office for launching a full-scale – and expensive – punitive expedition to remove Mackiah, Crawford, who was in charge of a troop of Frontier Police at Sulymah, proposed leading an offensive of his own. Although Crawford had no mandate to undertake such operations, he had the backing of Governor Hay, who left Freetown with reinforcements to support the endeavour. Hay was also accompanied by the aforementioned Captain Mackay, who was equipped with Hale rockets, which – from the British perspective – proved a highly effective weapon against local defences.

On the morning of 2 January 1889, Crawford led the march from Bandajuma, which he had previously recaptured from Mackiah, to Fanima. In addition to the Frontier Police force, he was joined by a large contingent of local 'warboys', led by the friendly chiefs Momoh Jah of Pujehun and Gbanah Gumbo of Sahn. They arrived at Fanima before noon. The town was surrounded by a mudbrick wall and stockade. Crawford takes up the narrative of his assault in a report of 7 January 1889:

> At 11.50 a.m. I formed up the police for attack and opened fire with rockets upon the town, at a range of 250 yards.
>
> The advanced guard worked round to the left, whilst the rocket party after having set fire to the town passed round to the Largo gate and cut off the enemy's retreat in that direction.
>
> The rear guard supported this movement. The Native levies encouraged by the noise of the rocket quickly surrounded the town.
>
> Half-a-dozen rockets were discharged from the north side of the town when the Native contingent tore down the stockades and the place was entered over the mud wall.
>
> The western portion of the town was taken about the same time by the advanced guard. The whole of Fanima was in our hands at 1.10 p.m. [. . .]
>
> Mackiah was himself present early in the day, but he effected his escape before the place was surrounded. [. . .]
>
> The enemy's loss could not be accurately ascertained, as the greater part of the town was in flames; 85 bodies, however, were counted, one being that of Fonie Kimbo, the lead warrior of the town. (House of Commons 1889: 66–7)

Crawford goes on to detail the number of captives that were recovered, including a large number who had been taken during Mackiah's raid of Sulymah in 1887. His report then describes the advance on Mackiah's headquarters at Largo on 3 January. The town – which was actually a cluster of six stockaded settlements and three open villages – had been abandoned and was taken without resistance. As Captain Mackay notes in his own report, 'We subsequently ascertained that after the fight at Fanima, Makiah was deserted by most of his people, who felt that they could not hold Largo against us. They were in great dread of the rockets, which they had seen for the first time' (House of Commons 1889: 69). Over the next days, all nine of Largo's settlements were torched. Mackiah fled inland and remained at large for a further three months before being handed over to the British. He was eventually deported to the Gold Coast.

The colonial archive, from which this account can be reassembled, is a significant site of memory in the Sierra Leonean memoryscape. While episodes such as the attacks on Fanima and Largo have not entered national historical consciousness in modern Sierra Leone, the 'memory' of these events is lodged in the vast accumulations of telegrams, letters and reports that were once crucial instruments of colonial governance (Stoler 2009). These mnemonic traces, materialised in ink, typescript and occasional photographs, are important because what they reveal goes beyond the textbook narrative of colonial expansion to reveal the complex workings of power relations. The British attack on Mackiah was only possible through collaboration with friendly chiefs such as Momoh Jah and Gbanah Gumbo. Yet, as Jones argues, their alliance with the British against common enemies 'was not a token of submission to foreign rule, but a positive effort to manipulate outside forces in propping up their own power' (1983: 159). At the same time, there is no doubt that such alliances, together with the removal of non-compliant chiefs, hastened the progress of British indirect rule throughout Sierra Leone. Within weeks of the attacks on Fanima and Largo, for example, a police barracks had been established at Bandajuma, and, when the Sierra Leone Protectorate was declared in 1896, the town became the district headquarters and thus the seat of colonial administration in the region.

But, of course, the colonial archive is not the only site at which these events are recalled. Following the story 'remembered' in the colonial archive to the localities of present-day Fanima and Largo – to oral traditions of the attacks, or to the landscapes in which the attacks took place – raises a host of fascinating issues, both concerning consistencies and inconsistencies in the story itself, and relating to the significance of these past events in the present. In Largo, many stories are told about Mackiah himself. He was not a native of the place, but came *'as a stranger'* from Gorahun and was allowed to settle in a new section of the town, which was called Ngukpebu. He had twelve wives, and if he suspected any man of cuckolding him he would cut his throat. If a pregnant woman set eyes upon Mackiah when he wore his warrior's gown, she would miscarry. He is said to have owned a dog named Banbangleh, which he carried under his arm and for which he cared more than any person. He is even said to have challenged the authority of the omnipotent Poro society, threatening to cut the Gɔbɔi (a masquerade figure representing the powerful spirit of the society) in two. Stories are also told about Mackiah's response to British attempts to make a treaty with him:

> *Queen Victoria sent a message to Mackiah that if he stopped fighting she would make him king of Sierra Leone. She also flattered him that she would make him her husband. He was defiant. The messenger was hesitant because he knew this would make Mackiah angry. He said 'go tell them!' and he gave a statement to the messenger to take back to the white people, which made them angry.*

The account of the attack on Largo is consistent with Crawford's account: '*When the town was attacked, everyone ran away. People left and the white man came in and burnt the town*'. The remains of the various settlements that made up the historic town (the six stockaded settlements and three open villages described by Crawford) are still discernible as undulating earthworks and house mounds in the surrounding forest floor. None but the main settlement of Largo itself was repopulated after Crawford's attack, but their names are still remembered – *Njomorwihun, Ngiehun, Bendu Tomboihun, Tigbesse, Njegor, Koribundo, Ngukpebu* – and they, too, function as powerful sites of memory in the landscape.

The attack on Fanima, which preceded the taking of Largo, also survives in cultural memory through stories passed down from grandparents and great-grandparents. This is more complicated since it was not in fact Fanima that was attacked, but nearby Yanihun. Fonie Kimbo was indeed a warrior and ally of Mackiah who hailed from Fanima. According to local tradition, with the coming of the whites, Mackiah invited Fonie Kimbo and other local warriors to join forces to repel the invaders. At this time Fonie Kimbo left Fanima to establish a new settlement at the more strategic location of Yanihun. Mackiah and Fonie Kimbo were repeatedly invited to meet with the white men, the 'colonial masters', but they refused to comply with their terms. Locally, it is felt that those who sided with the British did so as a way of getting revenge on their enemies. According to the oral tradition, on the day that Crawford's attack came, the townspeople of Yanihun were rethatching their houses and singing as they did so. When the whites arrived, they inquired what was going on and the Frontier Police and native war-boys of Momoh Jah and Gbanah Gumbo who accompanied them told them, '*They are laughing at you*'. With that,

> *the white men ordered those with the cannons to fire on Yanihun. The bullet hit one of the cotton trees and the top of the tree fell to the ground, causing*

the thatch to catch fire. The top of the tree fell on Fonie Kimbo, killing him and the town itself caught fire. When people heard that Fonie Kimbo was dead they all ran away to Mackiah in Largo.

The same story of the cotton tree being hit and the crown of the tree falling onto the town is repeated in other local accounts, but this also resonates with a much more widespread tradition, which associates the cotton tree (a magnificent species that towers above the surrounding forest) with chiefs and elders. When a branch of a cotton tree falls, it is reckoned that an elder will die (Basu 2007b). Thus, there is a symbolic association between the destruction of the cotton tree and the destruction of Fonie Kimbo (in one account I have collected, it was said that the '*head of the cotton tree was severed*' by the cannon fire). It is interesting to note the vividness with which the rocket attack, in particular, is remembered in oral tradition. This is certainly consistent with Captain Mackay's view that the spectacle of rocket fire had not been encountered before and was so dreaded that Largo was given up without resistance. Although they are described as 'cannon' or 'tracers' in local accounts, there is no doubt this refers to the rockets. One informant explained that the '*whole sky was lit up with tracers*'.

It is common throughout Sierra Leone to find that the location of a particular settlement has moved around the physical landscape as one site has been abandoned and another established. As Ferme argues, the naming of later settlements after an original settlement may itself be understood as an act of memorialisation (2001: 42). Yanihun, for example, moved to its present location in 1957. This is the fourth location that Yanihun has occupied, and the sites of the three earlier phases of the settlement are still known and still visible in the surrounding bush. Like the deserted settlements of Largo, the remains of Fonie Kimbo's original Yanihun survive as clusters of overgrown house platforms and concentric earthworks that mark the lines of the mud-brick wall and stockades that once formed its defences. It was not reinhabited after Crawford's attack. Although such sites are not necessarily the locations of explicit commemorative rituals, they continue to be part of the community's 'mental landscape' and actively presence the past in everyday life. Indeed, in contrast to Fonie Kimbo's Yanihun, it could be said that the site of Mackiah's settlement, Ngukpebu, at Largo has been *actively abandoned* and allowed to be taken over by the forest. Rather than perpetuating the remembrance of a hero, one suspects this is a conscious strategy for hastening cultural forgetting: an attempt to erase the memory of a figure who is felt to have brought shame on the town. It is, say the people of Largo, thanks to the wickedness of Mackiah that the town has been unable to modernise and develop. The town has been cursed by its past.

MATERIAL CULTURE AND MEMORY – REMEMBERING ANCESTRAL POWER

In most societies material culture plays an important role in the transmission of cultural memory. In Sierra Leone, this is particularly true of objects associated with prominent hunters or warriors, founding ancestors, and powerful chiefs, whose 'relics' are often endowed with the potency of the ancestors themselves, and are usually subject to strict rules prohibiting access. This is perhaps most powerfully expressed in the customary rituals that accompany the installation of paramount chiefs in Temne chiefdoms in the north of Sierra Leone. These installation rituals are regulated by members of the *Ragbenle* society and include the transference of a basket or box – the *akuma ka məsəm* – containing the 'sacred things' of chieftaincy, which are passed from one ruler to the next (Dorjahn 1960: 118; Hart 1986: 41–2). Through acquiring the right to possess the chiefdom's sacred objects, the person of the paramount chief becomes an important site of memory himself – an embodiment of the chiefdom's cultural memory – and a site of continuity between past, present and future (Dorjahn 1960: 119).

Researching such aspects of the Sierra Leonean memoryscape is extremely difficult since access is highly restricted and, indeed, part of the power of these objects and associated knowledges is derived from their being 'secret' (Murphy 1980; Bellman 1984; Ferme 2001). There are, however, occasions when it is possible to gain insight into the potency of particular objects as media that connect past with present, and carry the memory – and the power – of ancestral figures into the future. At Madina, on the Mabole River in northern Sierra Leone, for example, I was privileged to be shown the sword of the town's founder, a warrior named Kemoh Yiraman Touray. The sword, which carries the Mandingo name '*Jawoo-faa*' (*faa* = to kill; *jawoo* = enemy), is in the possession of the current section chief, a direct descendant of Kemoh (Figure 7.2). The holder of the sword is the holder of this chiefly office, and both are hereditary within the founding ancestor's lineage.

The production of the sword during my visit to Madina occasioned the telling of the story of the founding of the settlement, which in turn relates to the wider narrative of Mandingo migration into what is now Sierra Leone in the mid-nineteenth century. The story is a good example of what Elizabeth Tonkin describes as 'geochronology', the narration of the past in terms of a sequential movement in space (1992: 34), and it tracks the Mandingo settlers' journey southwards over a number of generations, establishing settlements as they progressed. Kemoh emerged as a powerful warrior at this time and split away from the main group with a number of followers. He founded the settlement of Madina beside the Mabole River and defended it against the local Loko population by enclosing it within a high mudbrick wall with a ditch

Figure 7.2 Ali Turay, son of Section Chief Alhaji Almamy Bangalia Turay, bearing the sword of his ancestor. The sword carries not only the history of Madina and its founder, but tells of the coming of Islam to the region. Paul Basu.

surrounding it. The settlement grew as people from the surrounding area took refuge in the town under Kemoh's protection. A photograph of Madina's impressive gatehouse survives in the UK's National Archives and, as with Largo, it was this archival site of memory that initially prompted my visit.

Stories are told about the failed attempts of the Loko warrior, Kobaawa, to expel the Mandingo settlers. According to one tradition, Kemoh's men were aided by a woman named Mammy Janneh Bah, who was gifted with second sight. The Mandingo warriors would consult her before a fight and, through divination, she would tell them whether or not they would be victorious in battle. If anyone went against her advice, they would be defeated. Mammy Bah also had a piece of iron out of which she could squeeze water. The warriors would wash in this water before going into battle and they would be protected by its magical properties. The Mandingoes were Muslim, and Kemoh's sword and its many stories therefore also 'remember' the spread of Islam into this region. Indeed, the use of the Arabic toponym, *madīnah* (town), testifies to this, and it is likely that the settlement was named after the holy city of *al-Madīnah al-Munawwarah*, the home and burial place of the Prophet Muhammad. (Among the families that established Madina with Kemoh were the Sillahs, who were and continue to be the hereditary 'Alpha-men' or Islamic scholars and scribes of the community.)

Another fascinating example of such a portable site in the Sierra Leonean memoryscape is the iron and bronze staff held at RoPonka in the coastal chiefdom of Kafu Bullom. Similar figural staffs are known throughout the wider Mande region and, as Patrick McNaughton argues, their significance and potency is rooted in the 'rich interface between Mande beliefs about the world and the powers [black]smiths possess to manipulate it' (1988: 121). According to McNaughton these staffs had overlapping political and spiritual uses: they were employed, for example, in initiation ceremonies, funeral rites, and as chiefly insignia. Supernaturally powerful devices, they might be placed in sacred groves and shrine houses, or stuck in the ground to demarcate the grave of a town's founding ancestor; they have protective powers and could be used to ward off attack by enemies (ibid.: 123–5). Among the Fula, in coastal Guinea and Guinea Bissau, the staffs are known as *sonoje* (singular *sono*) (Bassani 1979). They are said to have been brought to these coastal regions from the inland Mali Empire, and have since served 'as emblems of political authority and religious objects within . . . non-Muslim cults' (McNaughton 1988: 128).

According to tradition, the *sono* at RoPonka was given to the local ruler, Bai Kumaka, by the Portuguese some time in the late seventeenth or early eighteenth century (Koroma 1939: 25). At this time there was a thriving kola nut trade along the West African coast, and it is suggested that the staff was brought to Kafu Bullom from Farim in present-day Guinea Bissau by Portuguese traders as a sign of friendship and in recognition of Bai Kumaka's authority (ibid.; McNaughton 1988: 128–9). In this way, the staff became part of the insignia of the rulers of Kafu Bullom. Oral tradition relating to the RoPonka staff was first collected in the 1930s by a Sierra Leonean from the region named U. H. Koroma. His account was published in 1939 in the journal *Sierra Leone Studies*, which was edited and published by the colonial government in Freetown (Koroma 1939). It is interesting to note that an off-print of Koroma's article is now kept with the staff itself and together they form this important site of cultural memory. While the oral tradition relating to the staff survives, the hereditary guardians of the staff now refer to their grandfathers' earlier oral account, as published in *Sierra Leone Studies*, for the finer details. This reminds us that oral and written accounts are often complexly interfused (e.g. Goody 1987).

Aside from its more ancient history relating to the Mali Empire and interaction with Portuguese traders, the staff tells a fascinating local story regarding the chieftaincy of Kafu Bullom. Bai Kumaka, the chief who was given the staff, ruled for many years, but on his death no successor was immediately crowned. Instead, Kumaka's cousin, Bai Shera of RoGbane Bana became Regent. Since

Bai Shera was not crowned, he did not have the right to take custodianship of the staff, and it was left in the keeping of Kumaka's heirs at RoPonka. On the death of Bai Shera, a powerful man named Bai Sherbro Gbere of Yongro assumed the chieftaincy. While Bai Sherbo Gbere was widely recognised as the new ruler, Kumaka's descendants refused to acknowledge him as such, claiming that their lineage alone had the right to the chieftaincy. And so the story continues down two centuries, with the descendants of Kumaka using the staff, which remains in their possession, to contest the chieftaincy and assert the legitimacy of their own claim to the Kafu Bullom crown. In 1918, for example, Koroma records that a member of the RoPonka house made a strong bid for the chieftaincy and on this occasion the staff was 'brought to light and exhibited in evidence before the Assessor Chiefs and Political Officer who presided over the election' (1939: 27). Alas, the crown returned to Yongro, but to this day, as hereditary keepers of the staff, Bai Kumaka's descendants insist that the chieftaincy rightfully belongs with them. The site of memory is the site of power.

MULTI-SITED AND MULTI-DISCIPLINARY METHODS

My intention in outlining these examples is not to provide an exhaustive account of Sierra Leone's cultural memoryscape, but merely to illustrate something of its multi-sited character. Even in these few cases, one can begin to discern the 'logics of relationship, translation, and association' discussed by Marcus (1995: 102). At each site – textual and photographic archival traces, landscapes, objects, oral traditions – one encounters a different form of remembering, and, as Young evocatively phrases it, each form 'generates a different meaning in memory' (1993: viii). This diversity of mnemonic form and meaning requires considerable methodological dexterity on the part of the researcher, not least since the memory studies scholar may approach these 'sources' in quite different ways to other researchers. By bringing an 'ethnographic sensibility' to the colonial archive, for example, Ann Stoler is led to ask 'how oral and vernacular histories cut across the strictures of archival production' and how this refigures 'what makes up the archival terrain' (Stoler 2009: 33–4). Such sensibilities open the way for new approaches to researching the archival trace, both following the complex circuits of colonial bureaucracies and their paper trails (paying as much attention to unofficial marginalia as official inscriptions), but also following the narrative out into 'the field'.

Similarly, in the field, there is a clear correspondence between the methods one uses and the understanding one gains. A two-hour oral history recording session produces one kind of knowledge, while the sustained presence of the ethnographer, cautious of relying on explicit narrations of cultural memory, may produce knowledge of an entirely different order (see Argenti 2007, for example). But even in oral history collection there is an art to elicitation based on developing a trusting relationship with participants, as well as thorough prior preparation, so as to know both what to ask and how to inquire. Where images exist, photo-elicitation can be a powerful tool, but must be carefully handled, since, as we know, photographs are not objective representations of reality any more than written accounts (or oral traditions), and the 'reading' of images is also culturally-specific (Niessen 1991; Harper 2002). As I have tried to illustrate in the Sierra Leonean context, it is equally important to engage with material sites of memory, including portable objects and the landscapes in which events occurred. How are such sites regarded? How are their stories told? Are they maintained or protected in some way? Are they visited? Do they form part of explicit commemorative practices? How do they live in the minds and everyday activities of people?

As the diversity of academic traditions represented in this book attests, the study of memory is a multi-disciplinary endeavour. Given the wide variety of individual and social forms of memory, the range of media through which remembering – and forgetting – take place, and the numerous explicit and implicit ways in which memory can be active in the present, this multi-disciplinary perspective is not only a strength, it is a necessity. In many respects, researchers concerned with memory are called upon to synthesise these different academic traditions and their respective methodological practices. This is especially true if the object of study is as expansive as the cultural memoryscape, which embraces a plurality of mnemonic phenomena. Even in the few instances I have outlined in this chapter, a high degree of multi-disciplinary fluency and methodological adaptability is required. How much more so if one extends the scope to include those less obvious sites where memory is not explicit or verbalised, but is 'embedded in habits, social practices, ritual processes, and embodied experiences' (Shaw 2002: 7).

To accomplish this would seem to require an act of disciplinary bricolage, with the researcher borrowing the tools of the historian, the oral historian, the art historian, the ethnographer, the linguist, the archaeologist, or whatever, as the context dictates. On the one hand, such an approach might attract accusations of methodological dilettantism, with researchers working beyond the limits of their core disciplinary training or expertise. On the other hand, however, researchers must be free to innovate their methods in response to the changing objects of their study, and not be forced to restrict their analytical purview by cleaving to methodological orthodoxies (Amit 2000: 17). In a widely-cited contribution to a qualitative research methods handbook, Valerie Janesick cautions against a tendency towards 'methodolatry', which she defines as a 'slavish attachment and devotion to method' (Janesick 1994: 215). A preoccupation with particular methodological conventions, she argues, ultimately distances the researcher 'from understanding the actual experience of participants in the research project' (ibid.). Instead, Janesick likens the research process to a dance: something that requires skill, practice, careful choreography, and indeed creativity and imagination (see also Emke 1996). Rather than forging new methodological orthodoxies for the field of memory studies, therefore, I suggest we not only follow the 'paths, threads, conjunctions [and] juxtapositions' between the multiple sites of the cultural memoryscape (Marcus 1995: 105), but also that we learn to dance between our multiple disciplines and their various methodologies.

SUMMARY: KEY POINTS

- Pursuing the spatial metaphors that dominate memory studies, the 'cultural memoryscape' may be understood as comprising multiple sites of memory connected by a particular associational logic (e.g. national, ethnic, religious, village, etc.).
- Memoryscapes include a plurality of different forms of mnemonic phenomena, ranging from individual acts of remembrance to transnational contexts. As well as different 'sites of memory', they may include different 'regimes of memory' and both explicit and implicit (embodied) forms. Examples explored in the chapter include written and photographic archival traces, oral traditions, landscapes and portable objects.
- Due to the pluralistic and dispersed character of the memoryscape, multi-sited research methods are particularly useful. These involve discerning 'logics of relationship, translation, and association' between multiple sites of memory.
- Researching cultural memoryscapes is a multi-disciplinary endeavour. Rather than forging new methodological orthodoxies, an argument is made for retaining a pluralistic approach.

FURTHER READING

On ethnographic methods and the development of multi-sited ethnography see Amit (2000), Atkinson et al. (2001), Coleman and von Hellermann (2011), and Marcus (1995). For an example of the application of multi-sited ethnographic methods in the context of memory/heritage studies see Basu (2007a); this includes an extended methodological discussion. For an introduction to visual research methods and photo-elicitation see Niessen (1991) and Harper (2002); for an introduction to material culture studies see Tilley et al. (2006). Recent ethnographic monographs exploring cultural memory in West African contexts include Argenti (2007), Ferme (2001), Shaw (2002), Stoller (1995), and Tonkin (1992). For more detailed discussions of particular sites in the Sierra Leonean cultural memoryscape see Basu (2007b, 2008, 2011, 2012, 2013).

CHAPTER 8

Ethnicity and Memory

Amanda Kearney

INTRODUCTION

Ethnicity is the ultimate memory project. Memory and collective consciousness mesh with self-identification to shape a sense of belonging and affiliative membership within a real or imagined community. This communion becomes a lifelong project and constructs itself through varied cognitive and emotional interactions with memory. Memories are made and require the negotiation of shared histories through acts of remembrance. The nature of memory is contested in the literature, and it is variously treated as an individual and group project; shared yet deeply personal. For the purposes of this discussion I envision memory as the product of both individual and collective decision making around what is valued, recalled and actioned in the world today.

Present realities of ethnic strength or vulnerability are often key to understanding contemporary political movements articulated around ethnically prescribed boundaries. So too, understanding memory is key to unpacking these articulations. Ethnic studies has generated several approaches to the study of ethnicity, with the most prominent models being primordialist, constructionist and instrumentalist approaches. In this chapter I engage with each approach, seeking a conceptual framework to better understand the role of memory in making ethnicity within the contexts of memory and African-descent in Brazil. I explore the reality of undertaking ethnographic fieldwork aimed at unpacking elements of complex identity politics constructed around ethnicity and the particularities of group and individual memory. Witnessing ethnic identities in their early stages or moments of politicised action in fieldwork contexts in both Australia and Brazil has led me to understand something of the process of negotiation undertaken when 'making our selves'. This has necessitated a method capable of accessing inter-subjective spaces, and conversational dialogue with the practices of 'making sense' of the self and collective along ethnic lines.

ACCESSING MEMORY AND WITNESSING ETHNICITY

By recognising the particularities of memory in the project of ethnic identifying we find a methodological framework for accessing the relationship between memory, national identities, processes of remembering and decision making regarding unity. Narrative and discourse analysis, along with ethnography, have been my methods to interact with memory as the cornerstone of a socially constructed and instrumentalist sense of ethnicity. By undertaking ethnographic research with indigenous families in Australia (since 2000) and African-descendant groups in Brazil (since 2008) I have witnessed the emergence of ethnic states that involve processes of remembering, and commemoration of a loyalty built around what is remembered and channeled into a politico-creative project.

What strikes me in these ethnographic moments is the degree to which this project is at once conscious and unconscious. Individuals and groups have articulated their ethnicity to me through shared dialogue in fieldwork contexts. Often they speak casually and candidly, other times passionately and with a strong political tone, and the process of making sense of the self takes place in front of the anthropologist, who wishes to better understand what it means to be this person or group. In the act of ethnographic recording and participant observation I witness a process of decision making around memory and its relationship to ethnicity. I am closer to the unself-conscious moment when decisions are being made about what is remembered and what is forgotten, and often those decisions or the difficulties they bring with them are expressed directly to me as the individual or group grapple with the project of becoming.

In the context of fieldwork and relationships built around ethical conduct and empathy I work with people as they come to express their ethnicity by negotiating difference and contradiction, fluidity, ambiguity and even vulnerability. From this an intersubjective understanding can emerge in which I might begin to appreciate, in its full complexity, just how an individual or a group makes choices in crafting ethnicity as an instrument for a 'good' or otherwise 'politicised life'. I have encountered this complexity throughout the course of ethnographic research over a decade, in instances where people express (both clearly and with uncertainty) who they think they are, who their ancestors were, and who they wish to be into the future. This has been particularly so for young indigenous Australians shaping their indigeneity in post-colonial Australia, the expression of which differs significantly to the ways of their old people. Similarly, in Brazil, contentious public debate around racial quotas in universities and overall equity debates concerning African-descendants has drummed up individual and group negotiations as to who 'rightfully' qualifies as African-descendant and who does not. This is what drives me to find a methodology that is sophisticated enough to deal with the nuances found in post-colonial or post-imperial spaces in which a quality of woundedness marks the human experience of being one type of ethnic citizen or another.

Through ethnographic research I have also come to encounter the embodiment of memory as informing ethnic identity through public performance of cultural expressions such as dance, song, language and poetry. In these contexts I witness this as an audience, rarely privy to the decision making that establishes the character of public enactments of ethnicity. More self-conscious in its nature, this presentation involves decision making well in advance of the act and beyond the gaze of the audience. Observing this is vital for the anthropologist as it adds another layer to what can be understood through the process of ethnographic research. Moments of presenting memory as fact in the substantiating and performing of a certain ethnic identity, when combined with the inter-subjective insights we gain through dialogic fieldwork, allows for a richer understanding of ethnicity in wounded spaces.[1] These spaces carry particular histories that must be understood in terms of their remaining legacies in contemporary socio-political settings and memory making. Thus, my research also enters a realm of discourse analysis, as this allows light to be shed on the world that surrounds ethnic citizens – the world which celebrates or limits, contests or denies their character and legitimacy in society. This space is characterised by popular opinion, public debate, media representation and normative textual and visual representations of particular identities along ethnic lines. Discourse analysis offers the opportunity to interact with these narratives, which in themselves 'offer specifically rich opportunities to observe the cultural construction of meaning, locations, where we can see the social production of ideas and value happening before our very eyes' (Turner 1997: 203).

By taking a journey into a Brazilian ethnic landscape born of a cross-Atlantic slave trade, and post-imperial nation building, I have enriched my understanding of ethnicity as a work in progress. Ethnographic fieldwork has put me into contexts of working closely with individuals (both friends and new associates through the research) who identify as African-descendant, and collectives articulated around an African-Brazilian identity and activism kinship of Black Rights movements. My ethnography has involved participant observation and ethnographic recording in friendship, activist and academic contexts, with the Instituto Cultural Steve Biko, Centro de Estudos African-Orientais (affiliated with the Federal University of Bahia), and Ilê Aiyê.[2] I have carried out qualitative research using techniques of formal and informal interviewing, recording oral histories, as well as documenting organisational objectives. I engage in conversational dialogue with members of the public from a range of ethnic backgrounds and analyse Brazilian popular media. I turn to Schacter (2001: 9) to outline the dialogic nature of my methods for this research.

> We tend to think of memories as snapshots from family albums, that, if stored properly, could be retrieved in precisely the same condition in which they were put away. But we now know that we do not record our experience in the way a camera records them. We extract key elements from our experience and store them. We then recreate or reconstruct our experiences rather than retrieve copies of them. Sometimes, in the process of reconstructing we add on feelings, beliefs, or even knowledge we have obtained after the experience.

Using an ethnographic method that is continually informed by what individuals and collectives teach me about their experiences allows me to better engage with the field of memory studies for this project and brings me closer to identifying a methodology suited to expressing the relationship between memory and ethnicity in wounded spaces. I achieve a nuanced approach to the challenging questions that many individuals, families and communities face around themes of ethnicity. For example, in Brazil, in a time of increased affirmative action around African-descent, people ask: Who is black? When are you black enough? How is blackness defined and what constitutes black culture? (see Zabaki and Camargo 2007). Whether memory is selective, repressed, politicised, real or false, in this case it is undeniably at the core of the project of becoming one's ethnic self.

I craft a methodology that rethinks how memories are utilised in the process of self-actualisation and what role remembered histories have within the context of present lives. In the context of this research, ethnicity is a powerful element of local and national history and is likely to have arrived at its present state as something that is not merely a maintenance of what is remembered or drawn from social memory; nor is it exclusively a metaphor of unity drawn from ancestral connection and innateness. I turn to the experience of African-descent within the prevailing narrative of Brazilian nationalism and the state myth of social homogeneity – *sameness despite difference*. This is achieved by focusing on the implementation of Law 10.639, the *Law on Education of Racial-Ethnic Relations* in the Brazilian educational system. By examining the role of collective and social memory in the crafting and implementation of this law I argue that memory is instrumental when the project of ethnicity is constructed.

MEMORY

Most often memory, the result of remembering, is modelled in terms of retrieving stored data from a database of past human experience. According to this vision memory is defined as the past as it is lived by social agents (Berliner 2005: 199). Thus it is that we witness and encounter memory in many forms, as continuing cultural practices, in literature, performance, and the full range of cultural expressions – from oral history to song, dress, visual expression, language and bodily behaviour.

Memory, and the act of remembering, are human and subjective, and construct reality rather than represent it. The vitality of memory lies in the fact that it involves a process of meaning-making linked to cultural episodes that are differentially constructed by individuals, families, and cultural groups. Hoelscher and Alderman (2004: 348) identify this vitality in the continually unfolding nature of memory, and the importance of selection and forgetting in every act of remembering. For Berliner (2005: 200), people 'remember, forget and reinterpret their own pasts'. In this vein, 'memories of the *past* are shaped in accordance with a certain notion of what "we" or, for that matter, "they", really are' (Said 2000: 177). The wider literature on memory and memory studies acknowledges this inventing enterprise and affords memory looseness or interpretive quality, rather than a fixity and inherentness.

Elsewhere I have gone beyond a definition of memory as the past brought into the present through processes of remembrance (Kearney 2012). I have developed the notion of '*present memory*' in order to articulate a wider vision that has synergies with a range of epistemologies and ontologies (both indigenous and non-indigenous) and non-linear understandings of knowledge formation and time. Present memories, as I have come to understand them, involve a conception of memory in a temporal framework that is not dependent on a referral to the past, but rather is intimately linked to the present and what lies ahead. It is a present construction of ideas subject to what the individual or group knows now (including what they have learnt already) and what they wish to know in the future. In this configuration the past as something that is fixed and retrievable is not essential to the construction of present memories. What is essential is the present, the social world occupied now that generates the frameworks for understanding the self and collective identity. These frameworks delineate what matters, what is needed, and even what is absent in the world the individual or group occupies. Once we establish what is present (or absent in the present), a process of decision making begins, and what is known is brought to bear on our current lives. These decisions are often underscored by visions of an aspirational future that determines our present action of constructing and choosing memory.

ETHNICITY

It is memory as understood in its 'present' state that has its greatest resonance with ethnicity and therefore ethnic studies. Ethnic studies emerged internationally in the 1960s. In much the same manner as kinship, politics, economics and religion offered structure to the organisation of everyday lives, ethnicity became the lightning rod to define the theoretical and methodological approaches for persons to redefine the bases on which they construct a sense of social and moral worth (Williams 1989: 401). For Scott (2008: 175), 'in its broadest sense, ethnicity consists of social and cultural processes that are associated with a constructed group identity'. Thus, 'it is a relational construct, something that results when individuals feel a need to conform to a collective identity' (Scott 2008: 175). 'Importantly, ethnicity pointed to self-identified groupings formed on the basis of shared culture, not shared skin colour. It allowed for human agency' (Fozdar et al. 2009: 26). There is an 'agreed-to-ness' about ethnicity. 'You make your choice at least partly based on your knowledge of your ancestry.'

Ethnicity has come to signify processes of self-identification, wrapped up in perceptual encounters between the self, the other, presence, ancestry and an aspirational future. Its value as an interpretive tool for culture and sociality is highlighted through the realisation that 'ethnicity and ethnic identity can be extremely powerful and influential forces, sparking the development of pseudo-histories, claims of political autonomy and sovereignty or a propensity for social relativism' (Scott 2008: 175). It is the subjective loyalty of ethnic belonging that we witness in wounded spaces; they are what sustain platforms for self-determination, politics of exclusion and inclusion, nationalist political agendas, and racial violence (Scott 2008: 175). Ethnicity as an emergent phenomenon created by structural conditions was taken up throughout the 1970s (Yancey et al. 1976). Structural conditions (which are open to change), result in the formation and development of ethnic identities by reinforcing the maintenance of kinship, political and social group affiliation and networks (Yancey et al. 1976: 392). In which case, the capacity for pluralism is ever present.

In common usage, ethnicity is attributed to those groups who are located as a demographic or cultural minority within a majority state. Decolonizing methodologies and post-colonial theory have led the charge in deconstructing this notion, levelling critique at the normative power attributed to certain human groups (largely white and colonial powers) as a result of historical processes. Once imbued with normative power, all other identity positions deemed non-white were classified 'ethnic', despite the fact that to identify as 'white' is itself entirely an ethnic distinction. Ethnic identities may be referred to as wider categories such as indigenous and non-indigenous, white, or black, or as specificities such as Yanyuwa,[3] Australian, Brazilian or African-Brazilian.

There is no limit to the range of possible ethnic identities that exist and at any moment in time, and these labels and their parameters can be renamed, redrawn, or removed.

FRAMEWORKS FOR UNDERSTANDING ETHNICITY AND MEMORY

According to Levine (1999: 166) 'the primordial approach situates ethnicity in the psyche, so deeply that society and culture are bent to its will. Ethnic identities and hatreds naturally draw people into persistent identities and antagonisms'. This approach has formulated an 'understanding of ethnicity as rooted in deep-seated or "primordial" attachments and sentiment' (Brubaker et al. 2004: 49). Whether manifest as deep-seated passions that merit no explanation, or limited scope for a social existence beyond that which is circumscribed, memory, and very particular styles of remembrance, can work to create psychological essentialism around ethnic identity. Treating ethnic identity as primordial requires a particular relationship between the past and present, to be enshrined in the sense of one's self as an individual and member of a collective. This is a relationship of processual understanding in which memories are fixed narratives of the past, inherited and then used as governing structures for how 'to be'.

Memory and ethnicity in this case are bound by historical continuity with a distant past. Memory is seen as factual, an historical archive of accumulated events that has persisted and is knowable, and manifest in the form of a particular ethnic identity. Memories are understood as originary snapshots of an agreed-to past reality which can be stored, retained and recalled to inform present life and future direction. Acts of remembrance, which are also agreed to, ritually re-embed knowledge of a certain ethnic narrative into the consciousness of the collective.[4] This is bound by the logic of linear time in which what is 'present' cannot be disentangled from a remembered (or archetypal) past. Essentialised memory supports a type of primordial self that can be retrieved from the deep past in an almost archaeological quest for parameters of belonging and selfhood in the world today. Thus a primordialist approach to ethnicity allows us to consider how deeply held and subjective loyalties come to be mandated and often powerfully defended. I argue that although naturalising of ethnic identities does occur through psychological essentialism, on behalf of those who claim a certain identity or by external entities that affect their presence, there is nothing primordial about the process of ethnicity itself. Change cannot be precluded from a discussion of the ways and means by which collectives arrive at an essentialised ethnic identity. While the ethnic arrival point may be claimed as primordial (in that it allegedly replicates what has always been), the journey taken to this destination is open to change as a result of historical particularities and contemporary conditions.

From the 1920s, Halbwachs sought to describe memory as a social phenomenon. The success of his project is seen in the prevailing view of ethnicity as a socially constructed identity (Yang 2000). As an extension of constructed identity, ethnic boundaries are flexible or changeable. In sum, ethnicity is dynamic (Yang 2000). In line with this dynamism, I argue that temporality is secondary in understanding the role of memory in the process of ethnicity. Distinguishing between distant and recent memory, Brownlie (2011: 5) states: 'In distant memory there are many instances of neutral attitudes, whereas in recent memory of a significant event we may find only negative or positive attitudes'. Whether memory be attributed to the distant or recent past (vague temporal measures at best) is irrelevant to the place of remembrance in the construction of a particular ethnic identity. We see distant memory and historical continuity with the distant past utilised in the construction and reconstruction of ethnic identities worldwide. We also see it as a coercive tool for alliances and hatred based on perceived ethnic difference. Whether from a proclaimed primordial and distant past, a recent traumatic past, or emerging sense of past and present (with the sudden assertion of an ethnic specificity) it remains that memory is an act of making meaning, which may or may not be based on invention and desirable loyalty.

In this vision of ethnicity the process is linked to existing socio-political structures and human agency. Ethnic identity becomes the product of actions undertaken by groups as they shape and reshape their self-identification, often actions set against a background of external social, economic and political processes (Nagel 1994). In sum, the process of ethnicity is highly relational and rarely fixed. According to Hoelscher and Alderman (2004: 348) there is a continually unfolding quality to memory and, for this reason, memories exist as part of a frame of understanding, or worldview, in which the present is the governing temporal episode for all aspects of life. The present delimits what we know, and therefore how we understand our position in the world relative to group and individual identity. Once we establish what is present (or absent in the present) a process of decision making begins, and what is known is brought to bear on our current lives. This notion is followed up by instrumentalists who emphasise the social construction of ethnicity and its annexation as an instrument for gaining resources (Comaroff and Comaroff 2009). This view is underscored by the proposition that costs and benefits associated with ethnic group membership partly determine ethnic affiliation (Yang 2000). According to an instrumentalist (also termed situationalist) position, when an ethnic choice becomes available, the costs and benefits of ethnicity play a pivotal role in determining the options. Alternative assertions of ethnic identity become possible only when an ethnic status quo is challenged and superseded, and from this is born something distinct – not altogether new, but distinct from an earlier form. According to this view not all ethnic choices are rational and materialistic. Some people choose an ethnic affiliation not for material gains, rewards, or access to resources and services, but for emotional, intellectual and political satisfaction, which includes states of well-being, self-fulfilment, social attachment or recreational pleasure (Yang 2000: 47).

Comaroff and Comaroff (2009: 38) point to 'looseness' as a definitive quality of ethnicity as an organisational category or mechanism of affiliation for human groups in today's world. I contend that swinging the pendulum so far that ethnicity becomes a loose organisational structure may render it meaningless (or, more tragically, powerless) as a means to distinguish cultural specificity born of challenging circumstances as, for example, found in Brazil. For human groups that occupy marginal spaces, and for those groups whose cultural specificity is born of a political project based upon wounding and reclamation, the capacity to create and emerge in ethnic form remains an essential component of survival.

When modelling memory on similar instrumentalist or situationalist terms, we encounter a discourse of the 'inventing enterprise'. Imagination, repression and selection are central to an understanding of the relationship between memory and ethnicity as a process governed by principles of meaningful choice. Remembrance on instrumentalist terms also implies the opportunity to forget. According to this framework, memory involves deliberate and thoughtful choices as to what is remembered and what is forgotten. From this decision making are born normative memories or criteria to forge or dismantle ethnic and other political identities. The subjective and contested loyalties that may be born of ethnicity as an instrumental process require an understanding of memory which acknowledges its plasticity. What is remembered and what is forgotten are subject to the weighing up of costs and benefits in light of material and emotional well-being. The complexity involved in this process is at the core of important work in memory studies, such as Connerton's (2008) work on forgetting, which recognises repressive erasure, prescriptive forgetting, forgetting as annulment, and forgetting as humiliated silence. Similarly, remembrance and commemoration come to be complicated by way of understanding a complex suite of types of memory: explicit and implicit, sensory, autobiographical, episodic, procedural or repressed. These possibilities in the way we remember, or the way we choose to understand memory and its purpose in our present lives, indicates that wherever we find memory at the centre of identity construction we enter an arena of emotional and political magnitude. If indeed ethnicity is the ultimate memory project, then the need for a methodology that charters the subjectivity of personal and political lives is emphasised. It is to this that I now turn in my discussion, bringing to bear an approach to memory and ethnicity in Brazil that combines a constructionist approach to ethnicity and an instrumentalist approach to memory.

AFRICAN-DESCENT AND MEMORY IN BRAZIL

In Brazil, many social and structural conditions have functioned as catalysts for ethnic consciousness (Yang 2000: 53). Ancestry, self-interest, and the larger economic, political and social structures all underlie the social construction of African-descendant identity in northern Brazil. The Brazilian Census of 2009 provided five options for self-declared 'race', along colour lines.[5] These were 'preto' (black), 'branco' (white), 'pardo' (brown), 'amarelo' (yellow) and 'indigena' (indigenous) (Instituto Brasileiro de Geografia e Estatística). Leaving aside the obvious deconstruction demanded of how colour relates to race, and in turn relates to ethnicity, these colour declarations, and that of 'indigena', can be seen to represent five more generalist ethnic identities. In 2009, 6.9 per cent of the Brazilian population self-identified as *preto* (black) (Instituto Brasileiro de Geografia e Estatística). For many who identify as such, life is framed by 'deep disparities in income, education and employment between lighter and darker-skinned Brazilians', and these 'have prompted civil rights movements advocating equal treatment' (Wideangle 2007). Making up a considerable proportion of the total population, African-Brazilians constitute a majority of the nation's poor. The declaration of one's self as black sits in relationship to declarations of ethnic identity such as African-descendant and African-Brazilian. The differences or similarities between these monikers require attention, but this goes beyond the depth and breadth of this discussion. When referring to ethnicity in this discussion I refer to African-descendant as the ethnic identity which collectively holds those who self-declare an identity linked to an African heritage through kinship and African cultural expressions. This may include biological and cultural ancestry. What is key here is self-declaration, as many individuals who have African ancestry do not identify themselves as African-descendant in Brazil, with individuals opting to identify as either 'branco' or 'pardo' (or a range of other self-declared classificatory terms).

Discussions of ethnicity and memory in Brazil are inflected by the historical particularity of a population with ancestral connections to a cross-Atlantic slave trade that brought generations of African descendants into Brazil. Today, many Brazilians identify as African-descendant, yet the manner in which they do so is highly contingent and dependent on a range of complex variables ranging from individual choice (self-declaration), family history, socio-economic status, location of residence, and imposed categories used in demographic data collection by national bodies. For the purpose of this discussion I draw attention to this African heritage, traced through a history of slavery in Brazil set to the rhythm of imperialism and nation-building. Beginning in the mid 1500s, the Portuguese traded enslaved Africans into Brazil, a practice which would continue until its official abolishment in 1888 with the passing of the *Lei Áurea* (Golden Law), and for some time after that through illegal channels of human enslavement and trading (see Klein and Luna 2009). According to Baranov (cited in Wolfe 2001: 901) the decree involved 'abolishing the slave while simultaneously failing to emancipate the African', thus planting a seed which would grow into a complex of inter-ethnic relations still being heavily negotiated in contemporary Brazil. The majority of Africans enslaved and brought to Brazil were from West and West Central Africa, including the Yoruba, Ewe, Fanti-Ashanti, Ga-Adangbe, Igbo, Fon and Mandinga peoples and Bantu people from across Angola, Congo, and Mozambique (see Karasch 1987; Verger 1976).

While slavery became the mainstay of the economy throughout all parts of Brazil, the northern regions are particularly regarded for having retained African influences and cultural expressions as a result of a rich history of African cultural presence (see Nishida 2003).[6] The history of African slavery in Brazil sits prominently, if not uncomfortably, in contemporary narratives of nationhood and cultural origins. This is due partly to the nation's failure to reconcile a difficult and traumatic past,[7] and the historical tendency for Brazilian nationalism to be prefaced on the notion of 'sameness' and blurring of ethnic distinctions. The beating heart of Brazilian nationalism was prefaced on the myth of social homogeneity (*sameness despite difference*), and social homogeneity has been regarded as the lynchpin for racial democracy (Schwartzman 2007; Wolfe 2001). Today, assertions of racial plurality, 'difference amidst claims to sameness', have taken flight, in an era of burgeoning affirmative action. Critiquing the narrative of social homogeneity, Ramos (2001: 2) writes:

> The Brazilian nation has been constructed on the basis of two main premises: one is its territorial and linguistic unity; the other is its purported social homogeneity resulting from the combination of three 'races' – Indians, Blacks and Europeans. While the first premise, especially regarding territoriality, has been empirically sustained, the second is a clearly mystifying ideology.

The desire to find the essence of Brazilian identity is fraught, and brings about inevitably varied and inconclusive results over time and space. For Ramos (2001: 3) the desire to find an essence, or rather, create an essence, came down to the imperial project of *branqueamento* or 'whitening'. What masks as harmonious ethnic encounters or 'social memory' of accommodation and assimilation in the annals of imperial history is, for Ramos (2001: 3), best understood as a process of creating 'a recipe for homogenous nationality', 'an amalgam of whitened races with a unique and uniform national flavour'. 'Rather than having differences sorted out in a separate-but-equal ideological pattern, one would have a mixed-though-unequal national design' (Ramos 2001: 3). The singularity of Brazil has been a point of national reflection since the Declaration of Independence in 1822, which brought about the beginnings of questioning around national identity.

In 2003, the Brazilian government implemented Federal Law 10.639 (Presidência da República), which positioned cultural plurality as a 'transversal theme' (Nascimento 2007: 236). This was the result of activism for Black Rights and efforts to bring the issue of racism to the minds of educational policy makers (Nascimento 2007: 236). The law establishes 'guidelines for national curriculum for teaching ethno-racial relations and African-Brazilian and African history and culture' (UNESCO). It extends to elementary and middle school levels, as well as higher education. The curriculum covers the Atlantic slave trade, sixteenth-, seventeenth- and eighteenth-century African history, and studies of contemporary Africa. The text also establishes the need for teachers to be trained in these subjects (Nascimento 2007: 239). Initiatives of intervention in school curricula and in the classroom have also been carried out by non-governmental organisations and black movement organisations for some time now (Nascimento 2007: 236). These include 'African-Brazilian religious communities, and cultural groups like the African-Reggae Cultural Group in Rio de Janeiro and the Olodum and Ilê Aiyê Blocos in Salvador, Bahia' (Nascimento 2007: 236). Much of this has sparked concern as to the impact that increased recognition and valorisation of ethnic diversity within Brazil might have on Brazilian nationalism and inter-ethnic relations (Centro Cultural Orunmilá). The Centro Cultural Orunmilá, a non-profit Black Rights organisation, which declares its function as 'the elevation of the human condition through the promotion of citizenship, the search for elements of the sociocultural identity, the regaining of dignity and self-esteem of black people in particular' has raised the following questions of Law 10.639: 'Who will teach black culture?' and 'Who is trained/qualified to transmit black culture?'

Emergence of an African-descendant ethnic particularity, shaped through processes of social memory and the politics of affirmative action, involves collective coordination of ancestral lineage, agreed-to social memories, and contemporary events. If the aim of educational initiatives is to strengthen the 'African identity', and its associated memories and cultural expressions, then there has to be agreement over a normative view of African identity and culture in Brazil. This requires a suite of memories and narratives to be identified that might best inform the construction of this normativity. It is the constructed part of this process that is most complicated and interesting. The instrumental logic behind both Law 10.639 and more general Black Rights movements in

Brazil involves the weighing up of the costs and benefits involved in certain aspects of being African-descendant. We see this in the streets of major cities like Salvador with the use of African-Brazilian cultural symbols such as capoeira, Candomble and samba, Carnaval blocos (groups), dress and personal aesthetics of styling, attendance at African-educational facilities (such as the Instituto Cultural Steve Biko and Centro de Estudos African-Orientais) to craft the personality of African-Brazilian ethnic identity (Nishida 2003; Pinho 2010). For Pinho (2010: 1), 'reinventions of Africa have been tremendously important for black communities in the diaspora and have frequently spurred black resistance'. Simultaneously they corroborate pre-established notions of blackness, keeping Africa alive though memory projects which require the enactment of songs, music, literature, foods, dance forms, and myths, along with the embodiment of an aesthetic linked to African inspired fashion, beauty and style (Pinho 2010). There are those who agree to and accept these symbols and terms of identifying, and those who do not. Self-declaration is central and suggests it is individual decision making (as sanctioned by the collective) that leads to the embodiment of elements of African descent and the choice to subscribe to an ethnic identity with full knowledge of the politics and aesthetics this implies. Even outsiders participate in the process of setting the limits to what being an African-descendant might involve. Judgements of what constitutes a black person, or a brown or white person for that matter, are keenly debated in Brazil.

The decision to move towards the teaching of black culture in Brazilian schools involves the construction of a pan-African diaspora, history and subsequent identity. This overlooks the specificities of ethnic group experiences in Africa, a diversity of experiences matched by the diverse ethnic representation found among those enslaved and brought to Brazil. It does however, instrumentally, create unity in shared ancestry made of a pastiche of different historical experiences and specific cultural identities. What I argue is that this is entirely reasonable, and is often at the core of individual expressions that I have recorded ethnographically. This may be a middle-aged woman who clearly articulates her Africanness by tracing her ancestry to individuals enslaved in Benin, West Africa and brought to Brazil. She embodies her African-descent by choice, through an African aesthetic of dress, physical appearance, music, and politics, alongside a proud expression of her mother's indigenous descent. It is also a younger man who politically articulates his ethnicity as African-Brazilian, and takes inspiration from African-Brazilian music and Carnaval practices for a kinship with this political identity, while at the same time not wishing this to define his personal life. Or it may be the young woman who chooses to identify as African-descendant for the first time in official documentation, in order to qualify for application of university entry under racial quota programmes. Memory can only be understood at the very moment of its construction, the instance in which a choice is made regarding what and how to remember and therefore 'how to go on'. In the crafting of African and African-Brazilian history, we see in action what is known in the present and what is desired in the future as negotiated and expressed by individuals in the moment of ethnographic description or as expressed by organisations in the presentation of an African-descendant identity. In this configuration the past is not essential to the construction of present memories. What is essential is the presence of a population within Brazil that asserts a connection to Africa through kinship and cultural expression, and the tragic reality of documented inequity and disadvantage for this collective.

The social world, which is occupied now, generates the frameworks for understanding what being black, African-descendant, or African-Brazilian means. In the case of African-descendant interventions into social and political realities in Brazil we see a deliberate project to assert a collective identity along ethnic lines, with the goal of creating a space within the national consciousness and the deliverance of rights. The decision of what constitutes an African-descendant in this moment is underscored by visions of an aspirational future of equity and rights. This is what influences memory and prompts the call for black autonomy over who teaches African and African-Brazilian history, which, according to the Centro Cultural Orunmilá, cannot be 'learned in books and in the academy' (Centro Cultural). If this is the case, then can it be that the essence of black culture lies in the mind, the body, the spirit – the elements that constitute identity politics and the construction of our 'selves' in reference to an agreed-to set of memories, values and expressions?

OVERVIEW

In this chapter I have argued that the instrumentalist approach to ethnicity acknowledges emerging and new forms of ethnicity as valid, powerful and legitimate. The key to understanding African-descendant ethnic identity as an emerging and powerfully articulated social position has been adopting this approach. It allows for a greater connection between anthropological understandings of emerging and politicised ethnicities. The methodology I adopt is one in which I argue that memory is instrumentalist when the project of ethnicity is underway and politically charged. This in no way dilutes the power of memory; nor does it render it false. Instead, it is about realising that memory is an instrumentalist project in that its construction and reformulation is instrumental to making sense of our place in the world right here and right now. 'The past', while entirely relevant to our present states (albeit in more complicated ways than we think) is, as L. P. Hartley states in the opening to *The Go-Between*, 'a foreign country'. The present is our home, and present memories are what we make and remake in the act of establishing an ethnic identity. This means that states of emergence in identity politics do not diminish the value and importance of certain ethnic identities, however much they might challenge the status quo, or appear to be 'born overnight' or opportunistically engaged for some form of benefit. Critique of affirmative action and identity politics around African-descent often cites its emergent quality and perceived opportunism as argument against the rise and vigour of a Black Rights movement in Brazil. Viewing political action around ethnic identity as 'trouble making', as often witnessed in media and political debate around certain ethnic identities and their 'privileges', or threatening the stability of national identity, is flawed, not only because it is racist, but also because it disregards the current state of play in any given country or region. The state of play is what is 'present' and, for many African-descendants in Brazil, this is inequity and disadvantage. It is the present and its form as a persistent memory that needs addressing in wounded spaces. Realising this brings us closer to understanding the social and political motivations that underscore ethnicity and identity politics more generally.

SUMMARY: KEY POINTS

- In this chapter I have revisited the relationship between memory and ethnicity.
- I argue that the instrumentalist approach, which enables research into emerging and new forms of ethnicity as valid, powerful and legitimate, allows us to understand human agency as underscored by complex motivations.
- The benefits of this approach far outweigh a primordialist or essentialising approach to ethnicity, which might position qualities of emergence or newness as invented or even disingenuous.
- By marrying ethnographic methods of dialogic research and intersubjectivity with an instrumentalist approach we find the best method of working with ethnicity in wounded spaces.

FURTHER READING

Comaroff and Comaroff (2009) offer a contemporary analysis of ethnicity in a range of ethnographic settings. They explore instrumentalism in its fullest sense and raise important questions regarding the use of memory as a deliberate project for the delivery of benefits according to ethnic identity. This resonates with consideration of the role of memory and identity in a globalised world. Halbwach (1992) is a foundational text for recent work on theorising memory as a collective exercise and act. Sociological in its disciplinary focus, the work can be used to guide more general interactions with the role of memory in cross-cultural frameworks. It sets an important precedent for the study of memory as it identifies memory as culturally determined – therefore as a cultural construction that is linked to group consciousness. Pinho (2010) is a rich ethnography of ethnicity and 'blackness' in Bahia, Brazil. Focusing on contemporary manifestations of ethnicity, it draws on the history of Africa in Brazil, while also examining the role of remembering in contemporary enactments of a Black identity. This is a very engaging text which comments on affirmative action and the politics of memory and identity. Yang (2000) is an excellent introduction to ethnic studies. It provides background to the theorising of identity, ethnicity, prejudice, discrimination, politics and ethnicity in the future.

NOTES

1. By wounded space I refer to those geographical spaces that have witnessed human suffering, violence, and exile as a result of political intervention (see Rose 2004: 34). This includes colonial and imperial frontiers, which contain traumatic histories for different ethnic groups, whether in the form of enslavement, genocide, or dispossession of land and culture.
2. The Instituto Cultural Steve Biko, named after South African anti-apartheid revolutionary Steve Biko, is an organization working to assist African-descendant students' transition through educational phases into university. The institute expresses its objective as seeking to 'arm and equip students to use education as a weapon against oppression' (Instituto Cultural Steve Biko).
   Ilê Aiyê was founded in 1974, as a carnaval group in the neighbourhood of Liberdade in Salvador, Bahia. Members work to raise consciousness around the Bahian black community and strive to reinvent 'the meanings of Africa and Africanness as a basis for constructing new cultural and aesthetic symbols' (Pinho 2010: 2).
3. An indigenous Australian language group (ethnic group).
4. By 'agreed to' I mean any type of sanctioning of knowledge (called memories) or processes for articulating this knowledge that becomes normative (for example, language, dress, appearance, social codes of behaving, or national holidays and monuments).
5. There is a history of documented colour/ethnic classifications in Brazil. Wolfe (2001: 895) remarks on Harris' (1970) identification of 490 such classifications. He states that while these are not all in contemporary usage

throughout Brazil, they reveal a complexity of social classification and stratification in a post-imperial era.
6. As Wolfe (2001: 895) notes, slavery was not homogenous in Brazil. In fact different types of slavery occurred in different parts of Brazil in relation to different industries (sugar, mining, coffee, domestic slavery). The sugar industry largely dominated in the north-eastern parts of Brazil, and in Bahia, where much of my ethnographic fieldwork has been carried out. For comprehensive discussions on the history of slavery in Brazil, see Klein and Luna (2010) and Mattoso (1993).
7. Brazil is not alone in this, and much of my work as an anthropologist has been concerned with similar issues in Australia.

SECTION FIVE

Disturbed Memory

CHAPTER 9

Painful Pasts

Emily Keightley and Michael Pickering

INTRODUCTION

While memory studies has emerged as a diverse and heterogeneous body of work, a common issue over the last two decades has been with the ways in which the past is reconstructed in the present, regardless of whether this involves macro-structures such as the nation-state or the everyday minutiae of personal experience. The different perspectives and their associated scales of analysis which are brought to bear on this concern may be various, but they share a concern with the use of the past as a resource in making experience and social life meaningful, in producing or challenging cultural norms and conventions, and in reproducing or subverting established orders of power. In post-Halbwachsian explorations of memory processes, the consensual nature of these processes is rarely taken for granted. Often the pasts involved in these negotiations and struggles involve heavy emotional investment, and entail experiences of exclusion, discrimination, loss and bereavement. Under these circumstances, the stakes are high. Through remembering displacement can be redressed, victimisation recognised, and pain acknowledged. Alternatively, claims for recompense can be silenced, losses denied and exclusions reinforced. Painful pasts of this kind have preoccupied memory studies research, as is evidenced by the extensive and continually expanding literature on the memorialisation of large-scale atrocities such as the Holocaust or 9/11, and the considerable attention paid to such painful past experience as childhood sexual abuse, exile or genocide.

In some cases, painful pasts are of such severity that they cannot be integrated into processes of remembering and contestation. They can be so disruptive or disorientating that they become disconnected from the present, unamenable to narrative form and so off limits as a resource for making sense of experience. Pain is nevertheless variable, and differences in the experience of and responses to difficult pasts must be accounted for if the specificity of the experience is to be respected. Alongside this, making sense of the past and its relation to the present depends upon establishing connections between different pasts and presents, identifying commonalities and developing meaning from past experiences in new contexts. Dealing with different types and intensities of painful pasts pose methodological challenges for memory studies. How, precisely, do we go about investigating and researching such pasts when they vary so much in nature and consequence? How can the various roles they have in processes of remembering be assessed? How should they be addressed on various social scales, from the individual to the global?

In thinking about such questions, this chapter focuses particularly on issues raised when we are dealing with painful pasts in empirical research. These include considering how we may investigate processes of remembering when the past itself is problematic as a resource for such processes, how we may make visible disturbances in routine oscillations between the temporal domains of experience, and how we may recognise and account for disruption of transactional relations between the tenses. These are methodological issues, but in approaching them we must start with the conceptualisation of painful pasts in memory studies. We must do so because one particular conceptualisation, based around notions of trauma, has dominated the treatment of such pasts in this field. This has, in our view, limited the range of methodological options open to memory studies scholars in doing research on difficult pasts. In particular, it has led to the profligate application of trauma beyond acute individual suffering to such research objects as material culture, population categories, entire periods of history, even history itself (see for example Caruth 1991, 1996; Neal 1998; Eyerman 2001; Edkins 2003). In this chapter we reject such ethically dubious uses of the concept of trauma and try instead to develop a more humanly sensitive methodological framework for dealing with the memory of painful experience.

CONCEPTUALISING PAIN

From its roots in psychiatry and psychoanalysis, there has been a remarkable academic uptake of trauma as a concept. As Kansteiner (2004: 98) notes, 'trauma is everywhere, or, to be more precise, everywhere in the humanities'. This is equally true of the social sciences, for it now occupies a prominent position, not only in literary and cultural studies, but also in media studies, sociology and history as well as in psychology. It is this trans-disciplinary mobility that has made trauma the go-to concept in memory studies for assessing the ways in which past pain features in individual experience, social life, and contemporary culture. Indeed, it has been argued that 'increasingly, memory worth talking about – worth remembering – is memory of trauma' (Antze and Lambek 1996: 2). In contrast to the broadly accepted definition of remembering as constituting our sense of successive selves, and therefore of identity, over the course of time, psychic trauma refers 'to any developmental event or crisis that overwhelms the ego's integrative capacities, compromising subsequent adaptive structures' (Pickering and Keightley 2009: 238; Haaken 1998: 68). Trauma is the disruption of the remembering process caused by an event or experience so at odds with our usual frameworks of remembering that it cannot be remembered in any conventional fashion. Instead of being assimilated into the continually developing story of a life, traumatic experience haunts the present by distorting memory's links to the past, leading to feelings of dissociation or panic, the re-experience of emotions felt during a traumatic episode but with no narrative connections to the episode, only terrifying flashbacks and malevolent images reverberating in the psyche of the affected person.

So far, so relatively uncontroversial: some people, from the shell-shocked soldiers of the First World War to contemporary survivors of childhood sexual abuse, have been unable to remember their painful experiences in a coherent fashion and put past experience to use in the interests of developing a durable identity in and through time. Yet the ways in which trauma has been taken up and applied in the social sciences and humanities has gone radically beyond this specific application in several ways. To begin with, trauma has been so loosely deployed that the concept is used to cover all recollections of painful pasts. When any violent or painful experience is labelled as traumatic, the distinctive features of trauma on the one hand, and remembering on the other, are casually but definitely elided. For example, Jenny Edkins talks of the ways in which traumas are 'inscribed and re-inscribed into everyday narratives' in the practices of remembrance, memorialisation and witnessing related to political events and processes (2003: 15). The notion that trauma is broadly embedded in and structures everyday memorial practices is problematic, and is so because it is 'amnesiac rather than memorial' in nature (Luckhurst 2003: 28). Trauma involves the abrupt failure of the remembering practices and processes central to the making of the self over time, or to the representational reinterpretation of the past in public culture.

While in some accounts distinctions between trauma and memory are collapsed into each other, in others the notion of trauma is stretched to such a degree that, while it denotes a condition that is unrepresentable in language or any other symbolic form, and is advanced as generic and 'unlocatable' in any given person or group, it can also be transmitted as experience from one generation to another and is 'something that can be shared by victims and non-victims alike' (Leys 2000: 304–5). The experience of someone suffering traumatic stress disorder is run together and made relative to one who hears their account second-hand. This is highly evident in Cathy Caruth's work. The paradox of this is that Caruth seems to suggest that trauma can be communicated and shared, despite the fact that it is beyond language. Trauma is characterised as the basic condition of historical experience, regardless of the various experiences of and responses to pain that this might involve for any given person or group; in her sweeping generalisation of the term, 'we are all victims and survivors of the trauma of representation' (Kansteiner 2004: 204). The radical relativism of this understanding of trauma as the key symptom of historical process utterly conflates victims and perpetrators of violence since both are conceived as survivors of a generalised traumatic condition (see Kansteiner and Weilnböck 2008; Leys 2000; Rothberg 2009; Keightley and Pickering 2012, Chapter 6, for further critiques of this position). Caruth places modern experience within an inescapable traumatic cage from which there is no escape.

As well as undermining historical analysis and the politics of memory, the analytical application of trauma is routinely accompanied by what can be considered as an 'aesthetic valorisation' of trauma (Kansteiner and Weilnböck 2008). In this sense trauma as a universal condition of victimhood becomes a 'form of cultural capital that bestows moral privilege' (Rothberg 2009: 87). This has the interesting effect of placing those who have experienced painful pasts beyond critique. The position of the witness, and in some theorists' accounts, the vicarious witness via mediated culture, becomes a subject position beyond critical assessment. Trauma becomes an indisputable way of knowing, one not subject to the inherent instabilities and polysemic qualities of representation. This raises the question as to whether it is desirable for trauma to be 'worked through' at all if it is the mode by which we can most authentically know the past. Narrative remembering as a continual process of making sense of the past, with its inevitable selectivity, contingency and temporariness, comes to be conceived, paradoxically, as a way of *not-knowing*, whereas trauma, a concept originally conceived to address the unrecoverable nature of the past, is positioned as its conceptual opposite. On this basis, a radical rupture between past and present is celebrated, and possibilities for renewal through a transactional relationship with the past are rejected. The possibility of working through pain, learning from it, using it as a resource in the present and for the future is conceived not only as impossible, but also as undesirable. This has an unavoidably atomising as well as politically nullifying effect.

It is our contention that instead of conceiving of trauma as either collapsed into remembering processes or radically divorced from them, we should see trauma as distinct from, but also linked to, these processes. While trauma involves the disruption of conventional processes of making sense of experience and adding to our store of knowledge, traumatic responses to painful pasts disrupt and problematise the remembering process in a variety of ways. Remembered narratives and representations can therefore be used as an empirical resource to identify the gradations of response to painful pasts, ranging from a complete inability to remember on the one hand, and a completely coherent remembered narrative on the other. In between these poles are representations of the past which we might consider as possessing traumatic features, as well as being characterised as remembering. It is through the examination of these examples that the tensions and difficulties involved in remembering painful pasts can be made visible.

TRAUMA, PAIN AND THE PROBLEM OF METHOD

The imperialistic extrapolation of trauma as the analytical framework *par excellence* for social and cultural memory poses serious methodological problems. If trauma is at the root of historical consciousness, but at the same time unavailable in representational form, there can be no method for its critical identification – still less for making analytical sense of the ways in which it is involved (or not) in relations between past and present. This double-bind is conveniently overlooked when the concept of trauma is applied as an interpretative frame, while the specificity of trauma as an uninterpreted response to a intensely disruptive experience is lost along with the struggle to bring it into the realm of conventional discourse and so begin the process of 'working through'. The cavalier metaphorical application of trauma obscures the relationship between remembering and trauma and the distinctive features of each. The problem memory studies is left with is that trauma identifies an important response to painful experiences at an individual level, but it is only one mode of response to past pain. A much broader approach is needed if we are to account for the wide variety of painful pasts and responses to them. What has made this difficult in memory studies to date is the woeful lack of empirical research attempting to investigate the specific ways in which individuals and groups remember painful pasts. This is compounded by a tendency to ignore empirical research from other fields of research which may contribute to this project, including studies of individual trauma victims and of collective suffering.

In moving beyond the limitations of the trauma paradigm, the methodological prerequisites for dealing with the remembering of painful pasts are threefold. Firstly, the integrity of traumatic suffering should be recognised and appreciated, and clearly distinguished from the variety of experiences involved in the remembering of painful pasts along with the rhetorical strategies and power relations they entail. This necessitates a close empirical focus on the key features of traumatic responses observable in accounts of painful pasts in contrast to the assimilation of such pasts in accounts which activate transactional relations between the past and present. In this respect, Gadi BenEzer has identified thirteen specific discursive features which 'signal' trauma, ranging from long silences and the loss of emotional control to changes in voice and body language (2004: 34–6). In being indicative of a specifically traumatic response to an event, such features mark uncontrolled disruption in the movement between experience as process to experience as product. Making this distinction means seeing trauma and remembering as existing along a discursive continuum in which, over time, traumatic features may decrease and the availability of past experience to the processes of remembering may emerge. This opens up the possibility for seeing trauma, not as a closed circuit of literal repetition, but a temporally specific response which may, in time, be moved beyond, so rehabilitating the possibility for renewal.

Secondly, we should attend methodologically to the different levels on which painful pasts operate, from the individual through to the cultural. This requires looking into the interplay between cultural representations of the past, the social practices involved in their articulation and the social frameworks of remembering that they draw on, as well as individual practices of interpretation in their reception (Irwin-Zarecka 2007). Rather than distantly 'reading off' a traumatic response from memorial sites, mediated representations, or a groups' proximity to a given event, the lived relationships between past and present that are performed through remembering practices need to be closely attended to.

Attending to oscillations between individual, social and cultural domains of engagement with painful pasts is intimately bound up with our third methodological requirement. This is that we should attempt to work ethically with the memory of painful pasts in empirical research. The wilful dismissal of the experiential relationship between the trauma sufferer and the original traumatic event in much recent literature on 'cultural trauma' has considerable ethical implications, as we and others have discussed elsewhere (Kansteiner 2004; Leys 2000; Luckhurst 2003; Pickering and Keightley 2009). The extrapolation of trauma to large categories of people on the basis of secondary or tertiary encounters with violent or disruptive pasts hugely dilutes the experience of victims and survivors, and in doing so empathy, as a response premised on the maintenance of critical distance, is transformed into a position of identification where the experience of suffering is appropriated at one remove (LaCapra 2001: 21–2). In order to redress this, memory studies needs ethically to dissociate the experiences of individual victims from practices of reception among those who engage with painful pasts at one (or more) remove(s). This is not to say that the transmission of painful experiences is impossible, but rather to argue that when exploring second-hand engagements with painful pasts and the interpretative practices that they involve, remembering rather than trauma is the more appropriate analytical framework since it requires critical engagement with the discursive and rhetorical processes involved in the articulation of the pain of others. This is precisely what Sontag recommends when she suggests that 'no "we" should be taken for granted when the subject is looking at other people's pain' (2003: 6). In addition, working with individual accounts of traumatic and painful pasts brings its own set of methodological dilemmas for the researcher with respect to the elicitation of accounts and the treatment of sensitive data. In attempting to develop ethical research practices in this regard, memory studies has much to learn from the more established practices of oral history.

It is to the ways in which these methodological imperatives can be performed in empirical research that we now turn. As has already been discussed, memories of painful pasts operate on a number of scales, from the intensely personal to the broadly public. Of course, each scale is implied in every other – the intensely personal account draws on publicly shared frames and discourses in order to be communicable, while public accounts are received and interpreted at an individual level. In this chapter we have chosen to focus on the increasingly overlooked iterations of personal pain in order to demonstrate the analytical strategies involved in working with trauma and painful remembering.

PERSONAL ITERATIONS OF PAIN

Empirical research on painful remembering involves the collection of personal narratives of painful pasts. This can be achieved in two ways. Firstly, it could involve the elicitation of accounts as part of the research process. Although quantitative methods such as surveys might provide important contextual data for assessing the prevalence and key features of memories of this kind, it is primarily qualitative approaches which provide in-depth, detailed accounts of how disruptive or disturbing experiences affect identity construction and processes of reconciling past and present over time. For example, Anna Reading collected gendered memories of the Holocaust articulated by generations of Jews with experience of the Holocaust at one or two removes, either through family narratives or cultural mediations. Reading used a life-history approach in order to elicit written and then verbal accounts of young people's memories of the Holocaust in order to 'give voice to and explore the meanings and constructions of socially inherited memories for the generation of people who would not have experienced the events of the Holocaust themselves, although they may have family or older friends who did' (Reading 2002: 20). The use of qualitative interviews to elicit memories of disturbing events generates data which both captures the content of painful memories but is also inscribed with the processes of remembering through which they are constructed and articulated.

In contrast, our own research investigates the use of everyday media in remembering practices rather than memories of a specific event or period. In this research we have utilised a variety of qualitative techniques. Our starting point was the in-depth interview in which one researcher, or sometimes two, initiated a guided conversation with participants about their remembering practices. As part of these interviews participants were asked to discuss particular photographs or items of music which were associated with important or particularly emotive memories. Inevitably this produced accounts where painful pasts, or more often pasts which had subsequently taken on a painful resonance with the passing of time, were described and discussed. The use of elicitation techniques provides a valuable anchor for the interview process, allowing sometimes intangible and nebulous memories to be articulated with more clarity and precision. This is of particular value to the researcher in the data-gathering process as it provides a focal point for elaboration. For example, when discussing a particular song which is associated with a painful past, researchers can go beyond asking about its mnemonic associations to ask when it is played in the present, the specific responses to it on listening, who one might listen to it with or where it is stored. These questions move us beyond a focus on the content of painful memories into the realm of their articulation in everyday remembering practices, and provide clues to their contemporary use and significance.

When eliciting mnemonic accounts of painful pasts, the presence of the interviewer can pose its own methodological challenges. Allowing an interviewee the required time and space for reflection on a painful experience without interruption can run up against or contravene the discursive demands of an in-depth interview, where extended gaps, silences, tears or long breaks disturb the flow of talk and may cause the interview process to break down. In our own research we have experimented with methods which remove the physical presence of the interviewer while maintaining the guided nature of elicited recollections. To do this we have used what we have called 'self-interviews', in which participants are provided with a guidance sheet which asks them to look through their photo albums, listen to their music collections, and narrate the experience of doing so using a Dictaphone (Keightley et al. 2012, and see Chapter 6). This partially frees the participants from the discursive and social demands of a conventional interview, allowing them to have reflective periods of silence, take breaks as necessary, and follow the path of their own recollections without the interjections of an interviewer. While the interviewer's presence is still felt through the guidance sheet, this mode of interviewing provides participants with a discursive space that is more sensitive to the demands of painful remembering than a traditional qualitative interview.

Gathering data on personal iterations of painful remembering does not necessarily involve the active elicitation of remembered accounts. Empirical research may involve the collection of pre-existing first-hand accounts of painful pasts, such as diaries, memoirs, and other autobiographical writings which have been self-produced outside of the research process. This kind of writing features heavily in both popular and academic literature, but for memory studies accounts – such as those of second-generation Holocaust survivors – has proved particularly fertile for the analysis of the performance and transmission of painful memory.[1] These accounts are qualitatively different from those produced through the research process as they have been created for different reasons in a variety of social and historical contexts, but, in common with elicited narratives, they contain both the content of painful memories and traces of the remembering process itself. These may be particularly useful if the painful event under investigation has passed out of living memory, or if the object of investigation is historically specific processes of remembering.

Although specific research objectives in analysing painful remembering using both elicited and self-produced narratives may vary, what they have in common is the need for an analytical approach which addresses the distinctive content of painful memories while attending to the specific mnemonic practices and processes they involve. In remembering we see the relatively successful reconciliation of experience with social schemas in the processes of making sense of the past, while traumatic accounts are characterised by an inability to communicate or fully represent painful experience using shared frameworks of meaning. In order to show how such differences may be manifest, we offer two brief examples.

The first example derives from an account which displays a number of traumatic features. It is taken from an interview we conducted with Gabor, a man in his seventies, in which he describes memories of his childhood in Hungary. The extract is taken from a lengthy interview in which he disjointedly recounts a poverty-stricken and abusive family life, his realisation that he was Jewish and possibly adopted, and his subsequent disowning by his family on his failure to send money back to Hungary after moving to London. In the interests of clarity, it should be noted that the extract is comprised of two sections of the original interview which, as they are a continuous part of the same story, we have placed together. Between them came a lengthy excursus on the process of coming to the UK. For reasons of space this has been removed from the example.

> Mainly small as my parents were – I myself personally had been adopted. I don't really like talking about that too much. Er, but I was adopted. I believe – not I believe, I know I was born Jewish. Having

spoke about that, it brings a tear to my eyes. Mm, ask me something else and go back because I'm going to cry. I can't cope with that. But of course we never came [to London] for the money, did we? Because, er, well I myself personally just absconded due to the row with my parents. As I touched on earlier, I was adopted. I think I – well, I not think, I know, I know, I just won't want to admit it even to myself. I was born Jewish and somewhere along the line my mother either – she either my birth mother or she's inherited me or somehow has got me. I'm not hundred percent certain, I've never been told the truth. And, er, and, er, I found out when I was a teenager. Other boys in our school called me Jew boy and things like that. And it's like a bullying – and when I find I – when I one day had enough courage to ask my mother she denied it. She said, 'they just bullying you, ignore them', this and that. But I knew she was lying, you could see on her face she was lying. And about two or three months later, or a year later, it was confirmed that I'm in fact been adopted, I'm Jewish. But how I ever was adopted or why, I don't know. [Break] Because if you can stop to think for a minute, I've told you that I was born Jewish, but that has an implication that my father, if not my mother – because I'm not a hundred percent certain that my mother is my birth mother, but I think she is. But my father went to the gas chamber and it's in your head all the time. I never shifted it, ever since I find out that I was Jewish. And I often thought to myself I'd go into the synagogue and ask if they could help. Then I thought, what the hell for? You know, what the hell for? What do I going to say? I don't even know a name of a person. You know, do as I've said to you earlier, if you would think on those lines when you approach any subject is a person is really made a part of their experience. What you are is really what you live through.

Gabor's narrative is intensely painful and hinges on his discovery of his Jewish identity and the identity-oriented affective disturbances associated with his sense of not belonging. The narrative is disjointed, ricocheting between the core element of the narrative (his Jewish identity) and a number of other events, both real, such as his re- or rather dis-location to the UK, or imaginatively engaged with, such as the manner of his biological father's death. His account demonstrates a number of features characteristic of traumatic experience, indicating the difficulty of assimilating elements of his past into a coherent narrative. In the first instance Gabor loses emotional control in the telling of his account at the point just prior to his request for the interviewer to 'ask me something else. . .'. In fact Gabor shed a silent tear just before this request was made. It is clear that he is reflexively aware of the potential for remembering to move him to tears, and also aware of his inability to control this emotional response without diverting away from the subject completely. But some aspects of his emotional account are unintended.

There is, for example, an observable shifting between the tenses. In recounting his experience of bullying at school he begins discussing it in the past tense, then the present tense ruptures the narrative with the phrase 'and when I find' as he attempts to formulate an account of asking his mother about his schoolmates' derisory references to his Jewishness. He quickly returns to the past tense in continuing his description, but this lapse in tenses provides fleeting evidence in the transcript of Gabor becoming momentarily re-submerged in the original experience. Slipping from remembering into reliving the past is given expressive form in the temporal dislocation of his story. Losing oneself in the original event, along with temporal disorientation, are features identified by BenEzer as indicative of a traumatic response (2004; see also LaCapra 1999). The past has not been fully assimilated, and so intrudes on the present, throwing Gabor back into the moment of his original pain. In the face of that again, the temporal domains of past and present become radically unstable rather than retaining their integrity as narrative touchstones. Temporal duration is either vague or variable: phrases such as 'somewhere along the line' and 'about two or three months later, or a year later' make clear that narrative coherence has not been achieved, even at this distant remove, with Gabor's narrative being marked by lacunae and imprecision, its meanings still elusive after all these years. Along with this lack of clarity is the shifting between 'thinking' and 'knowing' which characterises the narrative. Gabor searches for stability in his revision to his original statement that he 'thinks' he was adopted, changing it to his 'knowing' that he was adopted. He searches for a referential relationship with the past, but his ontological claims are built on shaky experiential foundations which threaten to give way at any point and plunge him once again into a state of 'not-knowing'. In all these ways the events of his past remain unmanageable in his remembering.

The unknowable nature of Gabor's past is most evident in his description of the supposed manner of his father's death. He says that 'my father went to the gas chamber and it's in your head all the time. I never shifted it, ever since I find out that I was Jewish'. His father's death in the Holocaust and his own Jewish identity are inextricably linked, but this connection cannot be made clear sense of. He is unable to hinge his narrative either on public discourses of anti-Semitism as his Jewish identity remains in question, or on the historical narratives of the Holocaust as he is unable to establish, factually or imaginatively, a referential link between his experience and that historical event.[2] As BenEzer suggests, 'life stories include an exposition of the relations between the private and the collective context' in which they are lived, but in this case that relationship is not fully formed (2004: 30). The socio-cultural frames through which Gabor might marshal his experience and make sense of it remain out of reach. Instead he is left to piece together disparate elements of his own and his inherited past without shared frames of memory through which to interpret them. Under these circumstances, his past remains atomised and alienated from a collective past, and so speculation on his father's death is left to inhabit his mind without narrative settlement.

There is anger as well as confusion and doubt in this. Gabor considers going to a synagogue for help in tracing his father, but then repeatedly asks 'what the hell for?' Past experience is not a resource for renewal in the present because he has no way of situating his own experience within a wider collective Jewish memory. He has no point of entry into the Jewish community of memory; his experience remains on the margins, with shared interpretative frames just out of reach. The resulting incoherence of his narrated experience does not provide him with a site from which to build the story of himself and integrate new knowledge about the past into it. Gabor's harrowing childhood experience is made all the more poignant as he concludes that 'what you are is really what you live through'. Without the possibility of creatively reconstructing his past into a meaningful remembered narrative, Gabor's very sense of self is disharmonious.

In contrast to the extract from the interview with Gabor, the second example is taken from Brian Dillon's memoir of his troubled childhood, which articulates the experience of painful remembering generated by the viewing of a photograph of his childhood home.

> I am looking now at the photograph I took of a house which was no longer my house. I have never noticed before that from the junction of the pavement and tarmac, where there was once a gate on which I was forbidden to swing, there radiates a pattern of cracks that stretches out to the very edge of the image. There was a time when I knew every one of those striations, and all the similar scars and contusions that marked my passage towards the house as I turned off the main road and into the quiet curve of ours. I remember now that as I approached the house that day, I remarked how familiar each and every crack still looked and how at the same time they seemed to have recomposed themselves into a new and startling arrangement: they all led to a house I could no longer enter, a house that in some sense was simply no longer there. The house in the photograph seems to define the centre of a web of memories that have obliterated its actual, concrete presence. It is the meeting place, and the vanishing point, of the lines that make up my perspective on the past. (Dillon 2005: 45–6)

Dillon's account deftly traces the experience of remembering. His narrative shuttles back and forth between his childhood experience and the contemporary foreignness of this once familiar place. In this shuttling back and forth, the temporal tenses of his experience retain their integrity despite the pain of loss he experiences in the act of remembering. This is in direct contrast to Gabor's accidental slippage into the present tense which is indicative of the instability of his own temporal positioning in relation to his experience. Dillon's movement between past and present is a productive one, as the tension he constructs between the remembered past and the remembering present opens up a critical space in which absence and loss are rendered meaningful.

The photograph Dillon narrates is situated as the 'meeting point' of past and present, and through his telling he weaves these different temporal states together to produce an account of absence in the present. This provides a stable referential anchor for his narrative, the most notable missing feature in Gabor's account. Dillon crafts an account of the relation between past and present as one of painful absence and loss, but in doing so communicates the complex transformations in meaning of the lived places of his childhood. The 'scars and contusions' that once marked his imaginative possession of that place are now 'recomposed', forming new markers of meaning in the present. Dillon's narrative is also stable in terms of the positioning of his subject position in relation to the past. He resolutely inhabits his remembering self, despite reflecting back on the perspective of his remembered self. In doing so the past is creatively used, not only to narrate his past experience but cumulatively to construct the rememberer himself. Dillon's account works up to a point where he can articulate 'my perspective on the past'; he successfully deploys a cultural framework of meaning which relates to the meaning of the 'family home' in order to make his past experience communicable. The detailed references to the textures and topology of the family home using the familiar images of the garden gate, the pavement and the quiet curve of the side street render Dillon's past recognisable to readers, and so the account of painful loss turns on the reader's shared understanding of the nuclear family and the spaces in which it is located.

Through his account, Dillon actively constructs a culturally and historically specific meaning of the childhood home through an imaginative return to it. In this sense it is characteristic not as an instance of trauma, but of painful remembering utilising effectively shared tropes and discursive strategies to render meaningful a painful legacy and represent that meaning in the public domain. In his painful remembering, the past is not hived off from the present but used in connection with it to make sense of experience over time. The past, although painful, is an accessible resource for the remembering subject.

In both accounts, loss and absence are articulated, but in Gabor's account the past is unavailable for the satisfactory construction of negotiated meaning, whereas in Dillon's account the past and present are brought into active dialogue with one another and in this process accumulated experience is made communicable. While the two accounts are produced in the quite different contexts of the in-depth interview and the literary act of constructing an autobiographical account, subsuming them both under the umbrella term of trauma would risk losing sight, not only of their individual narrative features, but also the renewal they provide (or not) in the present. While visible in the process of remembering, the 'unworked through' experience doesn't feature as a harmonious constituent of the narrative, and instead exists in the narrative only in a halting and disordered form. Contrary to Caruth's suggestion that traumatic experience is completely beyond representation, it is visible here precisely in the ways in which it breaks through and interrupts the representation of the past in the present. It is in the process of Gabor's struggle to order his experience into a coherent remembered narrative that we can identify trauma as distinct from, but also as acting upon processes of everyday remembering. To talk of Dillon's account as 'traumatic' would be to annul the possibilities his account creates for thinking through the experience of family life and the losses it entails and then acting on the qualitatively new knowledge that this remembering of childhood might allow. In addition, to equate the two accounts would diminish the very real psychic disruptions experienced by Gabor in his failure to achieve reconciliation with his deeply troubled past through the process of remembering.

CONCLUSION: WORKING WITH PAINFUL PASTS

In working with personal accounts of painful pasts it is crucial that analytical techniques are able to distinguish between traumatic disruptions to memory in which the meaning cannot produce a synthesis of past and present experience, and ways of reconciling past and present experience in order to make past pain meaningful and communicable through the synthesis of personal experience with social frameworks of meaning. Analyses of painful remembering should therefore take account of two interconnected axes which underpin remembering as a process of making sense of the past: the temporal axis along which the success or failure of trafficking between past and present occurs, and the social axis of transmission along which the success or failure to reconcile personal experience with social frames of meaning occurs. It is their radically different operation along these two axes that we are using to draw out the distinction between these two examples as characterised by traumatic experience on the one hand, and painful remembering on the other. In doing so the specificity of each traumatic or remembered experience can be attended to without running together qualitatively different responses to pain and the outcomes they involve, so preventing mnemonic responses being read off from the event itself. In each case this requires attending to specific instances in personal accounts where temporal distinctions are either collapsed and blurred, or identified and maintained, where the past is either uncontrollably repeated or creatively recomposed, and where social and cultural conventions are successfully or unsuccessfully deployed in making painful experiences meaningful.

Attending to these two axes of transmission prevents the bland universalising of trauma to the remembrance of any painful past experience and refuses the bracketing off of experiences which disrupt and challenge everyday remembering practices as intrinsically unknowable. Indiscriminate use of the term trauma renders questions about the rhetorical deployment of such pasts redundant, and annuls the possibilities they might provide for the construction of new meaning and action premised upon it in the present. If we are to develop methodological tools for investigating the politics of memory, our use of trauma as an analytical framework should be limited to those cases where there is clear empirical justification for its application. Using trauma outside these specific contexts, whether in personal accounts of painful pasts as we have seen in the examples explored in this chapter, or in more public representations of widely shared painful pasts, crucial questions relating to meaning and agency, victimhood and perpetration, the personal and the collective will be subsumed into descriptions of traumatic repetition. The transactional value of the past will be overlooked. Instead, as we hope to have shown here in our graded distinctions between painful remembering and traumatic accounts, the presence of pain in and of itself does not render the past sterile as an imaginative resource. That is why we need more refined analytical tools which will allow us to recognise and explore how painful pasts are manifested in everyday remembering practices.

SUMMARY: KEY POINTS

- In this chapter we have identified painful pasts and the ways in which they are remembered as a core concern for memory studies.
- We identify the prevalence of trauma as a concept in memory studies and discuss the ways in which it has been extended beyond its psychoanalytic and psychiatric origins into explorations of social and cultural memory.
- We argued that, as a concept, trauma has been extensively misapplied in memory studies, and noted its analytical limitations when exploring the remembering of painful pasts.
- We propose that trauma and painful remembering should be distinguished from one another in order to assess the gradations of response to painful experience by attending closely to the ways in which painful pasts are creatively used in processes of remembering, or remain unavailable for the imaginative work of memory.

- Using empirical examples we demonstrate how trauma and painful remembering can be distinguished in the process of analysis and the ways in which this opens up the possibility of accounting for the ways in which some painful pasts can be used rhetorically or as sites for renewal in the present, whereas some remain disruptive to the processes of remembering.

FURTHER READING

Cathy Caruth (1996) and Shoshana Felman and Dori Laub (1991) are perhaps the most widely cited proponents of the trauma paradigm in memory studies and provide good examples of the transposition of trauma into the cultural realm. Despite the widespread uptake of trauma in memory studies there have been a number of scholars who have provided critiques of the ways in which trauma has been applied. Wulf Kansteiner has produced a number of publications in which he develops a broadly based appraisal in this regard (see for example Kansteiner 2004). Ruth Leys (2000) provides a wide-ranging genealogy of the concept of trauma, and in doing so provides a critique of its culturalist applications. Likewise, Roger Luckhurst (2008) provides an excellent account of the origins of the concept of trauma and the emergence of 'trauma culture' in the 1980s. Michael Rothberg's work on multi-directional memory is an excellent example of research that moves beyond the trauma paradigm to explore in more detail the complex processes of transmission involved in remembering painful pasts (2009).

NOTES

1. See, for example, second-generation accounts by Fass (2011), Hoffman (1998, 2005) and Karpf (1997).
2. Elsewhere in the interview he talks of the possibility that his father was shot, or simply absent.

CHAPTER 10

Disrupted Childhoods

Jo Aldridge and Chris Dearden

INTRODUCTION

Until relatively recently, children and young people were left out of research studies that took as their focus macro themes and dimensions such as politics, citizenship and human rights. Alderson has argued, for example, that in the past adult-centred research was conducted 'with little reference to children' (1995: 40). However, in the last decade or so there has been something of a sea-change in the ways in which children and young people are viewed and understood that has meant the views and 'voices' of children themselves have been heard in more diverse settings – in social research studies, for example, as well as, increasingly, in health and social care consultations and in the formulation of policy (see Hill et al. 2004; Redsell and Hastings 2010; The Children Act 2004). Such revitalised perspectives and practices have been informed and underpinned by an internationally mandated children's rights agenda, which has included children's right to participation (see UNCRC 1989), as well as epistemological advances that have witnessed real shifts in the discourse on childhood and in the ('new') sociology of childhood specifically (see Wyness 2006).

While this shift towards a more equitable and inclusive approach to children, and the phase of childhood more generally, is undoubtedly welcome, it also brings with it a number of challenges when working with children and young people in social research studies. Heywood (2001) argues that we knew little about the nature of childhood until the late eighteenth century, primarily because children's views and perspectives through first-hand accounts were largely missing from the historical record. However, recognising the need for such testimony is only the first step in the far more complex process of obtaining children's first-hand accounts for the purposes of social research, public record, posterity and so on. This is not because children's abilities to contribute their views, experiences and recollections are in question; rather, the ways in which their contributions are sought and recorded require careful consideration in both design and implementation terms precisely because, from a research governance and ethical perspective, children are perceived to be 'vulnerable' and are categorised as such.

VULNERABILITY, 'VOICE' AND YOUNG CARERS

Children's vulnerability has also been described as, and assigned to, a range of factors and characteristics relating to their developmental and safeguarding needs in respect of UK health and social care policy and practice agendas. Vulnerability here is associated with children's lack of capacity for self-protection or for developing resilience or coping strategies (see Parrott et al. 2008). While, in many respects, most children are willing and able to participate in research studies and contribute their views and experiences despite these challenges, the (adult imposed) 'vulnerable' status conferred on all children under the age of eighteen can make access, permission and consent procedures in research investigations much more challenging; thus the opportunity to represent and present children's perspectives and 'voices' in research is also further problematised. This is particularly true of young carers who are often doubly or multiply vulnerable because of their age, level of responsibility and circumstances (that is, because they live with and care for a parent with a chronic illness or disability).

Young carers are children under the age of eighteen who provide care for a sick or disabled adult in the home, usually a parent (see Becker 2000). These children are also identified as children in need in UK health and social care policy because of the extent and impact of their caring responsibilities (see Dearden and Aldridge 2010). Such responsibilities can mean that young carers are often denied the opportunity for independence and making successful transitions into adulthood because of the demands of caring and the long-term and disproportionate effects of parental chronic illness or disability on children and their families (see Dearden and Becker 2000).

Much of what we know about children's experiences of caring emerged from a number of important investigations pioneered in the UK which used both qualitative and quantitative methodological approaches to uncover children's caring experiences, which had remained hidden for many years. The qualitative investigations in particular championed children's 'voices' in research studies that generated powerful and emotive personal testimonies from children, many of whom had been caring, unsupported, for a number of years. This is illustrated in the following extract from the 1993 *Children Who Care* study (Aldridge and Becker 1993: vi) in which sixteen year-old Jimmy recalls his experiences of caring for his father, who was terminally ill:

> When I think about all those years I cared for my dad, it makes me angry, not because I had to care for him – I wanted to care for him – but because I was left alone to cope with his illness for so long. I wasn't just doing ordinary tasks like other kids might do around the house. I was having to cook for him, beg for money and food parcels so I could feed him, take him to the toilet . . . no one should have to see their parents like that.

Despite the success of this approach – evidence from this study, for example, led to an Early Day Motion in parliament calling on the government to address the needs of young carers in the UK – following a number of later studies it became clear that some children and young people either do not want to, or feel unable to take part in research studies that rely on their verbal accounts and testimonies, and locate them only as the subjects-objects of research. Thus, methods need to be more adaptive and creative to ensure that these children aren't overlooked in social research studies simply because they present as difficult to recruit or unwilling to participate.

A key objective of research studies that include vulnerable groups, such as children and young people, must also be to provide evidence of meaningfulness for these groups, and thus to allow insight into their past or present 'inner worlds' (see Radley and Taylor 2003). The methods used must then be faithful, not simply in illustrating and representing experience, but also in testifying to it. They should involve adopting (and adapting) strategies that facilitate such testimony in ways that are flexible, useful, and valued by participants themselves. The field of memory studies research provides a diversity of methods to the social science researcher that can help develop and advance new techniques for working more creatively with research participants; such methods are especially useful in eliciting memorial recall among participants who are vulnerable or hard to reach in some way. In both of the research studies described and discussed in this chapter, creative visual techniques with vulnerable children and young people, as well as retrospective interviews with adults about their memories of caring, explore *autobiographical* memory performance (as opposed to the retrieval of memories that are procedural, semantic or cognitive – see Misztal 2003: 9).

PARTICIPATORY RESEARCH AND 'VOICE'

The notion of 'voice' in participatory research methods locates the narratives and the rights of participants centre stage in research agendas and processes by enabling participants to recall and recount their stories and experiences in their own words and in ways that enhance memory performance. Participatory visual research is not new, but its application in these different contexts has emerged more recently as a result of the need to address the particular, and even individualistic requirements (see Goodley and Moore 2000), of certain vulnerable groups in social research who want and need to tell their stories in different ways (see Greek 2005; Thomson 2008).

Drawing on Britzman's (1989) multi-conceptual understanding of 'voice' (literal, metaphorical and political), Thomson's participatory visual research with children and young people, for example, attempts to 'find ways to bring previously unheard voices into scholarly and associated professional conversations' (2008: 3). By conferring competency and agency on children in research by engaging with them in more direct and inclusive ways, Thomson attempts to 'give voice to the voiceless' (ibid.) by enabling children and young people to elicit their experiences and recall through visual 'voice'. For both Thomson and her colleagues this involves giving children cameras, video equipment, art materials and so on, in order for children to collect their own evidence and present their own memorial testimonies (see also Kaplan 2008; Leitch 2008; Sutton et al. 2007).

Sempik and colleagues (2005) also used photographic participatory methods in their study on the effects of social and therapeutic horticulture for people with learning disabilities (see also Aldridge 2007). The authors concluded that the participatory element of the study – and particularly the fact that the photographic data had been produced by the participants with learning disabilities themselves – provided a highly personalised dimension to the study that other methods would have missed, and that the method, uniquely, gave participants with limited verbal capacity or skills the opportunity to give visual testimony to their experiences and thus facilitated visual 'voice'.

A number of researchers and commentators have proposed that visual methods can also provide insight into unseen or hard-to-reach locations and hidden experience and that they can help to 'bridge gaps between researcher and researched' (Joanou 2009: 214). Notably, photographs themselves can be used as aids for recall or as visual prompts in memory studies research (see Kuhn 2010; Langford 2008) in order to stimulate elicitation and further discussion (in interviews, for example). Sutton et al. (2007), for example, used children's own photographic data of family and friends and experiences and memories that were important to them as visual cues in their study of children's perception of social difference. When children are engaged in studies such as these – as the co-researchers and co-producers of visual data – notions of past and memory are located in their more recent or contemporary personal histories, rather than in the further or distant past, which is more often the case in research that uses family photographic albums or museum collections, for example (see Kuhn 2010).

Photographic records or testimonies also capture present or 'snapshot' moments (Langford 2008) that immediately transform into past or memorial record as soon as the picture has been taken. In this respect, photographic data in social research also become historical or archival records in and over time. Such visual evidence can be useful, not just collectively (socially, culturally and politically, for example), but also personally, from the point of view of participants themselves for whom photographic data may also have (lasting) personal significance and meaning. This is particularly the case where participatory photographic methods facilitate collaboration and ownership in research production processes and engage participants as the co-producers of research.

PICTURES OF YOUNG CARING

Uncovering the silent and hidden aspects of children's lives as carers using photographic testimonial methods was one of the main objectives in the participatory study with children who care for parents with serious mental health problems (for a full discussion of the findings see Aldridge and Sharpe 2007). The children who took part in the study were not asked to recall and verbally record their past experiences of caring; rather, they were asked to show, through the use of photographic diaries, what their lives were like as carers when caring was an ongoing responsibility in their lives. A further objective was to gauge the usefulness of the methodology itself as a way of capturing children's visual testimonies of caring.

Sixteen young carers participated in the *Pictures of Young Caring* study, each of whom was caring for a parent (or parents) with serious mental health problems. Over the course of two weeks, the children and young people produced photographic diaries using disposable cameras and visually recorded aspects of their caring and family lives that were meaningful to them. Boddy and Smith (2008: 63) have argued that diary compilation research methods such as these can provide rich data, 'of acceptable validity', in terms of recording events in 'everyday life'. This approach is more often referred to in methods terms as Photovoice, although descriptors here in the research literature vary considerably (see Catalani and Minkler 2010).

The photographic data produced during the diary phase were analysed for content as well as thematically, and also used in the elicitation phase of the study as visual prompts and to aid recall. The children themselves were involved as active participants in the study as co-researchers and co-producers of the visual data, but they also owned the photographs themselves and chose to keep their photographic diaries as a visual record of their caring experiences and family life. In this way, the photographic data also served as personal keepsakes or souvenirs from the study (see Langford 2008).

A total of 287 photographs were analysed thematically based on content and location (subject and place) and focusing on the 'internal' and 'external' visual narratives produced, drawing on Banks's visual analytical framework (2001: 11). Banks defines the internal narrative as 'the story that the image communicates', and external narrative as, 'the social context that produced the image, and the social relations within which the image is embedded at any moment of viewing'. Sub-categories relating to external narratives in the photographic data were identified as 'play and leisure', 'social networks', 'home', 'school' and 'play/recreation'. The internal narratives identified in the data related to the more abstract autobiographical elements of the images – the children's highly personalised and subjective experiences and emotions relating to caring, feelings of responsibility, and duty and love for the parents they provided care for. In many respects these internal narratives could only be confirmed and validated during the elicitation phase of the study when the children used the photographs as visual prompts or cues for story construction and story*telling*.

In this sense, the photographic data provided what Prosser and Schwartz (1998: 112) describe as 'extra-somatic memory' aids for the children to use as prompts for recall and explication during the elicitation phase of the study (see Aldridge and Sharpe 2007: 10). Kuhn (2010: 303) also acknowledges that the use of family photographs in visual research can serve two important functions: 'prosthetically as substitutes for remembering' and 'as prompts for performances of memory in private, interactive, collective, and sometimes even public, contexts.'

The children were also involved in the selection and thematic categorisation of the photographic data, which were based on their descriptions and groupings of selected images, and which produced the final visual autobiographies of caring. Thomson argues that it is important children are involved in selection and editing processes when they are engaged as data collectors and producers in visual projects, 'so that their assumptions are also made explicit and available for discussion' (2008: 9). Indeed, the elicitation phase of the young carers study was an important stage in the research process intended to ensure that the internal or autobiographical narratives attached to the visual data were evinced entirely from the perspectives of the children themselves, and that this process then conferred ownership (of the visual data) on them as photographer-participants. This process also served to confirm and validate their experiences and memories of caring, as well as the importance of their ongoing caring contributions in the home. This was an important element of the participatory visual approach given that much of the research to date on young caring has highlighted children's need for recognition of their caring roles (see Aldridge and Becker 1993, 2003; Becker et al. 1998).

Although the intention from the outset of the study was always to allow the children and young people who took part to do so without reliance on their verbal testimonies during the data collection phase, it was interesting to note that all of the children involved in the selection and editing process identified images that were important to them and participated willingly in the elicitation phase of the investigation. Using the printed copies of the photographs as memorial aids and storytelling clues or prompts during the elicitation phase enabled the children to record, identify and discuss aspects of their caring and family lives that were important to them. In this sense, the children were engaged in what Kuhn describes as 'memory performance', where visual media are used to 'unpick interconnections between the private, the public and the personal' (2010: 298).

What was also notable from the study was that the children's selection and editing of the photographic data – that is, of their own personal visual diaries or autobiographies – did not always result in linear or chronological organisation of the data in order to tell or 'show' a story. Furthermore, not all of the children who took part wanted to annotate their photographs with textual narratives or explanations; nor did they want them to appear in this way in any of the outputs from the study.[1] Thus, some of the photographs were presented as they were, with no accompanying textual narratives or descriptions from the children who took part. In this respect, these photographs were simply left to 'speak for themselves' and for viewers to make of them what they would. This is perhaps best illustrated in the image below which was taken by Fiona, 13, who cared for her mother who had depression and physical health problems. Fiona selected the image for inclusion in her visual story, but did not want to talk about the photograph, explain it, or attach particular meaning to it in terms of its subject matter, content and so on:

A number of other visual projects have adopted similar approaches in that they simply present the photographic or visual image *as is*, rather than explicate images with accompanying textual narratives. An example here is Raine's (1994) visual project that looked at the production of home movies. Focusing on visual interpretations of home life through the use of video, Raine concluded: 'I don't want people to worry about whether it's true or whether it's fiction, I just want them to kind of live in this work – enter it, exist in it, enjoy it'. However, while commendable in many respects, and particularly from a participatory perspective (see Hart 1992), these kinds of approaches can be especially problematic in the context, say, of social policy research, where evidence is used to inform both policy and practice but which, as Walker et al. recognise (2008: 164), 'tend to be more cautious in [their] response to this type of evidence'.

However, in many respects the textual narratives produced by the children involved in the young caring project – where these were provided – helped both 'explain' the subject-content of the photographs themselves as well as demonstrate the effectiveness and emotive power of the visual-textual coupling. This is perhaps best illustrated in the following photograph of Lucy and its accompanying narrative:

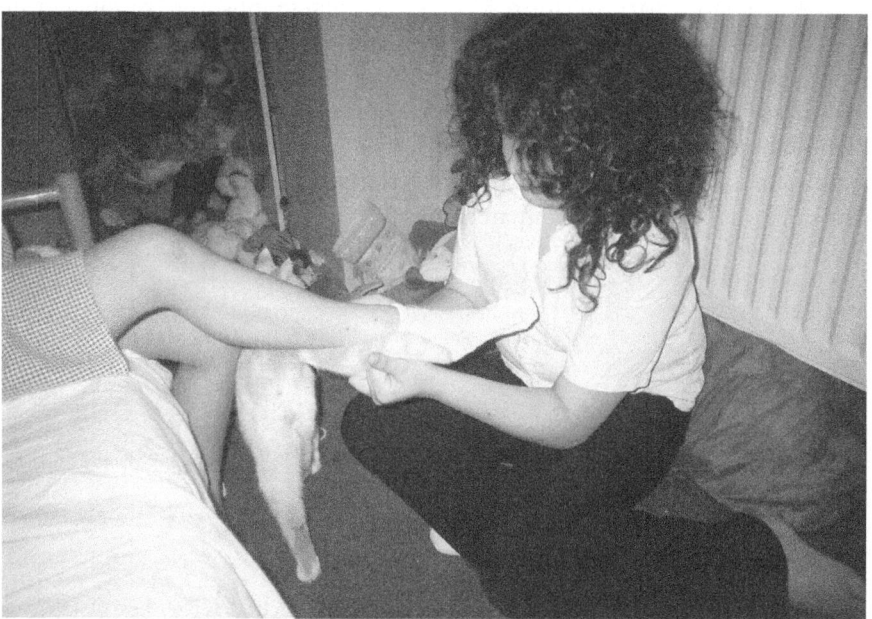

Some of the things I do are look after my younger sisters and I have to rub my mum's feet, because you have to push the circulation through. They showed me how to do it . . . to relieve mum's pain. I have to help my mum with her medication and injections. That's me helping the girls get ready for school in the morning. We take it in turns washing the pots from Sunday dinner. We take it in turn during the week, me and Ben as well. We all take it in turns. (Lucy, 14, who cares for mum who has schizophrenia) (ibid.: 12)

CHILDREN'S VISUAL 'VOICES' AND TESTIMONIES

Thomson (2008: 5) argues that children's 'critical voices' in research are essential in order to ensure that, as speakers, they exercise 'some agency and control of circumstances which previously felt beyond reach'. In respect of vulnerable children and young people, the use of participatory research methods can help challenge fixed perceptions and assumptions about their lack of competency as decision makers or active citizens. Photographic participation methods can also prove useful in a number of other ways. First, they can help overcome the inherent difficulties involved in accurately representing the 'reality' or lived experiences of participants – and vulnerable participants in particular – as interpreted through the researcher as photographer or researcher as memory data collector. Second, the use of photographic participation methods with vulnerable children who care recognises the importance of their caring contributions and lends a powerful visual dimension to the personal and sometimes intimate nature of their caring responsibilities (see Aldridge and Sharpe 2007).

More generally, using photographic methods among vulnerable children provides an effective showcase for these groups of participants to demonstrate their 'strong present-orientation' (Booth 1996) as well as their capacity for memory performance. It also allows children to overcome the participative barriers in research; if the participants in research cannot or do not want to *tell* us about their experiences, but are able to demonstrate them visually through the use of photographic participation methods, then this only serves to emphasise the positive, inclusive advantages of using such techniques, particularly *from the point of view of the participants themselves.* As Kuhn (2010: 312) argues, visual methods need to be not only scientifically credible, but also 'crucially, meaningful to those involved.'

Such approaches can also help to address and resolve, to some degree, the somewhat thorny dilemma of third-party representation. In the study of young carers, the data were generated and, importantly, also owned, by the children themselves; they were involved collaboratively in data selection and editing processes and also made important contributions to the content and thematic analyses. Walker et al. (2008: 170) recognise the importance of this type of inclusive, emancipatory approach with vulnerable children. In their four-country study of abandoned and orphaned children, for example, the authors 'learnt the importance of children being deeply involved in the process of interpretation and analysis,' and that children gain a sense of ownership and contextual understanding of research studies through the 'control they [have] over the process of selection and interpretation' (ibid.).

ETHICAL CONSIDERATIONS IN (PHOTOGRAPHIC) PARTICIPATION STUDIES

The use of photographic techniques in social research methods isn't new; but participatory methods that embrace inclusive and emancipatory approaches with and among vulnerable respondents – and in ways that also facilitate recall and testimony without reliance on verbal input alone – are less commonly used in social research studies. This may be explained to some extent by the number of ethical challenges involved in using participatory visual methods, and particularly with vulnerable groups. Such challenges can be amplified by the use of photographic techniques, in the main because of the potential intrusiveness and loss of privacy involved when using cameras and photography, and particularly when participants are asked to adopt the role of data collector/photographer (because they may not be as sensitive to privacy and confidentiality issues, for example – see Aldridge 2007). These matters can be further problematised for researchers when trying to design confidentiality and consent procedures for participants who may have little understanding or insight into the meaning of these concepts and the implications of taking part in studies that use potentially intrusive methods. As Donaldson (2001: 4) has argued, 'designing confidentiality and informed consent procedures that take into account photography's loss of privacy will be especially troublesome'.

In the young carers study, a precondition for the provision of funding, as well as access to participants via the two young carers' projects involved, was that all ethical considerations had to be addressed with respect to gaining informed consent from participants and ensuring they understood the implications of taking part in studies that used photographic methods (including the right to withdraw from the studies at any point; see Department of Health 2000). Verbal and written consent were obtained from the children who agreed to take part, as well as from their parents and/or legal guardians, and in line with the British Psychological Society Code of Conduct (British Psychological Society 2000: 3) pertaining to legal authority. Ethical issues were also discussed with project workers who were working with and providing services for the young carers (at the two participating young carers' projects).

However, in following recognised procedures for ethical clearance, it is also obvious that a number of dilemmas remain regardless of the extent to which, and how formally, ethical requirements have been met. For instance, it is particularly challenging to try and explain to participants the consequences of taking part in research studies that use visual methods such as photography, for example, when it is impossible to predict these fully (and also when working with vulnerable participants whose capacity to understand these issues may be limited – see Aldridge 2007). This is certainly important when considering issues of privacy, and its loss thereof, in studies where the primary intention is to make the private public through the visual presentation of photographic data in a range of public outputs.

In respect of working more directly and collaboratively with vulnerable groups in visual research projects, the rights of participants are of critical importance, and particularly the right to withdraw from studies. Thomson (2008: 3) argues that the rights of participants to informed consent and to withdraw from participation in research at any time, while essential, might also be seen as 'a somewhat minimalist version of voice'. Nevertheless, the opportunity to exercise their rights and make choices is especially important for vulnerable participants whose capacity for agency might be restricted, or where they may not have access to these opportunities in other areas of their lives. In the context of social policy research, adopting ethical approaches that are rights-based at each stage of research design and production can also provide avenues for vulnerable individuals and groups to give their views and opinions on matters that are directly relevant to their lives, but on which they may not have been given the opportunity to comment before.

In many respects, the photographic study with young carers would always present a challenge in terms of achieving the right balance between the emancipatory, inclusive aims of the study and its transformative objectives; that is, to use children's visual recall and testimonies of caring to further inform health and social care policy and practice. The purpose of the former was to ensure that children's experiences and memories of caring – as both past and present occurrence – could be more readily translated into (visual) testimony through the use of a more appropriate, rights-based participatory method that would both encourage and enhance memory performance. Such an approach recognises that children do not always want or feel able to contribute their testimonies in the same ways that adults might in looking back retrospectively on their childhood experiences.

GROWING UP CARING

This is demonstrated in the difference between the photographic study and the retrospective study with young adult carers conducted in 1999 (Dearden and Becker 2000). Sixty young adults took part in this study, all of whom had been carers throughout their childhood, and some who continued to care into adulthood. The aim of the study was to identify ways in which caring as a child might have an impact on their transitions into adulthood, and to use the findings from the research to influence policy and practice in supporting young carers and their families.

In this research, semi-structured interviews were conducted with sixty young people between the ages of sixteen and twenty-five. The interviews covered a range of issues such as family structure and the nature of parental illness/disability; type and extent of participants' caring responsibilities; education, training and employment; income and benefits; receipt of and experiences of services; housing, leaving home and family separations; and becoming an adult. This type of interview, which Lindlof (1995) terms a 'conversation with a purpose', is particularly useful in allowing participants unrestricted time to recall experiences and memories that have meaning for them (see Aldridge and Becker 1993; Dearden and Becker 1995, 1998). Furthermore, as was clear during the recruitment phase of the study, older children and young adults are often more willing and able to participate in conventional methods, such as qualitative interviews, and to make informed decisions about consent and whether to share their experiences with others.

Using interviews among this age group (16–25) to obtain retrospective data about experiences that are in the *recent* past (in this case, childhood caring) can help facilitate recollection and memory performance, while at the same time allowing for a degree of evaluative distance and objectivity; participants can consider and appraise the impact of certain experiences in the process of looking back. In the *Growing up Caring* study, the young people who took part were asked to consider the impact of living with and caring for a parent with a serious illness or disability on their childhood experiences, and in particular on that critical transitional period for those participants who had crossed the threshold into young adulthood.

While loss of immediacy can undoubtedly have an impact on memory performance and recollection in retrospective studies such as these, in this study not only was caring a very recent experience for some of the participants, but for others it was also an ongoing responsibility in their lives; here, retrospective methods are not so much about memory performance as they are about rendering the here and now. On the other hand, retrospective studies that focus on past events and experiences can provide important dissociation from what might be painful episodes in participants' lives. For young carers, such episodes often relate to parents' illnesses or disabilities, how these progress or deteriorate, the impact of bereavement, and so on (see Aldridge and Becker 2003; Becker et al. 1998).

What was clear from working closely with the participants in the study was that any distress or anxiety caused by their recollections of past experiences were ameliorated by a number of factors, including their age and level of maturity, the strength of parent-child relationships, the end of caring, and altruistic considerations that participation in the study – regardless of how difficult this might be for them personally – might help other young carers in the longer term.

In many ways, this study enabled us to contrast existing knowledge about childhood transitions into adulthood (see Barnardo's 1996) with the experiences of children and young people whose childhoods are interrupted, disturbed, or even curtailed by caring. In the UK, the phase of childhood is protected by a range of policies, practices and safeguarding legislation and it is expected that children will make transitions into adulthood through the *gradual* assumption of responsibilities and independence, which is 'a healthy and normal process [where children] seek to be in control of their own lives . . .' (ibid.: 9). And yet it is this measured progression into adulthood that is so often missing in the lives of young carers.

Through their recollections of childhood caring, the children and young adults in the *Growing up Caring* study were able to evaluate the impact of caring on their lives and provided valuable insight into their transitional experiences. Many of the participants reflected on the disruptions to their childhood caused by the premature and often sudden onset of caring responsibilities, as illustrated in the following example:

> 'I feel I became an adult when I was 15, when I had to live on my own and support myself [while mother was in hospital for an extended period].' (Trish, 16, caring for a mother with mental health problems – Dearden and Becker 2000: 42).
> 'I think I became an adult overnight when that [stroke] happened to mam. I think it was just, I was thrown into being responsible then.' (Diana, 23, caring for a mother with physical health problems – ibid.: 41)

Participants also described the effects of what can be described as precocious competence, or the early maturation of children who take on the type of caring responsibilities we usually associate with adulthood (for example, cooking, cleaning, nursing sick or disabled parents):

> 'I'm the more mature one out of me and my sister. I ended up taking on the role of the parent, trying to cook, trying to feed us . . . I mean it was mainly cereal and jam sandwiches 'cause I couldn't cook 'cause I was only nine.' (Melanie, 16, caring for her mother with physical and mental health problems and alcohol misuse – ibid.: 16)

What was also notable from the findings was participants' willingness to talk openly about painful episodes and experiences from the past, as well as the ways in which they used the process of memory performance to try and make sense of these during interviews. This was particularly the case when participants described incidents or episodes from the past that had required them to make critical adult-type decisions (as children):

> 'Last time she was ill I don't know whether I did the right thing or not
> ... I rang ... mum's psychiatric social worker and told them to check
> up on my mum ... because my mum went into hospital ... me and my
> sister had to go into foster care, and I feel as though it was all my fault.'
> (Laura, 17, caring for a mother with mental health problems – ibid.: 36)

Overall, evidence from the study showed that, as children, participants had little choice but to take on caring roles and that, when caring was a constant in their lives, transitions into adulthood were less marked by conventional milestones or the gradual accession to independence; the majority of participants continued to live with and care for their parents, for example, even when they became adults (in legal terms) and continued to be dependent on their parents financially. Previous research on young caring has shown that families affected by parental illness or disabilities often lack appropriate and effective health and social care services; furthermore, more recent research suggest that adults with disabilities do not have access to effective parenting support. This means that children are often compelled to take on caring responsibilities in the absence of alternative forms of professional support (Social Services Inspectorate 2000).

Thus, the messages from the *Growing up Caring* study in terms of policy and practice were that young carers' transitions into adulthood are not always linear: they are often characterised by the precocious assumption of responsibilities that we usually associate with adulthood, but without the status or recognition that being an adult brings. In the literature on young caring, this has been referred to as the duality of caring (see Aldridge and Becker 2003). Furthermore, while caring can often result in early or precocious transitions into the realm of adulthood it may also tie children to the parental home – and dependency – for longer, in the absence of alternative arrangements.

CONCLUSION

A fundamental aim of social policy research should be to use evidence in transformative ways – that is, research findings should be used to inform and shape policy and practice and to make a difference to people's lives. This is particularly pertinent when working with vulnerable people who may not have the same opportunities as others to have their voices heard. In which case, research methods need to be flexible, creative and even individualistic if such transformative objectives are to be met. The ways in which the stories or narratives of people's lives can be told and collated for social research purposes are manifold and diverse, and especially so in the field of memory studies research. Most research participants, including vulnerable individuals and groups, will want to participate and contribute if they are given appropriate opportunities to do so, and in ways that are both accessible and meaningful to them. Retrospective interviews and visual research methods of the kinds discussed here are just two of the ways in which research participants can successfully engage in research projects that enhance and endorse memory performance and participation. But it is also worth noting, as Cubitt (2007) acknowledges, that there are many different kinds of remembering or mental performance. Thus, a key objective for social researchers here is not only to identify ways in which memory performance can be enhanced methodologically, but also how the evidence from memory studies can be used in transformative ways for vulnerable or hard-to-reach groups.

SUMMARY: KEY POINTS

- More flexible and creative methods are needed when working with vulnerable research participants in order to facilitate and enhance memory performance and participation.
- Visual methods and retrospective interviews are two examples of the ways in which *autobiographical* memories can be retrieved in social research studies.
- Participatory research with vulnerable groups can present a number of ethical challenges, and strict adherence to rigorous confidentiality and consent procedures are essential.

FURTHER READING

As a starting point for researchers planning to use visual methods in their research projects, Collier and Collier's (1986) *Visual Anthropology: Photography as a Research Method*, covers essential aspects of using photography as an empirical tool, including photographic surveys, photographic participant observation and photographs in interviews. Developing this emerging visual anthropological method further, Thomson's (2008) exploration of visual media in research with children and young people provides excellent case studies and examples of how visual methods can lend new dimensions and generate new insights into the experiences and needs of vulnerable children. In her work with children who live and work on the streets of Lima in Peru, Joanou (2009) suggests that visual methods can help bridge the gaps between researchers and vulnerable research participants, while at the same time lending a note of caution with respect to the ethical challenges and dilemmas presented when using participatory photographic methods.

NOTES

1. All of the children who took part in the study gave their permission and consent for their photographs to be used in various outputs from the study. These included a final report to the Economic and Social Research Council as well as a gallery of the photographs to be included on the Young Carers Research Group Website. However, the children kept the original hard copies of the photographs and decided themselves which ones they wanted – or did not want – to be included in reports or websites for public viewing.

SECTION SIX

Confessing and Witnessing

CHAPTER 11

Apologia

Cristian Tileagă

'I have failed as a scientist, as a researcher. I have amended my research data and faked research. Not once, but several times and not for a brief moment, but for a prolonged period. I realise that this behavior has shocked and angered my colleagues and my profession, social psychology. I am ashamed and I regret this . . .' (social psychologist Diederik Stapel's response to interim report on academic misconduct)

'As the director of S-21, I did not dare to seek any alternatives to obeying the orders from the upper echelon, despite knowing that carrying them out would lead to the loss of thousands of lives. At present, I have the deepest sorrow and regret, and I feel ashamed and uneasy. As a perpetrator, I know that I am personally guilty before the entire Cambodian people and nation, before the families of all the victims who lost their lives at S-21 and before my own family, some of whom also lost their lives.' (Kaing Guek Eav, alias Duch, Khmer Rouge executioner)

'We are sorry. The *News of the World* was in the business of holding others to account. It failed when it came to itself. We are sorry for the serious wrongdoing that occurred. We are deeply sorry for the hurt suffered by the individuals affected. We regret not acting faster to sort things out. I realise that simply apologising is not enough. Our business was founded on the idea that a free and open press should be a positive force in society. We need to live up to this . . .' (signed by Rupert Murdoch, full-page *News of the World* 'sorry' ad)

'I informed the Securitate in writing about some of [my] friends and some of my acquaintances, without warning them, without confessing to them *post-festum* until my writing of this text, without apologizing, without assuming publicly this shameful past . . . Ethically and morally, confession and repentance are coming too late: to the gravity of my deeds from 25–30 years ago, one can add the indefensible gravity of silence, of life lived in lies and duplicity ...' (Sorin Antohi, public intellectual, on his collaboration with the Securitate, the communist Romanian secret police)

We live in an 'age of apology' (Brooks 1999). The public expressions of 'regret' that open this chapter are only some examples of a broader trend that includes (but is not limited to) collective (formal) political apologies for historical injustice (Augoustinos et al. 2011; Celermajer 2009), individual contrition for past wrongdoing of public figures and politicians (Bauer 2009; Blaney and Benoit 2001; Payne 2008; Simons 2000; Tileagă 2009b, 2011), or apologetic efforts of organisations (Benoit 1995; Brinson and Benoit 1999). How do we go about researching these ubiquitous instances of public behaviour? This chapter critically appraises conventional ways of understanding and interpreting apologia and puts forward an alternative account grounded in understanding apologia as *discourse*. It will make the case for the merit and potential contribution of discourse analysis to understanding politics of 'regret' in action. In doing so, this chapter turns repeatedly to data that are part of a wider project investigating the social construction of the communist/post-communist past in talk and text (Tileagă 2009a, 2009b; 2012), especially a public apologia of collaboration with the Securitate – the former communist Romanian secret police.

It is usually argued that apologies occur in a range of forms, from 'canonically explicit to ambiguously indirect' (Lakoff 2001: 201). The conventional wisdom invites us to identify rhetorical strategies of self-defence (Benoit 1995) or explore the internal psychology of the person (Miller 1999, 2003). This chapter argues that apologias are more than the sum of ways of interpreting them. They express socio-cultural meanings, especially the meaning of what it means to be 'sorry' (LeCouteur et al. 2001). They point to the cultural norm of remedial work on social relationships through language (Goffman 1971; Owen 1983). The language of social and political life is primarily a language of events, social relations, categories, psychological states, stake, interest, etc. (Edwards 1997). Public apologies *mobilise* the past in the present: events, people, identities, categories, social relations, institutions, memory (individual/social/organisational). Apologia displaces the (confessional) self into the social, opening a public space of judgement. Apologia is a social activity; politicians, broadcasters, etc. *issue* apologies; they *release* statements: public apology is a *performative discursive order*.[1] Apologia is a social product – the product of social and discursive accomplishments, socio-communicative practices involved in social-relational (accountability) management. Making 'moral amends', or accomplishing 'moral repair', is part and parcel of reconstructing, refashioning and restoring moral relations between people (Tavuchis 1991; Walker 2006). Apologia is animated in socio-communicative contexts of use. It projects a variety of alignments (footings) in relation to utterances, arguments, personal and social identities and audiences.

IMAGE RESTORATION

In interpersonal contexts (relationships) the framework of apologies is the negotiation of personal (moral) responsibility and managing threats to face (Goffman 1971). Speech act theory and politeness theory concentrate on the 'felicity' conditions for apologies (e.g. Austin 1962; Jaworski 1994; Kampf 2009). In conversation analytic terms (e.g., Robinson 2004), the focus is mostly on 'explicit' apologies that are said to present a sequential organisation. In the public sphere, maintaining a positive 'image' is at the core of various attempts to understand (public) apologies. Rhetorical approaches to image restoration (see Benoit 1995 for an overview) distinguish between several stances of self-defence. In an attempt to integrate seminal interests in rhetorical strategies of image restoration and social psychological concerns with impression management, Benoit (1995) proposes a theory of 'image restoration' that starts from two vernacular truths: 'communication is a goal-directed activity' and 'maintaining a favorable reputation is one of the central goals of communication'.[2] Benoit reviews a plethora of image restoration strategies: denial (simple denial, shifting the blame) evading responsibility (through scapegoating, defeasibility, accident, good intentions), reducing offensiveness (bolstering, minimisation, differentiation, compensation, transcendence, attack accuser), corrective action, mortification, and charts the presence of these strategies in 'image restoration discourse' in a variety of contexts: press statements of politicians (Benoit 2006), corporate crisis management (Benoit 1997), government discourse on SARS (Zhang and Benoit 2009), or the Queen's 'image repair' discourse occasioned by the death of Princess Diana (Benoit and Brinson 1999).[3] Other researchers conceive of apologies as rhetorical 'events' (Simons 2000). They point to the existence of rhetorical, pragmatic and socio-cultural factors that constrain the speaker to construct his or her apology in a very specific way. Each linguistic and rhetorical choice has implications for other (potential) rhetorical choices (Simons 2000). What *could* have been said is as important as what was *actually* said. Simons (2000) takes the example of Clinton's August 1998 apology and, analysing what he calls the 'situational logic of strategic response' (ibid.:441), concludes that 'Clinton managed his predicament "not badly", but not as well as he could have, under the circumstances' (ibid.: 449; see also Fetzer and Bull 2012 on concerns with the communicative competence of politicians). Simons' analysis (as that of Benoit) retains a focus on prescriptive (felicitous) aspects of apologies, rather than a concern with situated rhetoric and actual use of language (Billig 1987/1996).

APOLOGIA AS DISCOURSE

Image restoration strategies and offence-remedial actions are part of the intersubjective arsenal of defensive rhetoric of individuals and organisations. Public apologies are part of 'rituals which leave space for dignified restoration of the harm resulting from wrongdoing' (Braithwaite 2000: 129).[4] The effectiveness or ineffectiveness of a 'remedial' action is a contingent, yet relatively stable, product of the multi-subjective rhetorical context in which it is produced. Social actors may approach the same issue from different perspectives: multi-subjective agreement, as well as disagreement, is the intimate fabric of social and political life (Billig 1987/1996). What Schudson (2004) calls 'multidimensional social resources', such as trust and reputation, a range of discursive devices, textual networks of testimonies and opinion (public and private), rumours, and personal and official documents, are available to social actors to construct version of events, selves, contexts, to manage personal, group or institutional responsibility. This opens the way for the study of public apologies as ways of managing moral identity and moral accountability (Tileagă 2009b, 2011), and for appreciating multiple 'confessional forms' (Payne 2008) and the multiple identities that social actors inhabit, enact, defend or deny.

Public apologies are perceived more as image restoration moves than as social performances engendering their own dialogical context, public response and associated social and ideological consequences for self and others. There are four methodological principles that inform treating and analysing apologia as discourse. Three originate in discursive psychology (Hepburn and Wiggins 2007; Billig, in press; Potter 2012; Edwards 2012). The last principle originates in socio-cultural psychology (Middleton and Brown 2005, 2007). I will briefly address these in turn.

Discursive psychology conceives of socio-communicative practice as moral order (Edwards 2003, 2006; Potter 2012; Edwards 2012) and is concerned with people's own perspectives, orientations to features of subjectivity and the objective world in the course of practical engagement with the world (Edwards 1997, 2006). What lies at the core of discursive psychology's intellectual and empirical project is a way of doing psychology that understands discourse as social action. Discursive psychology offers an alternative way of conceiving the mutual relationship between people, practices and institutions (Hepburn and Wiggins 2007).

The first methodological principle is that of relying on naturalistic data in studying psychological and social phenomena. According to Potter (2012), the notion of naturalistic marks a contrast from 'got up' materials such as vignettes, experimental protocols, discourse completion-tests, retrospective self-reports and role-play (see Meier 1998 for the range of elicitation methods in apology research). An emphasis is placed on the collection and analysis of naturally occurring, publicly available materials and accounts that (would) exist without the intervention of the researcher (letters to newspapers, talk shows, official documents, etc.). Naturalistic materials provide access to participants' own orientations and displays. The analytic topic is the description and treatment of disclosure, apology, expression of 'regret' by members of society, not its 'objectivity' for us as researchers (Eglin and Hester 2003). The second methodological principle follows from the first. Naturalistic materials facilitate the study of vernacular and elite social practices. Discursive psychology treats and studies talk and texts as social practices. Discourse psychologists start with practices themselves: people interacting with others in mundane settings, the writing of texts in institutional settings, etc.

The third methodological principle is linked to considering the discursive organisation and action-oriented nature of accounts, and taking into consideration how talk and text is organised so as to potentially persuade hearers and readers towards a specified set of 'readings' and 'interpretations' (see Potter 2012; Hepburn and Wiggins 2007). Discursive psychologists have focused their study on the subtle, complex, context-sensitive nature of talk and text and its orientation to social action. People do things with their talk: they make accusations, justify their actions, ask questions, excuse, persuade, etc. People use language to do things – to construct versions of the world depending upon the function of their talk.

The fourth methodological principle is related to how socio-cultural psychologists treat individual and collective memory. For socio-cultural psychologists, processes of remembering, forgetting, suppressing, distorting memories and histories are seen as public, culturally mediated experiences and actions (Middleton and Brown 2005, 2007; Wertsch 2002, 2007). Individual and collective representations of recent personal and national history are not seen as given, or pre-existing, but rather are multivocal and multimodal, circulating and circulated by active agents at various levels of social organisation (individual/group/institutional) through the use of material/cultural tools (e.g. narratives, written records, social technologies) (Wertsch 2007; Brown 2012). Socio-cultural psychologists propose a shift in our understanding of remembering. As Brown (2012) cogently argues, 'remembering is a social practice that enables the production of subjectivity rather than the exercise of a mental faculty alone. Persons invoke and collectively negotiate versions of the past, drawing on the accounts of others as well as a potential host of other mediating objects, including common narratives, "official history", and artefacts varying from mementos, diaries, and photographs to public records' (ibid.:239).

In addressing these methodological principles I draw upon data that are part of a wider project investigating the social construction of the communist/post-communist past in talk and text (Tileagă 2009a, 2009b, 2011, 2012, in press). The context is that of the (ongoing) public release of the Securitate's files in Romania, and ensuing revelations and public debate around moral/deviant 'careers' created and negotiated out of engaging with personal and institutional accountabilities in relation to the communist recent past. A society's hierarchy of respectability and credibility came under scrutiny when, under the threat of detection or simply from a voluntary impulse to (finally) 'tell the truth', public confessions of collaboration flooded the public space. Most of the public confessions of collaboration featured in media and news interviews, newspaper articles, letters sent to newspapers, and radio and television panel debates. This chapter focuses on an exploration of a specific public confession (that of a Romanian public intellectual) of having been an informer for the Securitate (in an open letter to a national newspaper (on the case background, see Tileagă 2009b and 2011, on the broader context of coming to terms with the past in Romania, see Tismăneanu 2008).

DISCURSIVE ANALYSIS

By deciding to focus on an open letter to a newspaper I have followed two of the previously outlined methodological principles: using naturalistic materials and starting with social practices themselves, in this case, the writing of texts and management of public accountability. As argued earlier, naturalistic materials provide access to participants' own orientations and displays. I was mostly concerned with the discursive 'choices' that the writer himself makes in writing the apology, rather than my own assumptions regarding what counts or constitutes an apology. The letter is divided by the writer into two parts – the 'essence' and the 'existence'. The letter is described by the newspaper as a 'harrowing document'. It is placed under 'current affairs' (actualitate) with the gist prefaced by the author's name: 'Am turnat la Securitate' (I have been an informer for the Securitate). The letter (and apologia contained in it) is suggestive of an identity transformation. The writer declares himself to be a certain sort of degraded person, a person of a lower identity in the relevant group's scheme of social types – an 'informer'.

Extracts (1)–(3) below, come from the 'essence'. One can see how, from the onset, disclosure, apologia and moral identity are tied up through the use of organisationally relevant categories – 'informer' and 'Securitate'.

(1) I informed the Securitate in writing about some of [my] friends and some of my acquaintances, without warning them, without confessing to them *post-festum* until my writing of this text, without apologizing, without assuming publicly this shameful past.

(2) I informed on them sometimes, with death in my soul, but I never betrayed them: I have not been an agent provocateur, I have not received missions of any kind, I have not been promised and there have not been advantages created for me . . . during all this time, I remained hostile to the Securitate and the party-state.

(3) Ethically and morally, confession and repentance are coming too late: to the gravity of my deeds from 25–30 years ago, one can add the indefensible gravity of silence, of life lived in lies and duplicity . . .

Notice how in extract (1) moral accountability for actions and moral character are managed through the invocation of the membership categories 'friends' and 'acquaintances' that can be said to imply a set of category-bound activities and a locus for rights and obligations. The absence of moral courses of action in relation to *significant* others is made relevant. Public disclosure (or rather, its *absence*) is made accountable here. The orientation is to an underlying ethical issue (the sin of omission): *failing* to confess to those for whom the act (of confessing) matters.

Through the use of 'sometimes', the metaphor 'with death in my soul' and the extreme case formulation 'never' (see extract (2)) the reader is provided with a formulation of a general disposition to act in a particular way. 'Sometimes' serves to portray the relative character of the state of affairs, as well as the frequency of the practice. 'I never betrayed them' is a way of normalising actions and character by positioning the self in opposition to a potentially damaging moral identity: 'betraying your friends'. It is not the action of informing on close friends and acquaintances that is being denied here, but rather the potentially available/relevant moral inferences and moral identities attached to it. By using the term 'betrayal' the writer displays a reflexive awareness of a breach of a social moral order (what one could call 'trust'). 'Betrayal' is a members' lay term that is made relevant in the public language-game of constructing an explanation for wrongdoing, minimising and negotiating accountability for one's deeds. An alternative moral identity and moral character is constituted by denying other available characteriological formulations (e.g., 'agent provocateur'), morally implicative descriptions that can speak of one's 'tendencies, dispositions, moral nature, desires and intentions' (Edwards 2006: 498). We can see how the writer treats the social order of persons, actions, breaches, and underlying motives for action, as fundamentally a moral order. In doing so, he can build a platform for managing personal and public accountability.

Extract (3) can be seen as a display of a shared cultural understanding of the meaning of 'saying sorry' (LeCouteur 2001). The writer orients to the cultural relevance of the sequence of transgression – confession – penitence – absolution. He also orients to the idea that without a sense of moral self, without a morally penitent and redemptive narrative, there can be no confession; without both internal and external moral constraints, an exploration of selfhood and repentance is not possible. Confession permits both the staging and performance of self-disclosure and penitence; it produces the public scene of guilt and morality play. A play of self-disclosure and penitence is essential to the project of making a confession and constructing an apologia. There is a sense in which concerns with moral identity and moral character operate here as a background 'scheme of interpretation and expression' (Schütz 1967).

It would be relatively easy to identify the writer's account as grounded in image reparation or restoration strategies. But that would not tell the whole story. The discursive analysis of the kind I have been employing points to a different approach by which one can understand public apologies. Public apologies throw up matters grounded in our logical 'grammar' of using ordinary language concepts, and the particular common-sense assumptions about persons, memory, activities and social relations; as a consequence, they need to be studied in relation to those common-sense assumptions and activities. All three extracts point to and lay out the premises of a painstaking process of opening the self into the social – a process of identity transformation. The letter (and especially its second part, the 'existence') signals that it is time to take stock and revisit the biographical and commemorative underpinnings of that *identity* transformation. The 'existence' offers a chronological/biographical journey – from the first encounters with the Securitate, through becoming an informer to, ultimately, being put 'under surveillance'.

(4) I don't remember whether and about whom I was asked immediately for information notes. But I have found at CNSAS an Annex Report Note to nr. 00592/7 from 18.01.1979 written by cpt. Campeanu Corneliu, counter-information officer of U.M. 01241 Ineu (where I completed my military service between October 1978 and March 1980) the following paragraphs: On 29.03.1976 Antohi Sorin was recruited as a collaborator of the Securitate organ receiving the conspirational name of 'Valeriu' (in fact, 'Valentin'; my note) and has been used for information surveillance at the professional training course of Tehnoton plant in Iasi . . . Antohi Sorin has provided a number of information notes from 16.04.1976 to 15.05.1978, all containing general information about the general mood of the class.

Once the category 'informer' is on the record, category-tied activities, such as writing 'information notes', become relevant, and appear on cue (Eglin and Hester 2003). In (4), one can notice how retrospective knowledge claims are handled in sensitive ways (see Edwards 1997) and organisationally relevant products are used to substantiate the point ('I don't remember whether and about whom... But I have found at CNSAS[5] an Annex Report Note...'). The document is not a simple aid to remembering 'forgotten' details, but rather a *mediating* tool between the person's identity and biography and an organisational accomplishment of accountability. It is not presented unaccompanied by a reflective commentary. We find out that 'Ineu' is the name of the place where the writer has completed his military service (dates are relevant, biography is on the record, again) and that his conspirational name is in fact 'Valentin' and not 'Valeriu' (the name in the document is treated as a small mistake, but one without consequence). What is especially relevant in this case is the detail of the number of information notes written and the nature of their content. The document becomes significant for the inferences on the moral character of the person that it makes available (and is invoked to substantiate retrospectively his other claim from the 'essence', of not having harmed/injured anyone of those on whom he provided information notes). Although the narrator might be seen as evading remembering directly and faithfully, apparently the issue of how many notes were written, and their tone and content, is not evaded, but it is substantiated with reference to a relevant organisational product (an annex to a report). In this way, personal memory is indexed as 'practically unavailable' (Lynch and Bogen 1996) for scrutiny.

The official archive of the Securitate is a potential place of discovery (Featherstone 2006), a 'privileged space' (Lynch 1999), from where biographically and institutionally relevant products can be carefully selected to support the perspective offered by the narrator. We are not told about when and how discoveries took place, but what is important are the inferences that can be drawn from the adduced evidence with regard to dispositions, intentions, moral character and identity of the person. The narrator can point to documents for the inferences they make available. There is a clear sense that documents are being called upon, not simply as props to a sluggish and failing memory, but tailored precisely for the occasion of their use and with regard to current (and past) accountability concerns. In the apparent 'absence' of personal memories, documents constitute, and at the same create, a 'public standard of memorability' (Lynch and Bogen 1996).

(5) From Autumn of 1976, the Securitate officer who was in charge of me was a certain lt. Rotaru Vasile... I have found in one of my notebooks a note from 6 October 1976 from which one can infer that lt. Rotaru has been already looking for me: 'I am increasingly

concerned regarding my future. How on earth could I escape through their fingers?' On the 2nd of December I was writing that I was on Triumfului street to see lt. Rotaru, bumping into a colleague who was there for the same ill-fated reason; I quote: 'Despicable thing, but if, forced, I have joined the game, there is nothing I can do'. On the 14th of December 1976 I was to meet lt. Rotaru, at 10, in what looked like a bachelor's flat (his? a conspirative house?), just opposite 'Cotnari' restaurant. I have found a more elliptic mention on the same Rotaru towards the end of January 1977

The rhetoric of 'discovery' in extract (5) is similar to the one identified in extract (4). In extract (5) one can notice the use of the personal 'archive' as 'memory device' (Featherstone 2006). Information from the personal archive can be used to supplement, challenge and correct, the 'public record' of the official archive. The plausibility of recall and accountability of actions is grounded in, and fashioned by, the personal archive. The facts of the matter are not simply remembered, but, in a way, 're-thought' or 're-felt' to use Shotter's (1990) terms. Details 'retrieved' from the personal archive are brought into play rhetorically through reference to mental states ('I was *concerned ...*') and also contain moral positioning and evaluations (*Despicable* thing, but ...') that make available various inferences related to the writer's moral character and its agency.[6] The official and personal archives contain items with determinate, yet open, uses and readings. A certain kind of 'applied deconstruction' (Lynch and Bogen 1996) seems to be at work here. The writer exploits the personal and public record, notices gaps, and fashions an accountability space for justifying (accountable) actions (like having informed on others).

The account is framed as a self-dialogue or self-interrogation. The writer is the 'interrogator' who is trying to get himself to making admissions about his own past and biography. He dramatises, and 'stages' remembering as a vernacular activity. The written records need to be interpreted, especially as what the records 'say' is not decided beforehand. His self-interrogation provides the ground for managing moral inferences about the self. The various rhetorical questions used create ad hoc dilemmas and scenarios of experience. By turning oneself upon oneself, he is working up his own moral status as participant *and* witness to his own life. The standards he uses for working up his status are contestable, defeasible, etc., but they are nonetheless *public*. As self-interrogator he does not simply present the reader with biographical details, but rather uses his own utterances, notes and experiences as interrogative scaffolding for building a self-defence. He prods and enlists his own memory by relying on a previously experienced world of feelings, beliefs and moral emotions that carry implications for (his present) moral character. It can be argued that the role of textual interpositions (personal notes) is that of controlling the tension between remembering, responsibility and public record of wrongdoing.[7] He works *within* and *with* a 'dense intertextual field' (Lynch and Bogen 1996; see also Smith 1999), vernacular and official, that frames the dialogical (self-dialogical) production of the public apology. What he tries to do is to reconfigure, reset and subvert 'the relations of hermeneutic authority' (Lynch 1999: 82), forms of privileged access to knowledge, and modes of reading of biography from documents.

The analysis of extracts (4) and (5) shows how a different perspective on apologia can be obtained by taking into consideration how the text of the confession is organised so as to potentially persuade readers of the relevance of a particular 'reading'. These are examples of how one can learn more about apologia as a social practice by focusing on what the writer *does* with their writing, how the self, context and actions are justified, how different scenarios of action and accountability are introduced, and how particular versions of the world are constructed.

(6) I resigned myself to a lowest order morality, trying never to give information that would truly injure someone's interests, be it a friend or simple acquaintance. When the dossiers regarding the 1980–1982 period will surface, I shall be able to prove this claim; I shall be able to complete the story that I start telling now. Until then, everything remains a simple excuse of an informer.

In the particular case of having 'collaborated' with the Securitate, the narrator shows an orientation to how describing the past is not a neutral matter, but implicates a range of potential (and sometimes competing) accountable descriptions associated with being a certain *type of person*. The relationship to the past is an unfinished business and, in this particular case, the past and the identity of the person can only be made whole through the mediation of a documentary reality: the surfacing of 'dossiers regarding the 1980–1982 period' (see extract (6)). There is a sense that the label and negative inferences on moral character will stick until further documentary evidence is brought into play. Completing the story is a way of challenging the (deviant) identity 'informer' and the process of identity demotion itself. What is not present, *not yet available*, is more significant than what is *already* on the record.[8] As in the previous examples, individual memory is not the only 'support' for the account; official records are used to establish the interpretative frames 'for confirming and elaborating upon recollections' (Lynch 2009: 97). The narrator works backwards from the document to what must have been the case. He reflexively alludes to the idea that 'the past is not something a witness has available in the form of a concrete representation of an event; describing the past implicates a range of claimable, assertable, and disclaimable rights and responsibilities' (Lynch and Bogen 1996: 192).

> (7) A lot of . . . questions persist, the flow of remembering can't quite advance without new concrete elements. I will wait for a while for the documents from the CNSAS . . . here we are dealing with a commemorative beginning, where the essence has been told without rest, and the existence – the realm of nuances and details – has only been sketched.

'Mea culpa' is not just a simple confession of guilt or remorse; it is part of a process of rewriting identity and memory, a process that involves (and at the same time, *constitutes*) the various relationships and tensions that get established between individual and social/organisational memory. As in (6), in (7) it is intimated that organisational records (the official archives) contain the seeds of retrospective, as well as prospective histories. Extracts (6) and (7) show that remembering is a social practice, not only for the analyst, but for the apologist too. Apologists negotiate versions of their past experience by drawing on 'mediating objects' (documents, common narratives, diaries, etc.). Apologies are usually accompanied by 'pleas for closure', yet the narrator is unable to close the hermeneutic circle opened by the 'archive'. Public knowledge of a person's deeds has the power to demote the person to a lower moral type (Garfinkel 1956) and 'keep' it there. The narrator struggles against an imputation of a deviant moral essence. The moral of the story is that passage through institutions (like the Securitate) can have both dramatic and subtle effects. The moral self-portrait (and associated moral implications) is unfinished and yet undecidable. Individual memory needs to be complemented by organisational memory; the former is constructed as subjective, the latter presupposed to be objective. Organisational memory is there to confirm, use, erase, or deny the 'historical record', to promote a different version of identity – one that may bring absolution. As testimonies can be framed as 'remembered' or 'recalled',[9] so the public apology performs a 'theater of memory' (Lynch and Bogen 1996) as details from the past are adduced to complete the biographical and identity puzzle.

CONCLUSION

There are at least three major implications for analysing apologia as discourse. First, apologia can be studied as a public performative phenomenon, the outcome of complex discursive actions and discursive accomplishments. Second, the socio-cultural/discursive organisation of apologies can be studied as constructive of various argumentative and moral identity spaces and positions. Moral identity is not constituted in a vacuum, but through the use of 'open-ended' categories, cultural presuppositions about moral transgression, the workings of individual, social, institutional memory, textual mediation, etc. Third, individual memory can be studied as an active socio-communicative practice of instituting and tying the meaning of the past to ongoing relevant social activities in talk and text. If public apologies are ways of mobilising the past in the present, then one can investigate them in terms of the 'modes of access to the past' they open, and the forms of 'experience' in relation to self and others that are facilitated (Brown 2012).

It could be argued that it matters less whether public apologies are prospective or retrospective expressions of regret, 'anticipatory' or 'remedial'. The problem is less whether apologies are felicitous or not, but what they *do* in a space of public visibility. Although it is often assumed that apologia involves one person (the 'communicator') conveying a message to one or more others (the 'audience'), in practice the management of political communication, persuasion and image restoration is far more complex. As this chapter has shown, speakers and writers can project a variety of alignments (footings) in relation to the words they utter, the identities they are embodying, and the texts and intertextual fields in which they are operating. Social actors construct and mobilise multiple repertoires of self-protective or self-affirming rhetoric. In doing so, they perpetuate, defend or attack different (multiple) versions of lay morality and societal moral meanings.

SUMMARY: KEY POINTS

- The chapter outlines a methodological framework for researching apologia as a discursively and culturally constructed phenomenon.
- It argues that research should turn to the detailed and careful study of apologia as discourse and address it as a topic in its own right.
- Apologia is considered a social activity and the product of social and socio-communicative practices involved in 'image restoration' and social-relational accountability management. By *mobilising* events, people, identities, categories, social relations, institutions and memory, apologies participate in and mould the form and consequences of image restoration discourses.
- Researchers need to be concerned with the rhetorical structure of apologies and their effectiveness, as well as with the moral problems that public apologies raise for apologists and the communities to which they belong.

FURTHER READING

There are quite a few publications that deal with apologia and related issues. Tavuchis (1991) and Bok (1984) are classic texts, although depending on your orientation you may find them more or less relevant. Benoit (1995) includes a useful outline of rhetorical approaches to image restoration and social psychological work on accounts, accompanied by interesting case studies, mainly drawn from the United States. Meier (1998) is a systematic attempt at outlining the state of knowledge regarding apologies. Lakoff (2001) is a call for interdisciplinary ways of looking at apologies from the perspective of discourse analysis. Some other titles that offer valuable reflections on apologies of different kinds include Brooks (1999), Miller (1999), Blaney and Benoit (2001), Lazare (2004) and Payne (2008). In this chapter I have employed a discursive approach to analysing public apologies. For a general overview of the discursive approach (especially as it is developed in social psychology) see Hepburn and Wiggins (2007) and the September 2012 special issue on 'discursive psychology' of the *British Journal of Social Psychology*, edited by Augoustinos and Tileagă. On researching memory in socio-cultural psychology, see the excellent exposition in Middleton and Brown (2005). Tileagă (2009a, 2009b, 2012) and Augoustinos et al. (2011) provide useful examples of discursive studies on public apologies, and can be read in conjunction with this chapter.

NOTES

1. As Lynch and Bogen (1996) note, a pervasive feature of public avowals is that they are usually given 'for the record'. They can be summarised, quoted and 'recycled' in news reports, newspapers and so on.
2. Benoit treats apologies as communicative acts 'intended to attain goals important to the communicators who perform them' (Benoit 1995: 67). Simply put, what Benoit calls 'image restoration discourse' is about 'restoring or protecting one's reputation' (ibid.: 71).
3. Benoit's approach falls into what Meier (1998: 221) calls 'speaker-supportive' perspectives that conceive apologies as 'instruments of impression management or image restoration'.
4. Public apologies can be also seen as self-degradation or identity demotion ceremonies (Garfinkel 1956). The repentance rituals of politicians and public figures create and reproduce a very specific sort of restorative, community justice (Braithwaite 1999) where the apology is the necessary (and, sometimes, sufficient) condition for successful reintegration.
5. The CNSAS is the National Council for the Study of the Securitate Archives.

6. The writer can be said to reflexively problematise the natural tendency to treat what people say about the past as a report of an actual experience – a pre-existing 'memory trace' – what researchers refer to as the 'archival' model of memory (see Brockmeier 2010).
7. Using personal notes positions personal recollections into a (psychological) narrative of identity that can counter, as it were, the official version of the Securitate and manage the concerns of a potentially doubting, suspicious audience/readership. References to personal notes not only offer an alternative construction of 'facts', but also an alternative, moral-psychological perspective on the self – one which is not present in the 'official' records.
8. Akin to an ethnographer, the narrator retains the right to shift between the reflective commentary (the perspective of personal memory) and that of the organisationally ratified document in order to compare and contrast the personal 'inside' and the organisational 'outside'. Official documents and personal notes become 'dialogical objects' – an integral part of a conversation with the personal and political past. Invested with meaning and biographical relevance, they represent symbolic resources in the process of activating a reflexive/dialogical self (Bertau 2007).
9. For the role of memory in testimony, see Chapter 6 in Lynch and Bogen (1996) and Chapter 12 by Jovan Byford in this volume.

CHAPTER 12

Testimony

Jovan Byford

Over the past thirty years, testimonies from Holocaust survivors have become an indispensable form of Holocaust representation.[1] Footage of survivors recalling their experiences of suffering and endurance features prominently in most contemporary Holocaust-related museum exhibitions and educational programmes, and has a noticeable presence in popular culture through inclusion in films and TV documentaries. Since the 1980s, more than 60,000 such testimonies have been recorded, catalogued and archived, mainly thanks to the efforts of large-scale projects based in the United States.[2] When combined with smaller collections assembled in previous decades, or by institutions outside North America, primarily in Israel and Europe, the total number rises to as many as 100,000 (Kushner 2006). The large quantity and unprecedented public availability of Holocaust-related testimony has led to suggestions that when it comes to the representation of the suffering of European Jews under Nazism, we live in the 'era of the witness' (Wieviorka 2006).

The institutional collection of testimonies and the survivors' increasing presence in public life have opened up a number of questions about how testimonies should be understood, used and represented. Historians, sociologists, psychologists and scholars of literature have explored and discussed survivors' accounts in relation to a variety of issues, including trauma, identity, gender, memory, and the place of testimony in Holocaust historiography (see Browning 2003; Gerson and Wolf 2007; Bloxham and Kushner 2005). These multi-disciplinary explorations have thrown up numerous methodological and analytical challenges, some of which relate to issues considered elsewhere in this volume. For example, survivor testimony can be seen as a form of autobiographical memory (Chapter 1), and is typically evoked in the context of an interview (Chapter 3). Testimony collection as an institutional practice reflects the broader agenda of the genre of oral history (Chapter 2) in that it is underpinned by the assumption that systematic recording of a large number of personal memoirs represents a useful tool for capturing the voice of hitherto marginalised groups. Also, Holocaust survivor testimony inevitably poses questions pertaining to traumatic memory (Chapter 6), while its presence in the media (as a manifestation of televised remembering) reflects the growing role of film and television in the transmission of historical knowledge (Chapter 9).

However, there are aspects of testimony that distinguish this form of public remembering from other accounts of traumatic experiences or a typical oral history interview. For one thing, the term *testimony*, and the associated concept of *witnessing*, have strong legal and religious connotations, and are, in both contexts, inextricably tied up with the concept of 'truth'. A testimony, as a form of legal evidence, always attests to the veracity of some event or conduct, while in religious discourse, the term is associated with bearing witness to a higher truth, inaccessible to those who have not undergone some relevant transformative experience. Also, the witness who is called upon to provide testimony is seen as being in possession of some privileged, authoritative perspective which stems either from his or her proximity to facts, or from the immediacy of their experience. Finally, the term testimony is associated with remembering that has a pronounced moral dimension. Testimonies of the kind examined in this chapter are typically collected from, or proffered by, victims of injustice. In this context, bearing witness positions the survivor as a 'morally justified individual who speaks against unjust power' (Peters 2009: 30), and frames their testimony not just as a unique record of events, but also as a source of inspiration, affirmation, and historical lessons.

Within scholarly work on Holocaust survivor testimony it is possible to differentiate two broad conceptual and methodological approaches. The first, which I shall call the *event-centered approach*, focuses on survivors' narratives as potential sources of reliable information about specific events in the past. This perspective is typical of historical scholarship, within which there is an ongoing debate about precisely how testimonies should be utilised as historiographic evidence. The second, *witness-focused approach*, more common within other disciplines including therapeutic psychology and literary studies, looks beyond the evidentiary value of testimony. While its main focus is on how survivors perceive, work through and make sense of past experience (a theme that features in oral history generally – see Portelli 1998), this approach often drifts beyond the notion of subjectivity and incorporates the belief that survivor testimony offers unmediated access to some transcendent, 'unspeakable' essence of Holocaust experience, one that eludes conventional interpretative frameworks, narrative forms or modes of understanding.

In the sections that follow I provide a brief outline of the two approaches and explore the tensions that exist between them, especially in the context of continuing debates about the limits of Holocaust representation. I then discuss how insights from the discourse analytic perspective, already introduced by Cristian Tileagă in the chapter on apologia, might help to inform an alternative perspective on testimony, one that approaches bearing witness first and foremost as a socially and institutionally embedded discursive practice. Specifically, I consider the ways in which the analysis of testimony as discourse might help illuminate the complex interplay between individual and collective remembering which lies at the core of testimony both as a historiographic source and a commemorative form.

EVENT-FOCUSED PERSPECTIVE: HISTORIOGRAPHY, EVIDENCE AND THE RECONSTRUCTION OF THE PAST

In recent decades, historians have become increasingly mindful of the fact that the story of the destruction of European Jews cannot be fully told without taking into account the perspective of the victims of Nazi persecution. This is not just because, when it comes to specific events of the Holocaust, other relevant forms of historical evidence are often lacking, but also because the practice of writing history based solely on the material left behind by the Nazis (the so-called 'perpetrator history') has come to be considered both professionally and ethically questionable. Therefore, in addition to contemporaneous material recovered after the war, such as diaries, letters, reports, documents or personal possessions that had once belonged to the victims, scholars have turned to testimonies recorded years, sometimes decades, after the end of the Second World War. The use of such testimonies as a historiographic source remains controversial. This is primarily because of the inherent fallibility of human memory, which is known to be prone to errors, misremembering, embellishments, or even deliberate fabrication. Hence, when dealing with survivor testimony, historians face a conundrum, which one of the leading scholars in the field, Christopher Browning (2003: 39) articulated as follows: 'How may a historian of the Holocaust use a variety of different, often conflicting and contradictory, in some cases clearly mistaken, memories and testimonies of individual survivors as evidence to construct a history that otherwise, for lack of evidence would not exist?'

This challenge is especially important if we take into account that early and influential historians of the Holocaust, such as Leon Poliakov, Raul Hilberg or Lucy Davidowicz, were notoriously dismissive of survivors' memories, and preferred to rely on the more 'trustworthy' German documents. Their approach was not dissimilar to that which judicial authorities in the West adopted in post-war trials of Nazi criminals. Prosecutors at Nuremberg, for example, regarded survivor testimonies as inherently untrustworthy, and therefore as a largely irrelevant form of evidence (see Bloxham 2001;

Herber and Matthaus 2008; Browning 2010). Although later trials of Nazi officials (especially that of Adolf Eichmann) gradually shifted away from the exclusive reliance on documentary evidence towards a greater inclusion of oral testimony, the latter was seen (again because of the undependability of human memory) as pertinent primarily in the context of the 'correctional and educational' aspect of judicial proceedings (Hausner 1966: 292). This means that the guilt or innocence of the accused was established on the basis of documentary evidence, while the survivor as witness merely helped to personalise and concretise the process of destruction, provide evidence of its effects on the human body and soul, and in doing so 'touch the heart of men [sic]' the world over (ibid: 291).

For the most part, this approach persists in judicial practice, with some justification. This is not just because of the fallibility of human memory (see Wagenaar 1988) but also because of the complex legal and ethical challenges that arise when, in the course of judicial proceedings, an attempt is made to transform a survivor's personal memories of suffering and loss into pertinent, legally admissible, cross-examinable evidence (Hirsh 2001). History and law are built on different epistemological foundations however, so it is unsurprising that, over time, historians have developed a more flexible approach to oral testimony. In fact, as Ginsburg (1992: 85) points out, when it comes to rules of evidence, the analogy between the historian and a judge has acquired a 'definitely unfashionable ring'. There are several reasons why historians have found themselves compelled to consult survivor testimonies (above and beyond the fact that there are aspects of the Holocaust about which they constitute the *only* evidence). First is the realisation that archival documents – which are, also, ultimately of human origin – are not an infallible source. In fact, post-war testimonies have on some occasions proved more reliable than the seemingly 'objective' documentary records (such as the Gestapo files) which also contain misleading, erroneous or falsified information (Roseman 1999). Secondly, even if post-war testimony cannot always provide accurate information about specific facts or points of detail, it can offer insight into what protagonists of certain events *believed* to be true at the time, and how this determined their actions and choices. Thirdly, as Browning (2010) points out, the fact that the bulk of survivor testimonies were collected long after the events of the Holocaust is not always an impediment to their use as historical evidence. On the contrary, testimonies collected relatively late can be especially useful for purposes of historical reconstruction, because with time survivors overcome the reluctance to speak about sensitive or potentially controversial topics such as rape, revenge killings, or other examples of morally questionable conduct among inmates. With the passage of time, what initially were 'secret memories' can become part of publicly created accounts, thus illuminating dimensions of the Holocaust previously hidden from the historian's gaze.

Within contemporary Holocaust historiography there is an ongoing and productive debate about precisely *how* or *when* (rather than *if*) testimonies should be incorporated into historical writing. Although there are some who believe unequivocally in the absolute value of testimony – the Israeli historian Yehuda Bauer (2000: 24), for example, has argued that testimonies are 'at least as reliable as written documents of the time', and that survivors should be treated as '"documents" walking among us on two legs' – most scholars fit somewhere on the continuum between outright rejection and unequivocal acceptance. One common approach stipulates that testimonies should be considered a valid source only in so far as specific claims can be corroborated with other types of evidence. For those subscribing to this 'principle of correspondence' (Reissman 2008: 187) testimonies represent little more than a repository of illustrative examples, whose inclusion in historical writing can be used rhetorically to 'add colour' and authenticity to accounts based on other sources (e.g. Bankier 1992: 118, 124; testimonies are today used in a similar way in museum exhibitions – see Kushner 2006). Another approach states that survivors should generally be given the benefit of the doubt, and that their version of events should be treated as trustworthy unless there is convincing disconfirming evidence (e.g. Gross 2002). A third, and arguably more sophisticated approach involves identifying specific aspects of the Holocaust where testimonies constitute a particularly useful body of evidence (such as everyday life in, or the internal organisation of, a concentration or labour camp), adopting a critical stance that takes into account the conditions in which the testimonies were collected and the potential effects on recall of rumour or information acquired after the war, and then looking across multiple testimonies for a 'firm core' of mutually corroborated 'shared memory' (Browning 2003: 91; 2010).

While this, of course, is not an exhaustive list of approaches and heuristics used by historians, it illustrates the challenges posed by the need to balance the recognition that testimonies are a resource that cannot and should not be ignored, with the professional imperative that requires for survivors' attestations to be subjected to the same rules of evidence that apply to other sources. One thing which is clear is that, when it comes to determining the veracity of Holocaust survivors' memories, historians are not in possession of a methodological or analytic silver bullet. As Novick (1999) put it, some testimonies are undoubtedly true; the problem is that we don't know which ones. A historian must therefore rely on his or her expertise, judgement and insight that come from absorption in historical material, and make informed choices and, often, educated (and intuitive) guesses (Browning 2003, 2010).

This issue is complicated by the fact that engagement with survivors' memories is never solely about epistemology, or about dispassionate and detached evaluation of evidence. It is also about ethics and the acknowledgment that survivors, some of whom are still alive, have the right not to have their personal recollections scrutinised, interrogated, questioned and undermined by scholars. Especially as drawing attention to errors and inconsistencies in testimony has been a long-standing pursuit of Holocaust deniers and the cornerstone of their disreputable, revisionist ideological agenda. Moreover, in contemporary society, survivors of the Holocaust, but also of other acts of violence (9/11, cancer, rape, domestic abuse, etc.) are recognised as important sources not just of epistemic, but also *moral* authority. This widespread tendency to confer approval on those recognised as victims of suffering, and endow them with visibility and influence is referred to in the literature as the phenomenon of 'survivor identity' (McLaughlin 2011) or the 'culture of survivors' (Ballinger 1998; see also Stein 2007; Greenspan 2010). It is difficult to imagine that the increased sensitivity towards survivors shown by Holocaust historians, and their readiness to engage with testimony, is unrelated to the greater prominence of and public deference for those who have lived through the Holocaust, especially as the rise of Holocaust-related audio-visual testimonies and the emergence of the 'culture of survivors' are two closely intertwined cultural developments of the past forty years.

THE WITNESS-FOCUSED PERSPECTIVE: AUTHENTICITY, INTIMACY AND TRAUMA

Whichever approach to testimony a Holocaust historian happens to favour, their agenda is likely to be based on what Tozzi (2012) calls the 'court-witness' model of assessing its relevance. The key criterion for determining the value of a testimony is its perceived validity, credibility, and usefulness for establishing reliable facts about a historical event. And yet, if we examine closely the intellectual and institutional origins of the genre of audio-visual Holocaust survivor testimony, it becomes clear that accounts of suffering and survival were not collected primarily to be used as a historiographic source. Instead, the main aim has been to record 'personal reflections' about the past and 'accompany the witness on a journey back in time, in the most intimate manner possible', with a view to uncovering the deep-seated 'emotional layers of experience' (Beyrak 1995: 139). It was hoped that each survivor's unique language, life story and memories captured on video would 'rehumanise' the victims of Nazism and rescue the Holocaust from what Jean Amery called the 'cold storage of history'. As Geoffrey Hartman (1989: 55), the founder of the Fortunoff Archive at Yale (which began with the systematic interviewing of survivors in 1979) explains, audio-visual testimonies place the survivor centre stage, and focus on 'the mind as it struggles with its memories, making sense of or simply facing them, on transmitting in oral form, each version of survival'.

The emphasis on subjectivity and intimacy of experience (the 'human and psychological milieu' of the Holocaust – Hartman 1989: 55 and Beyrak 1995) and the conceptualisation of remembering as a 'struggle', gives the genre of audio-visual testimony distinct psychological overtones. Literature on testimony is replete with psychological jargon, with 'trauma' as the pivotal explanatory construct. There are frequent references to 'latent' or 'dissociated' memories, the need for survivors to exorcise the 'ghosts of the past', overcome trauma-induced repression and denial which 'contaminate' their lives, and uncover and confront the 'buried truths' that may have been bottled up (Felman and Laub 1992; Hartman 1989; Wieviorka 2006; LaCapra 2001).

This prominent psychological dimension is at least partly attributable to the fact that oral history – especially that which relates to traumatic historical events – has not been immune to the broader tendency, noted by Paul Thompson (2000: 173), to view psychoanalysis as the 'magic of our time', and those who practice it as having the power to both 'hear and to heal'. What is more, the drive to collect survivor testimonies in the 1980s coincided with the rise in awareness, in professional circles, of post-traumatic stress disorder, and the growing public concern, particularly in the United States, with the phenomenon of so-called 'repressed/recovered memories'. The latter refers to the belief, which continues to attract considerable controversy, that traumatised individuals with the help of a trained therapist might recover, and then overcome, previously repressed painful memories of abuse and victimisation (see Ballinger 1998).

The centrality of trauma in the discourse of Holocaust survivor testimony is also closely related to a specificity of the Holocaust which, in the eyes of many, distinguishes it from other instances of mass violence. It is the assumption that the tragedy of European Jews under Nazism is in some ways uniquely 'unthinkable', 'indescribable', 'incomprehensible' or 'unrepresentable' (see Lang 2005; Trezise 2001). According to this argument, the Holocaust is a tragedy that differs in both substance and consequence from other catastrophic events in history, and as such breaks the bounds of 'normal' philosophy of history and its established methods of analysis. Conventional paradigms of historical interpretation and the recognised historical, cultural and biographical modes of representation are believed to be incapable of capturing its essential truth and meaning (Stone 2006; Rothberg 2000).

On closer inspection, the thesis of 'unspeakability' reveals itself to be fraught with contradictions and ambiguities. For one thing, implicit in it is at least some idea (and therefore also a representation) of what it is that supposedly cannot be represented. Also, while some advocates of this view treat the Holocaust as *literally* unrepresentable, others use this trope more as a figure of speech, a hyperbole to draw attention to the moral and aesthetical challenges that working with the Holocaust inevitably poses (see Lang 2005; Hirsch and Spitzer 2009). The claim about the unrepresentability of the Holocaust is linked with the preoccupation with trauma in that one of the defining features of the latter is that it leads to a radical break with normal experience. Trauma prevents victims from articulating, making sense and giving shape to their past, either for the purposes of maintaining a coherent sense of self, or in interaction with others (Laub and Allard 2002; Pickering and Keightley 2009). This means that the fragmented, traumatic, inarticulable 'deep memory' of the Holocaust (Langer 1991), which cannot be represented narratively, needs to be transmitted *affectively*, by means of the survivors' body language, silences, grimaces, gestures and tears – the 'spectacle of pain' (Peters 2009: 30) captured on and communicated through video testimony. The claim that the Holocaust needs to be 'felt' through empathy, rather than comprehended intellectually, foregrounds the act of telling and sets up the figure of the survivor as the embodiment of the unspeakable essence of human suffering during the Holocaust. This is one of the main reasons why Holocaust survivor testimonies, unlike the majority of oral history collections, are mostly recorded in audio-visual format. The visual medium, recognised for its capacity to evoke emotion as well as articulate fact or opinion, is seen as capable of capturing the authenticity and actuality of testimony, and communicating a different, unique kind of 'truth' inherent in the act of bearing witness to the Holocaust – traumatic truth (Stone 2006), 'phenomenological truth' (Oliver 2004: 81) or the 'embodied truth of experience' (Assmann 2011: 110).

In their analysis of Holocaust testimony, exponents of the witness-centred approach tend to focus on the narrative styles, linguistic devices and modes of delivery which survivors deploy in the process of bearing witness (see, for example, Langer 1991). In doing so, writers will often emphasise the non-literal and non-factual in the accounts: the metaphors, similes and hyperboles – what Oren Baruch Stier (2003: 91) calls the 'vernacular poetics' of Holocaust testimony. The episode where a survivor, Bessie K., refers to her baby, which was taken away from her by the camp guards, as a 'bundle', Edith P.'s evocation of the memory of the sun being 'black' in Auschwitz, or Serena N.'s recollection of four crematoria being blown up during an uprising in the camp (instead of just one), are some examples of these 'still snapshots' or 'fragmentary sensations' (Herman 1992: 38, 175) which are frequently cited in the literature. One important reason for the prominence of the non-literal is that it epitomises both the eloquence and lucidity of survivors and the inherently incommunicable, traumatic reality of the Holocaust, of the kind that 'resists being domesticated through traditional historical comprehension' (Tozzi 2012: 2).

TESTIMONY AS DISCOURSE AND SOCIAL PRACTICE: BEYOND 'ACCURACY' AND 'AUTHENTICITY'

There are obvious tensions between the event-focused and witness-focused approaches to survivor testimony in terms of their respective epistemological assumptions, research agendas or methodological foci. The preoccupation with 'intimacy' and subjectivity sometimes even goes as far as explicitly pitting survivors' traumatic memories against historiography. Lawrence Langer (1991: 174) for example, describes testimonies as a cry against the 'totalitarian impulse of a historicism that believes it can account for everything' (see also Felman and Laub 1992). Conversely, a number of historians have argued that their discipline's aspiration to 'incite reflection, thought and rigour' when dealing with the Holocaust is consistently undermined by a testimonial genre that 'appeals to the heart and not the mind' (Wieviorka 2006: 143-4) and which encourages the sanctification of, rather than critical engagement with, survivors' memories (Waxman 2010). These differences in perspective have important methodological implications. Questions used to probe the survivors' memories in the context of a project whose focus is subjective experience are often very different to those that a historian would ask (Browning 2010). Also, audio-visual testimonies are rarely fully transcribed – that is, converted into a format that would facilitate their use for purposes of historical reconstruction. The reason is not just the cost involved in transcribing tens of thousands of interviews, but also the aforementioned contention that the value of testimony lies in a form of direct and emotional engagement which cannot be captured in a written record.

Bridging the gap that separates the two approaches represents an important methodological and professional challenge. Some steps in this direction have already been taken. For example, a number of writers have drawn attention to the fact that historical inquiry should become more attentive to the issue of memory, and encompass the exploration of how an event was experienced, remembered and passed on to successive generations (see Young 1997; Assmann 2006; Vidal-Naquet 1992). This is an extension of the much more widespread realisation that, while being the product of individual remembering, survivor testimonies are inherently *social*: they are contingent upon and mediated by circumstances surrounding their collection, by the established cultural and storytelling practices and by the broader discourses of collective memory. All of these factors inevitably determine the parameters – aesthetic, explanatory, cultural or ideological – of Holocaust representation in any given culture or historical period, including that which is materialised in survivor testimony (Young 1988; Wieviorka 2006; Waxman 2006; Kushner 2006, etc.).

Importantly, the recognition of the social nature of testimony does not imply an abandonment of history's overall empirical project and its quest for historical truth. Instead, it invites a more reflective enquiry, which turns inaccuracies in testimony, and the dynamic that produces them into an object of investigation (Roseman 1999). It is in this context that a discourse-based analysis offers itself as a useful methodological framework. The starting point of this approach, which draws on the established tradition of discourse analytic work on memory (Edwards and Potter 1992; Edwards 1997; Middleton and Edwards 1990; Middleton and Brown 2005; Lynch and Bogen 1996) is a fundamental reassessment of the two aspects of testimony which lie at the core of the other approaches – namely 'accuracy' and 'authenticity'. The object of discursive analysis is neither historical reality, which is more or less accurately represented in testimony, nor the way in which the person doing the remembering interprets, makes sense of, or deals with that reality. Instead, remembering is analysed as a *discursive act* through which both the events of the past and the understanding of those events are constructed (see Edwards 1997: 271–2). In the context of survivor testimony, this means that the true representation of the past and the insight into a survivor's authentic subjective experience are seen as more than just different aspects of testimony, accessible through the application of a particular analytical method. They are treated also as socially and culturally shared assumptions *about* survivors as witnesses, constitutive of the argumentative context within which survivors recall and speak about their past. Being positioned or interpellated as a 'survivor' comes with the expectation that the testimony will meet certain standards of plausibility and reliability, especially as it might, at some point, be compared for accuracy with other sources, including other testimonies. At the same time, survivors' accounts typically orient to, even if only implicitly, the widespread assumption about the Holocaust's inherent unrepresentability. The discourse analytic approach to testimony focuses on how survivors, in reconstructing the past, accomplish being simultaneously an (objective) eye-witness to historical facts, and the embodiment of an authentic 'truth about humanity and suffering that transcends those facts' (Oliver 2004: 8). From this vantage point, issues of 'accuracy' or 'authenticity' are, first and foremost, socially and culturally mediated concerns that survivors themselves attend to and negotiate as they construct a functional account of their lives – one that addresses both the interviewer who is physically present, and a hypothetical future audience of museum visitors, schoolchildren, scholars and other survivors (see Byford 2010, in press). Crucially, in this context, individual remembering is not conceptualised as an internal, psychic event, or a manifestation of mental processes like repression, denial, or trauma. The focus is on the act of remembering, its capture on tape or film, and subsequent dissemination and consumption as a set of dynamic, interacting social practices.

One advantage of the discursive approach, which I have examined in my own work, is that it provides a way of analysing the recurring inaccuracies and embellishments found in survivors' memories. For instance, it has been shown that testimonies of Auschwitz survivors recorded after the release of *Schindler's List* in 1993 are more likely to contain descriptions of events resembling the film's famous shower scene than those collected before that date (Browning 2003: 84). Similarly, undergoing selection by the notorious Nazi doctor Josef Mengele features with too great a regularity in testimonies of survivors of Auschwitz to be literally true in every case (Hartman 1996). In my case study I examined another, lesser known trope – namely the claim, frequently found in the testimonies of survivors of the Banjica camp in Serbia, that a gas van operated in that camp, even though there is persuasive documentary and circumstantial evidence to suggest that this was not the case (Byford 2010).

What is the nature and the origin of these and other 'iconic Holocaust tropes' (Browning 2010: 11), and how do they come to 'contaminate' survivors' recollections of the past? In my analysis of the gas van claim I proposed that, rather than dismissing them as products of cognitive error or traumatic memory, these tropes should be analysed as functional devices which survivors mobilise as they accomplish the task a being 'a witness' (see Byford 2010). It is well documented that an important challenge faced by many Holocaust survivors is that they feel they are expected to comment on events that lay beyond their immediate experience (Waxman 2006). Bearing witness often requires them to bridge the gap that separates what they experienced in the camps from their limited, individual vantage point, and the events to which they are summoned to bear witness years or decades after liberation (Peters 2009).

One route available to witnesses facing this predicament is to produce claims that are congruent with already available knowledge. By producing an account that corroborates rather than contradicts existing historical claims, survivors render their story more credible and strengthen their status as a reliable witness. They do so by confirming the audience's expectation about what someone in that position could and should have seen (Beim and Fine 2007; Byford 2010; also Byford, in press). This illustrates well the dilemma inherent in the practice of witnessing. Testimonies are valued if they provide previously unavailable information; that is, if they add to existing historical knowledge. At the same time, an established way of judging the plausibility of an account is by assessing whether it contains claims consistent with what is already known or believed to be true (Simon 1999). The fact that survivors incorporate in their personal narratives bits of camp rumour and hearsay, or reproduce claims found in textbooks, films, documentaries or other testimonies, is a product of this complex nexus of culturally rooted expectations which the survivors respond to and manage as they undertake the task of being a witness to the tragic past.

However, as was already noted, in testifying about the Holocaust, a survivor is never just a material witness to historical reality. Their testimony is the embodiment of what in the literature is referred to as the 'aporia of Holocaust testimony' (Hirsch and Spitzer 2009: 154) or the 'paradox of attestation' (Tozzi 2012: 5). This refers to the expectation that the survivor will describe events that are too traumatic to ever be fully represented or described, and too horrific to be understood by those who were not there. Once again, this is something that needs to be managed rhetorically. One way of doing this is through what Andrea Reiter (2005) calls the 'the trope of unutterability', a rhetorical device whereby the claim that an extreme experience cannot be put into language is followed by a description of that which cannot be described. Similarly, it is not uncommon for survivors to shift back and forth from a matter-of-fact, minimalistic and highly descriptive, affectless style characteristic of an 'objective', material witness who is conveying 'bare facts' about the past (see Clendinnen 1999; Dean 2010; Tozzi 2012), and an emotion-laden style full of silences, hesitations and abstractions, which relays the authenticity of unparalleled and unspeakable suffering – one that cannot be plausibly described using overly literal language. The task for the discourse analyst is to explore the rhetorical structure and function of these different styles, and the ways in which they are mobilised to conduct specific interactional and ideological 'business' (see Tileagă, this volume).

In the context of the 'paradox of attestation', it is worth reflecting also on another recurring motif in Holocaust testimony, namely the tendency among survivors to evoke the memory of 'a friend or relative who charges them, as the dying Hamlet does Horatio, to tell his story' (Hartman 1995: 200). This common trope has a number of different, overlapping dimensions. First, it could be seen as a manifestation of the imperative to remember (*zakhor*) enshrined in the traditions of Judaism. Second, it echoes the broader discourse of the 'duty to remember' which surrounds the Holocaust, and which is underpinned by its own complex ethico-political dynamic (Misztal 2003). Finally, it also has more immediate, rhetorical functions. As well as imbuing survival with meaning (which is important within the context of the well-documented phenomenon of 'survivor guilt' and the associated issues of accountability that also need to be managed in testimony), the direct appeal to the duty to speak on behalf of others and bear witness to their fate explicitly positions the survivor as a source of epistemic authority – someone who *can* give evidence to truth about the destruction of a community. Therefore, it contains an implicit and subtle argument against the assumption that the survivor, as a traumatised individual, can convey only their own inner turmoil, and intimate, subjective truth, and, instead, frames the Holocaust as an object of memory that can, and must be spoken about, described and represented. Furthermore, it opens up the space for the inclusion, in the testimony, of events that the survivor did not personally witness. The transformation of the witness into a messenger for the dead obscures the boundary between direct experience and other forms of knowledge, or between what the survivor actually saw and what they 'know' *happened*, either to themselves or to others.

CONCLUSION

It is important to emphasise that the broader point about the functional nature of remembering which is inherent in this analytic approach, and the focus on witnessing as a performative, culturally and historically situated social practice, is not intended to undermine the integrity of individual witnesses or to insinuate that they deliberately manipulate testimonies in ways that serve their self-interest. Remembering is an inherently (re)constructive, and *social*, process. It is not, as traditional psychology often argues, the product of the 'machinations of inner cognitive structures and processes', but a dynamic, performative, and rhetorical practice, aimed at producing what in a specific interactional, institutional and cultural context is 'an acceptable, agreed or communicatively successful version of what really happened' (Edwards and Potter 1995: 34–5). In weaving a story of their past, survivors inevitably address particular (real or imagined) audiences; they orient and react to actual or anticipated scepticism or challenges, and mobilise different discursive resources to construct versions of events that will be recognised as authentic, sincere, reliable and valuable.

Also, the analysis of survivors' memories of the kind proposed here does not imply that testimonies should be examined purely as pieces of text or a set of rhetorical devices. Analysis must always extend to the detailed exploration of the broader cultural and ideological context within which a specific act of bearing witness is embedded. For example, the narrative structure, thematic configuration and the overall tone of testimonies collected in the United States over the past 30 years reveal a discernible focus on feelings, the redemptive and heroic nature of survival, and the universal lessons of the Holocaust. This distinct 'vision of experience' (Young 1988) which is, for the most part, shared by survivors, the interviewers and their intended audience, and which helped to inform the development of the witness-centered approach to testimony, reflects a specific trajectory of post-war representation and understanding of the Holocaust in that country. In a recent article, I explored accounts of Holocaust survivors which US-based projects recorded in Serbia in the 1980s and 1990s (Byford, in press). The testimonies collected reflected very different assumptions about the nature of Holocaust experience and the educational and commemorative role of survivors and their memories. The emphasis on intimacy and trauma, for instance, or the assumption about the unrepresentability of the Holocaust, were almost completely absent in the Serbian collection. This is because the local culture of Holocaust memory was dominated by the motif of atrocity and an aesthetic of death which positioned the survivor, first and foremost, as a detached material witness and 'the accuser'. Their role was to describe and narrate the details of atrocities and suffering, rather than attempt to reconstruct or communicate their inner turmoil and emotion (Byford, in press).

The cultural contingency of Holocaust testimony and survivors as witnesses, which is often overlooked in the literature, highlights a broader methodological issue. The manner in which Holocaust experience is organised, interpreted and structured in testimony, reflects, while at the same time helping to shape, the ways in which a society, its institutions and publics (including scholars and academics) attribute relevance to, appropriate and utilise individual life histories. Therefore, details of rhetoric must always be analysed alongside and in the context of the wider question of how specific (and evolving) social, cultural, historical, and material conditions establish 'the survivor' as a source of epistemic and moral authority and a particular kind of witness, and how this helps to sustain, or challenge, established cultures of memory, collective identities and ideological agendas. Capturing the inherent complexity of the practice of bearing witness, which epitomises the interplay between, and mutual interdependence of, individual and collective remembering, requires insights from different disciplines – history, memory studies, sociology, psychology and others. It also calls for an analytic approach and a research agenda that transcends traditional disciplinary divisions, and moves beyond the preoccupation with either accuracy or authenticity.

SUMMARY: KEY POINTS

- The chapter began by discussing testimony and witnessing as a specific genre of remembering; one that as well as being tied up with the notion of truth, is also characterised by a strong moral dimension.
- Two different approaches to testimony apparent in literature on the Holocaust were contrasted with each other. The first considered survivor testimonies as a potentially useful historiographic source. The second focused on the intimacy and subjectivity of Holocaust experience and on the witness as the embodiment of that experience.
- The chapter then considered the tension that exists between the two approaches, especially in the context of debates about whether or not an event such as the Holocaust can ever be adequately represented. This is the tension between testimony as an accurate representation of the past, and testimony as an authentic voice of Holocaust experience.
- A discursive approach to testimony was introduced which views the act of remembering, its capture on tape or film and subsequent dissemination and consumption, as a set of dynamic, interacting social practices. This

approach moves beyond notions of accuracy and authenticity, and considers both of these as pragmatic concerns that survivors of the Holocaust attend to as they construct socially and interactionally relevant stories of their past.
- Finally, the chapter argued that as well as exploring the rhetorical structure and function of survivors' accounts, discourse-based analysis must encompass a detailed exploration of the broader cultural and ideological context within which a specific act of bearing witness is embedded, which establishes 'the survivor' as a source of epistemic and moral authority.

FURTHER READING

For a general overview of the rise of genre of Holocaust survivor testimony, see Annette Wieviorka's *Era of the Witness* (2006), the chapter on testimony in Bloxham and Kushner's *The Holocaust: Critical Historical Approaches* (2005), and a special issue of *Poetics Today* devoted to audio-visual testimony of Holocaust survivors. Browning (2003) offers a detailed and illuminating discussion of the dilemmas faced by historians when faced with survivor testimony, while Langer (1991) and Felman and Laub (1992) are representative of what I termed in this chapter the witness-centred approach. A discursive approach to memory is considered in Middleton and Edwards (1990), Edwards and Potter (1992) and, more recently, Middleton and Brown (2005). The book, *Spectacle of History*, by Lynch and Bogen (1996) deals specifically with testimony and the social and institutional practices of memory-making, but in a different context to that considered in this chapter. It focuses on (quasi-) judicial hearings held by the US Senate in the wake of the Iran-contra affair. Finally, on the notion of witnessing in the age of electronic media, see the different contributions in Frosh and Pinchevski (2009).

NOTES

1. Research presented in this chapter was made possible by the funds granted to the author through the 2010/2011 Charles H.Revson Foundation Fellowship at the Centre for Advanced Holocaust Studies, United States Holocaust Memorial Museum. The statements made and views expressed, however, are solely the responsibility of the author.
2. Among them are the Fortunoff Video Archive for Holocaust Testimonies at Yale, the Oral History Department of the United States Holocaust Memorial Museum (USHMM), and the University of Southern California Shoah Foundation Institute for Visual History, funded by Steven Spielberg.

Bibliography

Abraham, A. (1978) *Mende Government and Politics under Colonial Rule*, Freetown: Sierra Leone University Press.
Abrams, L. (2010) *Oral History Theory*, London: Routledge.
Alcoff, L. and E. Potter (1993) *Feminist Epistemologies*, New York: Routledge.
Alderson, P. (1995) *Listening to Children: Children, Ethics and Social Research*, Essex: Barnardo's.
Aldridge, J. (2007) 'Picture this: the use of participatory photographic research methods with people with learning disabilities', *Disability and Society*, 22 (1): 1–17.
Aldridge, J. and S. Becker (1993) *Children who Care: Inside the World of Young Carers*, Loughborough: Young Carers Research Group, Loughborough University.
Aldridge, J. and S. Becker (2003) *Children Caring for Parents with Mental Illness: Perspectives of Young Carers, Parents and Professionals*, Bristol: The Policy Press.
Aldridge, J. and D. Sharpe (2007) *Pictures of Young Caring*, Loughborough: Young Carers Research Group, Loughborough University.
Alexander, S. (2009) 'Memory-Talk: London Childhoods', in S. Radstone and B. Schwarz (eds), *Mapping Memory*, New York: Fordham University Press, pp. 235–45.
Allan, D. (2005) 'Mythologising Al-Nakba: Narratives, collective identity and cultural practice among Palestinian refugees in Lebanon', *Oral History*, 33 (1): 47–56.
Allen, M. J. and S. D. Brown (2011) 'Embodiment and living memorial: The affective labour of remembering the 2005 London bombings', *Memory Studies*, 4 (3): 312–27.
Allett, N., E. Keightley and M. Pickering (2011) 'Using Self-Interviews to Research Memory', Manchester: Realities at the Morgan Centre, University

of Manchester, <http://www.manchester.ac.uk/morgancentre/realities/toolkits/> (accessed 18 January 2013).
Amit, V. (ed.) (2000) *Constructing the Field: Ethnographic Fieldwork in the Contemporary World*, London: Routledge.
Antze, P. and M. Lambek (eds) (1996) *Tense Past: Cultural Essays in Trauma and Memory*, New York: Routledge.
Appadurai, A. (1990) 'Disjuncture and Difference in the Global Cultural Economy', *Public Culture*, 2 (2): 1–24.
Appadurai, A. (1991) 'Global Ethnoscapes: Notes and Queries for a Transnational Anthropology', in R. G. Fox (ed.), *Recapturing Anthropology: Working in the Present*, Sante Fe: School of American Research Press, pp. 191–210.
Argenti, N. (2007) *The Intestines of the State: Youth, Violence, and Belated Histories in the Cameroon Grassfields*, Chicago: Chicago University Press.
Assmann, A. (2006) 'History, memory and the genre of testimony', *Poetics Today*, 27 (2): 261–73.
Assmann, A. (2011) *Dugasenkaprošlosti.Kulturasećanjaipolitikapovesti* [Der langeSchatten der Vergangenheit], Serbian translation. Belgrade: XX vek.
Atkinson, P., A. Coffey, S. Delamont, J. Lofland and L. Lofland (eds) (2001) *Handbook of Ethnography*, London: Sage.
Augoustinos, M., B. Hastie and M. Wright (2011) 'Apologizing for historical injustice: Emotion, truth, and identity in political discourse', *Discourse and Society*, 22 (5): 507–31.
Austin, J. (1962) *How to do things with words*, London: Oxford University Press.
Baddeley, A. (2010) 'Concepts of memory', *Journal of Neurology, Neurosurgery and Psychiatry*, 81 e1 doi:10.1136jnnp.2010.217554.1.
Ballinger, P. (1998) 'The culture of survivors: Post-Traumatic Stress Disorder and traumatic memory', *History and Memory*, 10 (1): 99–132.
Ballinger, P. (2003) *History in Exile: Memory and Identity at the Borders of the Balkans*, Princeton: Princeton University Press.
Baltruschat D. (2002) 'Globalization and International TV and Film Co-productions: In Search of New Narratives', conference paper delivered at Media in Transition 2: Globalization and Convergence conference, Massachusetts Institute of Technology, 10–12 May, <http://web.mit.edu/cms/Events/mit2/Abstracts/DorisBaltruschat.pdf> (accessed 18 January 2013).
Bamberg, M. (2006) 'Stories: Big or small: Why do we care?', *Narrative Inquiry*, 16 (1): 139–47.
Banister, P., E. Burman, I. Parker, M. Taylor and C. Tindall (1994) *Qualitative Methods in Psychology: A Research Guide*, Maidenhead: Open University Press.

Bankier, D. (1992) *The Germans and the Final Solution: Public Opinion Under Nazism*, Oxford: Blackwell.
Banks, M. (2001) *Visual Methods in Social Research*, London: Sage.
Barnardo's Policy Development Unit (1996) *Transition to Adulthood*, Ilford: Barnardo's.
Barnes, H. E. (1998) *The Story I Tell Myself: A Venture in Existentialist Autobiography*, Chicago: University of Chicago Press.
Bartlett, F. C. (1932) *Remembering: A Study in Experimental and Social Psychology*, New York: Cambridge University Press.
Bassani, E. (1979) 'Sono from Guinea Bissau', *African Arts*, 12 (4): 44–7.
Basu, P. (2007a) *Highland Homecomings: Genealogy and Heritage-Tourism in the Scottish Diaspora*, London: Routledge.
Basu, P. (2007b) 'Palimpsest Memoryscapes: Materializing and Mediating War and Peace in Sierra Leone', in F. de Jong and M. Rowlands (eds), *Reclaiming Heritage: Alternative Imaginaries of Memory in West Africa*, Walnut Creek, CA: Left Coast Press.
Basu, P. (2008) 'Confronting the Past? Negotiating a Heritage of Conflict in Sierra Leone', *Journal of Material Culture* 13 (2): 153–67.
Basu, P. (2011) 'Object Diasporas, Resourcing Communities: Sierra Leonean Collections in the Global Museumscape', *Museum Anthropology* 34 (1): 28–42.
Basu, P. (2012) 'A Museum for Sierra Leone? Amateur Enthusiasms and Colonial Museum Policy in British West Africa', in S. Longair and J. McAleer (eds), *Curating Empire: Museums and the British Imperial Experience*, Manchester: University of Manchester Press.
Basu, P. (2013) 'Recasting the National Narrative: Postcolonial Pastiche and the New Sierra Leone Peace and Cultural Monument', *African Arts*, 46 (3), 10–25.
Batchen, G. (2004) *Forget Me Not: Photography and Remembrance*, New York: Princeton Architectural Press.
Bauer, S. (2009) *The Art of Public Grovel: Sexual Sin and Public Confession in America*, Princeton and Oxford: Princeton University Press.
Bauer, Y. (2000) *Rethinking the Holocaust*, New Haven: Yale University Press.
Baum, W. (1972) 'Oral history in the United States', *Oral History*, 1 (3): 15–30.
'BBC apologises as Dyke quits', BBC News, 29 January 2004, <http://news.bbc.co.uk/1/hi/uk_politics/3441181.stm> (accessed 18 January 2013).
Becker, S. (2000) 'Young carers', in M. Davies (ed.), *The Blackwell Encyclopaedia of Social Work*, Oxford: Blackwell, p. 378.
Becker, S., J. Aldridge and C. Dearden (1998) *Young Carers and their Families*, Oxford: Blackwell Science.
Beim, A. and G. A. Fine (2007) 'Trust in testimony: The institutional embeddedness of Holocaust survivor narratives', *European Journal of Sociology*, 48 (1): 55–75.

Belenky, M. F., B. M. Clinchy, N. R. Goldberger and J. M. Tarule (1986) *Women's Ways of Knowing: The Development of Self, Voice and Mind*, New York: Basic Books.

Bell, A. (1980) *Sydney Smith*, Oxford: Clarendon Press.

Bell, E. (2011) 'Television and memory: history programming and contemporary identities', *Image and Narrative*, 12 (2): 50–65.

Bell, E. and A. Gray (2010) 'History on television: charisma, narrative and knowledge', *European Journal of Cultural Studies*, 10 (1): 113–33.

Bellman, B. L. (1984) *The Language of Secrecy: Symbols and Metaphors in Poro Ritual*, Piscataway, NJ: Rutgers University Press.

Bendien, E., S. D. Brown and P. Reavey (2010) 'Social remembering as an art of living: Analysis of a "reminiscence museum"', in M. Domenechand and M. Schillmeier (eds), *New Technologies and Emerging Spaces of Care*, Farnham: Ashgate, pp. 149–67.

BenEzer, G. (2004) 'Trauma Signals in Life Stories', in K. L. Rogers and S. Leydesdorff (eds), *Trauma: Life Stories of Survivors*, New Brunswick, NJ: Transaction, pp. 29–44.

Bennett, J. (2008) 'Interfacing the Nation: Remediating Public Service Broadcasting in the Digital Television Age', *Convergence*, 14 (3): 277–94.

Bennett, J. and S. Holmes (2010) 'The "place" of television in celebrity studies', *Celebrity Studies*, 1 (1): 65–80.

Benoit, W. L. (1995) *Accounts, Excuse and Apologies: A Theory of Image Restoration Strategies*, Albany, NY: State University of New York Press.

Benoit, W. L. (1997) 'Image repair discourse and crisis communication', *Public Relations Review*, 23 (2): 177–86.

Benoit, W. L. (2006) 'Image repair in President Bush's April 2004 news conference', *Public Relations Review*, 32 (2): 137–43.

Benoit, W. L. and S. L. Brinson (1999) 'Queen Elizabeth's image repair discourse: Insensitive royal or compassionate queen?', *Public Relations Review*, 25 (2): 145–56.

Berdahl, D. (1999) *Where the World Ended: Reunification and Identity in the German Borderland*, Berkeley: University of California Press.

Berliner, D. (2005) 'The Abuses of Memory', *Anthropological Quarterly*, 78 (1): 197–211.

Bernard, H. R. (2011) *Research Methods in Anthropology: Qualitative and Quantitative Approaches*, 5th edn, Lanham, MD: AltaMira Press.

Bernsten, D. and D. C. Rubin (2004) 'Cultural life scripts structure recall from autobiographical memory', *Memory and Cognition*, 32 (3): 427–42.

Bertau, M.-C. (2007) 'Review symposium: Encountering objects and others as a means of passage', *Culture and Psychology*, 13 (3): 335–52.

Bertaux, D. and M. Kohli (1984) 'The Life Story Approach: A Continental View', *Annual Review of Sociology*, 10: 215–37.

Beyrak, N. (1995) 'To rescue the individual out of the mass numbers: intimacy as a central concept in oral history', in M. Cling and Y. Thanassekos (eds), *Ces visages qui nous parlent :actes*, Bruxelles: Foundation Auschwitz: Fondation pour la mémoire de la déporation, pp. 138–46.

Billig, M. (1987/1996) *Arguing and Thinking: A Rhetorical Approach to Social Psychology*, Cambridge: Cambridge University Press.

Billig, M. (1988) 'Methodology and Scholarship in Understanding Ideological Explanation', in C. Antaki (ed.), *Analysing Everyday Explanation: A Casebook of Methods*, London: Sage, pp. 199–215.

Billig, M. (in press) 'Undisciplined beginnings, academic success, and discursive psychology', *British Journal of Social Psychology*, 51 (3): 413–24.

Bishop, E. (2007) 'A Reflexive Account of Reusing Qualitative Data: Beyond Primary/Secondary Dualism', *Sociological Research Online*, 12(3)2, <http://www.socresonline.org.uk/12/3/2.html> (accessed 18 January 2013).

Blaney, J. and W. Benoit (2001) *The Clinton Scandals and the Politics of Image Restoration*, Westport, CT: Praeger.

Bloxham, D. (2001) *Genocide on Trial: War Crimes Trials and the Formation of Holocaust History and Memory*, Oxford: Oxford University Press.

Bloxham, D. and T. Kushner (2005) *The Holocaust: Critical Historical Approaches*, Manchester: Manchester University Press.

Boddy, J. and M. Smith (2008) 'Asking the experts: Developing and validating parental diaries to assess children's minor injuries', *International Journal of Social Research Methodology*, 11 (1): 63–77.

Bodnar, J. (1992) *Remaking America: Public Memory, Commemoration, and Patriotism in the Twentieth Century*, Princeton: Princeton University Press.

Bok, S. (1984) *Secrets: On the Ethics of Concealment and Revelation*, New York: Oxford University Press.

Booth, T. (1996) 'Sounds of still voices: issues in the use of narrative methods with people who have learning difficulties', in L. Barton (ed.), *Disability and Society: Emerging Issues and Insights*, New York: Sociology Series, Longman, pp. 237–55.

Bordo, S. (1990) 'Feminism, postmodernism and gender skepticism', in L. Nicholson (ed.), *Feminism/Postmodernism*, New York: Routledge, pp. 133–56.

Borland, K. (1991) '"It's not what I said": Interpretive conflict in oral narrative research', in S. B. Gluck and D. Patai (eds), *Women's Words: The Feminist Practice of Oral History*, London: Routledge, pp. 63–75.

Born, G. (2004) *Uncertain Vision: Birt, Dyke and the Reinvention of the BBC*, London: Secker and Warburg.

Bornat, J. (1992) 'The Communities of Community Publishing', *Oral History*, 20 (2): 23–31.

Bornat, J. (2004) 'Oral History', in C. Seale, G. Gobo, J. F. Gubrium and D. Silverman (eds), *Qualitative Research Practice*, London: Sage, pp. 34–47.
Bornat, J. (2008) 'Biographical Methods', in P. Alasuutari, L. Bickman and J. Brannen (eds), *The Sage Handbook of Social Research Methods*, London: Sage, pp. 344–56.
Bornat, J. (2010) 'Remembering and reworking emotions: the reanalysis of emotion in an interview', *Oral History*, 38 (2): 43–52.
Bornat, J. and H. Diamond (2007) 'Women's History and Oral History: developments and debates', *Women's History Review*, 16 (1): 19–39.
Bornat, J., T. Hunter and A. Green (2011) 'Woodberry Down Housing Estate: community representation and advocacy in print and film', *Oral History*, 39 (2): 107–16.
Bornat, J., P. Raghuram and L. Henry (2012) 'Revisiting the archives – opportunities and challenges: a case study from the history of geriatric medicine', *Sociological Research Online*, 17(2): 11.
Boroditsky, L. (2001) 'Does language shape thought?: Mandarin and English speakers' conceptions of time', *Cognitive Psychology*, 43 (1): 1–22.
Bourdieu, P. (1996) *Photography: A Middle-brow Art*, Cambridge: Polity.
Bourdon, J. (2003) 'Some Sense of Time: Remembering Television', *History and Memory*, 15 (2): 5–35.
Bradley, B. (2005) *Psychology and experience*, Cambridge: Cambridge University Press.
Braithwaite, J. (1999) 'Restorative justice: assessing optimistic and pessimistic accounts', *Crime and Justice*, 25: 1–127.
Braithwaite, J. (2000) 'Repentance rituals and restorative justice', *The Journal of Political Philosophy*, 8 (1): 115–31.
Bravo, A. (1985) 'Italian Women in the Nazi Camps: Aspects of identity in their accounts', *Oral History*, 13 (1): 20–7.
Brewer, W. (1988) 'Memory for randomly sampled autobiographical events', in U. Neisser and E. Winograd (eds), *Remembering Reconsidered: Ecological and Traditional Approaches to the Study of Memory*, New York: Cambridge University Press, pp. 21–90.
Brewin, C. R. (2007) 'Autobiographical memory for trauma: Update on four controversies', *Memory*, 15 (3): 227–48.
Brighton Ourstory Project (1992) *Daring Hearts: Lesbian and Gay Lives in 50s and 60s Brighton*, Brighton: QueenSpark Books.
Brinson, S. L. and W. L. Benoit (1999) 'The tarnished star: restoring Texaco's damaged public image', *Management Communication Quarterly*, 12 (4): 483–510.
British Psychological Society (2000) *Code of Conduct, Ethical Principals and Guidelines*, Leicester: The British Psychological Society.
Britzman, D. (1989) 'Who has the floor? Curriculum teaching and the English

student teacher's struggle for voice', *Curriculum Inquiry*, 19 (2): 143–62.
Brockmeier, J. (2010) 'After the archive: Remapping memory', *Culture and Psychology*, 16 (1): 5–35.
Brookfield, H., S. D. Brown and P. Reavey (2008) 'Vicarious and postmemory practices in adopting families: The construction of the past in photography and narrative', *Journal of Community and Applied Social Psychology*, 18 (5): 474–91.
Brooks, R. L. (1999) 'The age of apology', in R. L. Brooks (ed.), *When Sorry isn't Enough: The Controversy over Apologies and Reparation for Human Injustice*, New York: New York University Press, pp. 3–12.
Brown, C. (2006) 'Moving On: Reflections on oral history and migrant communities in Britain', *Oral History*, 34 (1): 69–80.
Brown, S. D. (2012) 'Two minutes of silence: social technologies of public commemoration', *Theory and Psychology*, 22 (2): 234–52.
Brown, S. D. and A. Locke (2008) 'Social psychology', in C. Willig and W. Stainton-Rogers (eds), *SAGE Handbook of Qualitative Research in Psychology*, London: Sage, pp. 373–89.
Brown, S. D. and P. Reavey (2013) *Vital Memories: Affect, Ethics, Agency*, London: Routledge.
Brown, S. D., P. Reavey and H. Brookfield (2013) 'Spectral objects: Material links to difficult pasts for adoptive parents', in P. Harvey, E. Casella, G. Evans, H. Knox, C. McLean, E. Silva, N. Thoburn and K. Woodward (eds), *Objects and Materials: A Routledge Companion*, London: Routledge.
Brown, S. D., P. Reavey, A. Kanyeredzi and R. Batty (2013) 'Transformations of self and sexuality: Psychologically modified experiences in the context of Forensic Mental Health', *Health*.
Brown, S. D. and P. Stenner (2009) *Psychology without Foundations: History, Philosophy and Psychosocial Theory*. London: Sage.
Browning, C. R. (2003) *Collected Memories: Holocaust History and Postwar Testimony*, Madison: University of Wisconsin Press.
Browning, C. R. (2010) *Remembering Survival: Inside a Nazi Slave-labor Camp*. New York: W. W. Norton and Co.
Brownlie, S. (2011) 'Does memory of the distant past matter?', *Memory Studies*, 1–18, available in R. Brubaker, M. Loveman and P. Stamatov (2004) 'Ethnicity as Cognition', *Theory and Society*, 33 (1): 31–64.
Bruner, J. S. (1990) *Acts of meaning*, Cambridge, MA: Harvard University Press.
Bruner, J. (1991) 'The Narrative Construction of Reality', *Critical Inquiry*, 18 (1): 1–21.
Bruner, J. (1995) 'The Autobiographical Process', *Current Sociology*, 43 (2): 161–77.
Buchanan, K. and D. J. Middleton (1995) 'Voices of Experience: Talk,

identity and membership in reminiscence groups for older people', *Ageing and Society*, 15 (4): 457–91.
Buckingham, D. and R. Willett (2009) *Video Cultures: Media Technology and Amateur Creativity*, Basingstoke and New York: Palgrave.
Buckingham, D., R. Willett and M. Pini (2011) *Home Truths? Video Production and Domestic Life*, Ann Arbor: University of Michigan Press.
Bullett, G. (1951) *Sydney Smith*, London: Michael Joseph.
Byford, J. (2010) '"Shortly afterwards, we heard the sound of the gas van!": Survivor testimony and the writing of history in socialist Yugoslavia', *History and Memory*, 22 (1): 5–47.
Byford, J. (in press) 'Remembering Jasenovac: Survivor testimonies and the cultural dimension of bearing witness', submitted to *Holocaust and Genocides Studies*.
Caldwell, J. T. (2008) *Production Culture: Industrial Reflexivity and Critical Practice in Film and Television*, Durham, NC: Duke University Press.
Campbell, S. (2009) 'Inside the Frame of the Past: Memory, Diversity and Solidarity', in S. Campbell, L. Meynell and S. Sherwin (eds), *Embodiment and Agency*, University Park, PA: Pennsylvania State University Press, pp. 211–33.
Carrier, P. (2000) 'Places, Politics and the Archiving of Contemporary Memory', in S. Radstone (ed.), *Memory and Methodology*, Oxford: Berg, pp. 37–58.
Caruth, C. (1991) 'Introduction to Psychoanalysis, Trauma and Culture', *American Imago*, 48 (1): 1–12.
Caruth, C. (1996) *Unclaimed Experience: Trauma, Narrative and History*, Baltimore: Johns Hopkins University Press.
Catalani, C. and M. Minkler (2010) 'Photovoice: A review of the literature in health and public health', *Health Education and Behaviour*, 37 (3): 424–51.
Celermajer, D. (2009) *The Sins of Nation and the Ritual of Apologies*, New York: Cambridge University Press.
Centro Cultural Orunmilá (no date) 'Centro Cultural Orunmilá and Law 10.639', <http://www.orunmila.org.br/blog/?p=28> (accessed 15 February 2012).
Chalfen, R. (1987) *Snapshot Versions of Life*, Bowling Green, OH: Bowling Green State University Press.
Chambers, D. (2003) 'Family as Place: Family Photograph Albums and the Domestication of Public and Private Space', in J. Schwartz and J. Ryan (eds), *Picturing Place: Photography and the Geographical Imagination*, London and New York: I. B. Tauris, pp. 96–114.
Chanan, M. (2007) *The Politics of Documentary*, London: BFI.
Chandler, M. J. and T. Proulx (2008) 'Personal persistence and persistent peoples: Continuities in the lives of individual and whole cultural commu-

nities', in F. Sani (ed.), *Individual and Collective Self-Continuity*, Mahwah, NJ: Erlbaum.

Chapman, J. (2007) 'Re-presenting war: British television drama-documentary and the Second World War', *European Journal of Cultural Studies*, 10 (1): 13–33.

Clendinnen, I. (1999) *Reading the Holocaust*, Cambridge: Cambridge University Press.

Code, L. (1993) 'Take subjectivity into account', in L. Alcoff and E. Potter (eds), *Feminist epistemologies*, New York: Routledge, pp. 15–48.

Coleman, P., D. Koleva and J. Bornat (eds) (2012) *Ageing, Ritual and Social Change*, Farnham: Ashgate.

Coleman, S. M. and P. von Hellermann (eds) (2011) *Multi-Sited Ethnography: Problems and Possibilities in the Translocation of Research Methods*, Abingdon: Routledge.

Collier, J. and M. Collier (1986) *Visual Anthropology: Photography as a Research Method*, Albuquerque: University of New Mexico Press.

Comaroff, J. and J. Comaroff (2009) *Ethnicity, Inc.*, Chicago: University of Chicago Press.

Connerton, P. (1989) *How Societies Remember*, Cambridge: Cambridge University Press.

Connerton, P. (2008) 'Seven types of forgetting', *Memory Studies*, 1 (1): 59–71.

Conway, M. (2005) 'Memory and the self', *Journal of Memory and Language*, 53 (2005): 594–628.

Conway, M. A. and C. W. Pleydell-Pearce (2000) 'The construction of autobiographical memories in the self-memory system', *Psychological Review*, 107 (2): 261–88.

Conway, M. A., J. A. Singer and A. Tagini (2004) 'The Self and Autobiographical Memory: Correspondence and Coherence', *Social Cognition*, 22 (5): 491–529.

Corner, J. (ed.) (1991) *Popular Television in Britain: Studies in Cultural History*, London: BFI.

Corney, F. C. (1998) 'Rethinking a Great Event: The October Revolution as a Memory Project', *Social Science History*, 22 (4): 389–414.

Coser, L. A. (1992) 'Introduction: Maurice Halbwachs 1877–1945', in L. A. Coser (ed.), *Maurice Halbwachs: On Collective Memory*, Chicago: University of Chicago Press, pp. 1–34.

Crace, J. (2012) *The Guardian* television review 24 May 2012.

Cubitt, G. (2007) *History and Memory*, Manchester: Manchester University Press.

D'Alisera, J. (2004) *An Imagined Geography: Sierra Leonean Muslims in America*, Philadelphia: University of Pennsylvania Press.

Deacon, D., M. Pickering, P. Golding and G.Murdock (1999/2007) *Researching Communications*, London: Hodder Arnold.

Dean, C. J. (2010) 'Minimalism and victim testimony', *History and Theory*, Theme Issue 49 (4): 85–99.

Dearden, C. and J. Aldridge (2010) 'Young Carers: Needs, Rights and Assessments', in J. Horwath (ed.), *The Child's World: The Comprehensive Guide to Assessing Children in Need*, 2nd edn, London: Jessica Kingsley, pp. 214–28.

Dearden, C. and S. Becker (1995) *Young Carers: The Facts*, Sutton: Reed Business Publishing.

Dearden, C. and S. Becker (1998) *Young Carers in the UK*, London: Carers National Association.

Dearden, C. and S. Becker (2000) *Growing Up Caring: Vulnerability and Transitions to Adulthood – Young Carers' Experiences*, Leicester: Leicester Youth Work Press.

de Groot, J. (2009) *Consuming History: Historians and Heritage in Contemporary Popular Culture*, London: Routledge.

Department of Health (DH) (2000) *Research Governance Framework for Health and Social Care*, 2nd edn, London: DH, <http://www.dh.gov.uk/en/Publicationsandstatistics/Publications/PublicationsPolicyAndGuidance/DH_4108962> (accessed 18 January 2013).

Dewey, J. (1938/1997) *Experience and Education*. New York: Touchstone.

di Bello, P. (2007) *Women's Albums and Photography in Victorian England*, Aldershot: Ashgate.

Dillon, B. (2005) *In the Dark Room: A Journey in Memory*, London and New York: Penguin.

Donald, M. (2001) *A Mind So Rare: The Evolution of Human Consciousness*, New York: Norton.

Donaldson, P. (2001) 'Using photographs to strengthen family planning research', *Family Planning Perspectives*, 33 (4): 176–9.

Dorjahn, V. R. (1960) 'The Changing Political System of the Temne', *Africa*, 30 (2): 110–40.

Drew, P. (1989) 'Recalling someone from the past', in D. Roger and P. Bull (eds), *Conversation: An Interdisciplinary Perspective*, Philadelphia: Multilingual Matters, pp. 96–115.

Edgerton, G. R. and P. C. Rollins (2001) *Television Histories: Shaping Collective Memory in the Media Age*, Lexington: The University Press of Kentucky.

Edkins, J. (2003) *Trauma and the Politics of Memory*, Cambridge: Cambridge University Press.

Edwards, D. (1997) *Discourse and Cognition*, London: Sage.

Edwards, D. (2003) 'Analyzing racial discourse: the discursive psychology of mind-world relationships', in H. van den Berg, M. Wetherell and

H. Houtkoop-Steenstra (eds), *Analyzing race talk: multidisciplinary perspectives on the research interview*, Cambridge: Cambridge University Press, pp. 31–48.

Edwards, D. (2006) 'Facts, norms and dispositions: Practical uses of the modal verb *would* in police interrogations', *Discourse Studies*, 8 (4): 475–501.

Edwards, D. (2012) Discursive and scientific psychology, *British Journal of Social Psychology*, 51 (3): 425–35.

Edwards, D. and D. Middleton (1988) 'Conversational remembering and family relationships: How children learn to remember', *Journal of Social and Personal Relationships*, 5 (1): 3–25.

Edwards, D., D. Middleton and J. Potter (1992) 'Towards a discursive psychology of remembering', *The Psychologist*, 5: 56–60.

Edwards, D. and J. Potter (1992a) *Discursive Psychology*, London: Sage.

Edwards, D. and J. Potter (1992b) 'The Chancellor's memory: Rhetoric and truth in discursive remembering', *Applied Cognitive Psychology*, 6 (3): 187–215.

Edwards, D. and J. Potter (1995) 'Remembering', in R. Harré and P. Stearns (eds), *Discursive Psychology in Practice*, London: Sage, pp. 9–36.

Eglin, P. and S. Hester (2003) *The Montreal Massacre: A Story of Membership Categorization*, Waterloo: Wilfrid Laurier University Press.

Eisenberg, A. (1985) 'Learning to describe past experience in conversation', *Discourse Processes*, 8 (2): 177–204.

Elliot, R. (2001) 'Growing up and Giving up: smoking in Paul Thompson's 100 Families', *Oral History*, 29 (1): 73–84.

Emke, I. (1996) 'Methodology and Methodolatry: Creativity and the Impoverishment of the Imagination in Sociology', *Canadian Journal of Sociology*, 21 (1): 77–90.

Enns, C. Z., C. L. McNeilly, J. M. Corkery and M. S. Gilbert (1995) 'The debate about delayed memories of childhood sexual abuse: A feminist perspective', *The Counseling Psychologist*, 23 (2): 181–279.

Erll, A. (2010) 'Cultural Memory Studies: An Introduction', in A. Erll and A. Nünning (eds), *Cultural Memory Studies: An International and Interdisciplinary Handbook*, Berlin: Walter de Gruyter, pp. 1–15.

Erll, A. and A. Nünning (eds) (2008) *Cultural Memory Studies: An International and Interdisciplinary Handbook*, Berlin: Walter de Gruyter.

Evans, G. E. (1956) *Ask the Fellows Who Cut the Hay*, London: Faber.

Evans, G. E. (1972) 'Flesh and Blood Archives: Some early experiences', *Oral History*, 1 (1): 3–4.

Eyerman, R. (2001) *Cultural Trauma: Slavery and the Formation of African American Identity*, New York: Palgrave Macmillan.

Fass, P. (2011) *Inheriting the Holocaust: A Second Generation Memoir*, New Brunswick, NJ and London: Rutgers University Press.

Featherstone, M. (2006) 'Archive', *Theory, Culture and Society*, 23 (2–3): 591–6.
Felman, S. and D. Laub (1991) *Testimony: Crises of Witnessing in Literature, Psychoanalysis and History*, New York and London: Routledge.
Felman, S. and D. Laub (1992) *Testimony: Crises of Witnessing in Literature, Psychoanalysis and History*, London: Routledge.
Ferme, M. C. (2001) *The Underneath of Things: Violence, History, and the Everyday in Sierra Leone*, Berkeley: University of California Press.
Fetzer, A. and P. Bull (2012) 'Doing leadership in political speech: Semantic processes and pragmatic inferences', *Discourse and Society*, 23 (2): 127–44.
Fiese, B. H., K. A. Hooker, L. Kotary, J. Scwagler and M. Rimmer (1995) 'Family stories in the early stages of parenthood', *Journal of Marriage and the Family*, 57 (3): 763–70.
Fivush, R. (2000) 'Accuracy, authorship and voice: Feminist approaches to autobiographical memory', in P. Miller and E. Scholnick (eds), *Towards a Feminist Developmental Psychology*, New York: Cambridge University Press, pp. 85–106.
Fivush, R. (2004) 'Voice and silence: A feminist model of autobiographical memory', in J. Lucariello, J. A. Hudson, R. Fivush and P. J. Bauer (eds), *The Development of the Mediated Mind: Sociolcultural Context and Cognitive Development*, Mahwah, NJ: Erlbaum, pp. 79–100.
Fivush, R. (2008) 'Remembering and reminiscing: How individual lives are constructed in family narratives', *Memory Studies*, 1 (1): 45–54.
Fivush, R. (2010) 'Speaking Silence: The social construction of voice and silence in autobiographical and cultural narratives', *Memory*, 18 (2): 88–98.
Fivush, R. and V. J. Edwards (2004) 'Remembering and forgetting childhood sexual abuse', *Journal of Child Sexual Abuse*, 13 (2): 1–19
Fivush, R., T. Habermas, T. E. A. Waters and W. Zaman (2011) 'The making of autobiographical memory: Intersections of culture, narratives and identity', *International Journal of Psychology*, 46 (5): 321–45
Fivush, R., C. A. Haden and E. Reese (2006) 'Elaborating on elaborations: Maternal reminiscing style and children's socioemotional outcome', *Child Development*, 77 (6): 1568–88.
Fivush, R. and K. Marin (2007) 'Place and power: A feminist perspective on self-event relations', *Human Development*, 50 (2–3): 111–18.
Fivush, R., K. A. Marin, M. Crawford, C. R. Brewin and M. Reynolds (2007) 'Children's narratives and well-being', *Cognition and Emotion*, 21 (7): 1414–34.
Forest, B., J. Johnson and K. Till (2004) 'Post-totalitarian National Identity: Public Memory in Germany and Russia', *Social and Cultural Geography*, 5 (3): 357–80.

Fozdar, F., R. Wilding and M. Hawkins (2009) *Race and Ethnic Relations*, Sydney: Oxford University Press.
Frattaroli, J. (2006) 'Experimental Disclosure and its Moderators: A Meta-Analysis', *Psychological Bulletin*, 132 (6): 823–65.
Freeman, M. (2007) 'Autobiographical understanding and narrative inquiry', in D. J. Clandinin (ed.), *Handbook of Narrative Inquiry: Mapping a Methodology*, Thousand Oaks, CA: Sage Publication, pp. 120–45.
Frisch, M. (1990) *A Shared Authority: Essays on the Craft and Meaning of Oral and Public History*, New York: State University of New York Press.
Frosh, P. and A. Pinchevski (2009) *Media Witnessing: Testimony in the Age of Mass Communication*, Basingstoke: Palgrave Macmillan.
Fyfe, C. (1963) *A History of Sierra Leone*, Oxford: Oxford University Press.
Fyle, C. M. (1981) *The History of Sierra Leone: A Concise Introduction*, London: Evans.
Garfinkel, H. (1956) 'Conditions of successful degradation ceremonies', *The American Journal of Sociology*, 61 (5): 420–4.
Gillespie, M. (1995) *Television, Ethnicity and Cultural Change*, London: Routledge.
Gillis, J. R. (ed.) (1994) *Commemorations: The Politics of National Identity*, Princeton: Princeton University Press.
Ginsburg, C. (1992) 'Just one witness', in S. Friedlander (ed.), *Probing the Limits of Representation: Nazism and the Final Solution*, Cambridge, MA: Harvard University Press, pp. 82–96.
Gluck, S. B. and D. Patai (1991) *Women's Words: The Feminist Practice of Oral History*, London: Routledge.
Goffman, E. (1971) *Relations in Public*. London: Allen Lane.
Goodley, D. and M. Moore (2000) 'Doing disability research: activist lives and the academy', *Disability and Society*, 15 (6): 861–82.
Goody, J. (1987) *The Interface between the Written and the Oral*, Cambridge: Cambridge University Press.
Gray, A. (2003) *Research Practice for Cultural Studies*, London: Sage.
Gray A. (2010) 'Contexts of production: commissioning history', in E. Bell and A. Gray (eds), *Televising History: Mediating the Past in Postwar Europe*, London: Palgrave MacMillan, pp. 59–76.
Gray, A. and E. Bell (2013) *History on Television*, London: Routledge.
Greek, C. E. (2005) 'Visual criminology: Using photography as an ethnographic research method in criminal justice settings', *Journal of Visual Culture*, 3 (3): 213–21.
Green, A. (2004) 'Individual Remembering and "Collective Memory": theoretical presuppositions and contemporary debates', *Oral History*, 32 (2): 35–44.
Greenspan, H. (2010) *On Listening to Holocaust Survivors: Recounting and Life History*, 2nd edn, St Paul, MN: Paragon House.

Grele, R. (1975) *Envelopes of Sound*, Chicago: Precedent Publishing.
Gross, J. (2002) *Neighbours: The Destruction of the Jewish Community in Jedwabne*, London: Penguin.
Gubrium, E. and M. Koro-Ljungberg (2005) 'Contending With Border Making in the Social Constructionist Interview', *Qualitative Inquiry*, 11 (5): 689–715.
Gubrium, J. F. and J. A. Holstein (eds) (2001) *Handbook of Interview Research: Context and Method*, London: Sage.
Haaken, J. (1998) *Pillar of Salt: Gender, Memory, and the Perils of Looking Back*, New Brunswick, NJ and London: Rutgers University Press.
Halbwachs, M. (1925) *Les Cadres sociaux de la mémoire*, Paris: Félix Alcan.
Halbwachs, M. [1925] (1992) *On Collective Memory*, Chicago: University of Chicago Press.
Halbwachs, M. (1941) *La topographie légendaire des évangiles en Terre Sainte*, Paris: Presses Universitaires de France.
Hamilton, C. (2008) 'On being a "Good" interviewer: empathy, ethics and the politics of oral history', *Oral History*, 36 (2): 35–43.
Hamilton, P. (1994) 'The Knife Edge: Debates about memory and history', in K. Darian-Smith and P. Hamilton (eds), *Memory and History in Twentieth Century Australia*, Melbourne: Oxford University Press, pp. 9–32.
Hamilton, P. and L. Shopes (eds) (2008) *Oral History and Public Memories*, Philadelphia: Temple University Press.
Hammersley, M. (2010) 'Can we re-use qualitative data via secondary analysis? Notes on some terminological and substantive issues', *Sociological Research Online*, 15(1)5, <http://www.socresonline.org.uk/15/1/5.html> (accessed 18 January 2013).
Haraway, D. (1988) 'Situated Knowledges: The Science Question in Feminism and the Privilege of Partial Perspective', *Feminist Studies*, 14 (3): 575–99.
Harding, S. (1993) 'Rethinking Standpoint Epistemology: "What Is Strong Objectivity"?', in L. Alcoff and E. Potter (eds), *Feminist Epistemologies*, New York: Routledge, pp. 49–82.
Harper, D. (2002) 'Talking about Pictures: A Case for Photo Elicitation', *Visual Studies*' 17 (1): 13–26.
Harris, M. (1970) 'Referential ambiguity in the calculus of Brazilian racial identity', *Southwestern Journal of Anthropology*, 26 (1): 1–14.
Harrison, B. (2012) 'College Servants in an Oxford College Forty Years Ago', *Oral History*, 40 (2): 40–58.
Hart, R. A. (1992) *Children's Participation: From Tokenism to Citizenship*, Innocenti Essays no. 4, Florence, Italy: Unicef, <http://www.unicef-irc.org/publications/pdf/childrens_participation.pdf> (accessed 18 January 2013).

Hart, W. A. (1986) 'Aron Arabi: The Temne Mask of Chieftaincy', *African Arts*, 19 (2): 41–5, 91.
Hartman, G. (1989) 'Preserving the personal story: The role of video documentation', in M. Littell, R. Libowitz and E. B. Rosen (eds), *The Holocaust Forty Years After*, Lewiston, NY: The Edwin Mellen Press, pp. 53–60.
Hartman, G. H. (1995) 'Learning from survivors: The Yale testimony project', *Holocaust Genocide Studies*, 9 (2): 192–207.
Hartman, G. H. (1996) *The Longest Shadow*, London: Palgrave Macmillan.
Harvey, J. H., K. Barnett and A. Overstreet (2004) 'Trauma growth and other outcomes attendant to loss', *Psychological Inquiry*, 15: 26–9.
Hausner, G. (1966) *Justice in Jerusalem*, New York: Harper and Row.
Hepburn, A. and S. Wiggins (eds) (2007) *Discursive Research in Practice: New Approaches to Psychology and Interaction*, Cambridge: Cambridge University Press.
Herber, P. and J. Matthaus (2008) introduction, in P. Herber and J. Matthaus (eds), *Atrocities on Trial: Historical Perspectives on the Politics of Prosecuting War Crimes*, Lincoln, NE: University of Nebraska Press.
Herman, J. (1992) *Trauma and Recovery*, New York: Basic Books.
Heywood, C. (2001) *A History of Childhood*, Cambridge: Polity.
Hill, M., J. Davis, A. Prout and K. Tisdall (2004) 'Moving the participation agenda forward', *Children and Society*, 18 (2): 77–96.
Hirsch, M. (1997/2012) *Family Frames: Photography Narrative and Postmemory*, Cambridge, MA and London: Harvard University Press.
Hirsch, M. and L. Spitzer (2009) 'The witness in the archive: Holocaust studies/memory studies', *Memory Studies*, 2 (2): 151–70.
Hirsh, D. (2001) 'The Trial of Andrei Sawoniuk: Holocaust Testimony under Cross-Examination', *Social and Legal Studies*' 10 (4): 529–45.
Hladnik-Milharčič, E. (2007) 'Zadnje leto meje', *Dnevnik*, 26 May 2007, <http://www.dnevnik.si/tiskane_izdaje/objektiv/247769> (accessed 10 June 2012).
Hobsbawm, E. (2002) 'Old Marxist still sorting global fact from fiction', *Times Higher Education*, 12 July, pp. 18–19.
Hoelscher, S. and D. Alderman (2004) 'Memory and Place: Geographies of a critical relationship', *Journal of Social and Cultural Geography*, 5 (3): 347–55.
Hoffman, E. (1998) *Lost in Translation*, London: Vintage.
Holdsworth, A. (2010) 'Who do you think you are?: family history and memory on British television', in E. Bell and A. Gray (eds), *Televising History: Mediating the Past in Postwar Europe*, London: Palgrave MacMillan, pp. 234–47.
Holstein, J. A. and J. F. Gubrium (1995) *The Active Interview*, London: Sage.
House of Commons (1889) *Sierra Leone: Further Correspondence Relating to*

Disturbances in the Native Territories Adjacent to Sierra Leone, London: Her Majesty's Stationery Office.

Humphrey, R., R. Miller and E. Zdravomyslova (eds) (2003) *Biographical Research in Eastern Europe: Altered Lives and Broken Biographies*, Aldershot: Ashgate.

Hutton, B. (2004) 'Report of the Inquiry into the Circumstances Surrounding the Death of Dr David Kelly C.M.G.', London: Her Majesty's Stationery Office.

Huyssen, A. (2003) *Present Pasts: Urban Palimpsests and the Politics of Memory*, Stanford: Stanford University Press.

Instituto Brasileiro de Geografia e Estatística (IBGE) Table 1.3.1, Populaçãoresidente, porcorouraça, segundo o sexo e osgrupos de idade, <http://www.ibge.gov.br/home/estatistica/populacao/censo2010/caracteristicas_da_populacao/caracteristicas_da_populacao_tab_brasil_zip.shtm> (accessed 15 February 2012).

Instituto Cultural Steve Biko <http://www.wix.com/cabralbete2/biko#!quem-somos> (accessed 24 April 2012).

Irwin, S. and M. Winterton (2012) 'Qualitative Secondary Analysis and Social Explanation', *Sociological Research Online*, 17(2)4.

Irwin-Zarecka, I. (2007) *Frames of Remembrance: The Dynamics of Collective Memory*, New Brunswick, NJ and London: Transaction.

James, W. [1890] (1950) *The Principles of Psychology*, New York: Dover.

Janesick, V. J. (1994) 'The Dance of Qualitative Research Design: Metaphor, Methodolatry, and Meaning', in N. K. Denzin and Y. S. Lincoln (eds), *Handbook of Qualitative Research*, Thousand Oaks, CA: Sage, pp. 209–19.

Janoff-Bulman, R. (2004) 'Posttraumatic growth: Three explanatory models', *Psychological Inquiry*, 15 (1): 30–4.

Jaworski, A. (1994) 'Apologies and non-apologies: negotiation in speech act realization', *Text*, 14 (2): 185–206.

Joanou, J. P. (2009) 'The bad and the ugly: ethical concerns in participatory photographic methods with children living and working on the streets of Lima, Peru', *Visual Studies*, 24 (3): 214–23.

Jones, A. (1983) *From Slaves to Pine Kernels: A History of the Gallinas Country (West Africa), 1730–1890*, Wiesbaden: Franz Steiner.

Kampf, Z. (2009) 'Public (non-) apologies: The discourse of minimizing responsibility', *Journal of Pragmatics*, 41 (11): 2257–70.

Kansteiner, W. (2004) 'Genealogy of a Category Mistake: A Critical Intellectual History of the Cultural Trauma Metaphor', *Rethinking History*, 8 (2): 193–221

Kansteiner, W. and H. Weilnböck (2008) 'Against the Concept of Cultural Trauma', in A. Erll and A. Nünning (eds), *Cultural Memory Studies*, Berlin and New York: Walter de Gruyter, pp. 229–41.

Kaplan, I. (2008) 'Being "seen" being "heard": engaging with students on the margins of education through participatory photography', in P. Thomson (ed.), *Doing Visual Research with Children and Young People*, London: Routledge, pp. 175–91.

Karasch, M. (1987) *Slave Life in Rio de Janeiro, 1808–1850*, Princeton: Princeton University Press.

Karpf, A. (1997) *The War After*, London: Minerva.

Kearney, A. (2012) 'Present Memories', in E. Keightley (ed.), *Time in Modernity: Changing Media, Alternative Temporalities*, Basingstoke and New York: Palgrave Macmillan.

Keightley, E. (2008) 'Engaging with memory', in M. Pickering (ed.), *Research Methods for Cultural Studies*, Edinburgh: Edinburgh University Press, pp. 175–92.

Keightley, E. and M. Pickering (2006) 'For the Record: Popular Music and Photography as Technologies of Memory', *European Journal of Cultural Studies*, 9 (2): 131–47.

Keightley, E. and M. Pickering (2012) *The Mnemonic Imagination: Remembering as Creative Practice*, Basingstoke and New York: Palgrave Macmillan.

Keightley, E., M. Pickering and N. Allett (2012) 'The Self-Interview: A New Method in Social Science Research', *International Journal of Social Research Methodology*, 15 (6): 507–21, <http://www.tandfonline.com/doi/abs/10.1080/13645579.2011.632155> (accessed 18 January 2013).

Kihlstrom, J. F. (1995) 'The trauma–memory argument', *Consciousness and Cognition*, 4 (1): 63–7.

Klein, H. and F. Luna (2010) *Slavery in Brazil*, Cambridge: Cambridge University Press.

Koleva, D. (2006) 'Memories of the War and the War Memories in Post-Communist Bulgaria', *Oral History*, 34 (2): 44–55.

Kopeček, M. (ed.) (2008) *Past in the Making: Historical Revisionism in Central Europe after 1989*, Budapest: Central European University Press.

Koroma, U. H. (1939) 'The Bronze Statuettes of Ro-Ponka, Kafu Bulom', *Sierra Leone Studies*, 22: 25–8.

Koshar, R. (1998) *Germany's Transient Pasts: Preservation and National Memory in the Twentieth Century*, Chapel Hill, NC: University of North Carolina Press.

Kuhn, A. (2002) *Family Secrets*, London: Verso.

Kuhn, A. (2010) 'Memory texts and memory work: Performances of memory in and with visual media', *Memory Studies*, 3 (4): 298–313.

Kushner, T. (2006) 'Holocaust testimony, ethics, and the problem of representation', *Poetics Today*, 27 (2): 275–95.

LaCapra, D (1999) Trauma, Absence, Loss. *Critical Enquiry*, 25(4): 696–727

LaCapra, D. (2001) *Writing History, Writing Trauma*, Baltimore: Johns Hopkins University Press.

Lakoff, R. B. (2001) 'Nine ways of looking at apologies: The necessity for interdisciplinary theory and method in discourse analysis', in D. Schiffrin, D. Tannen and H. Hamilton (eds), *Handbook of Discourse Analysis*, London: Blackwell, pp. 199–214.

Landsberg, A. (2004) *Prosthetic Memory: The Transformation of American Remembrance in the Age of Mass Culture*, New York: Columbia University Press.

Lang, B. (2005) *Post-holocaust: Interpretation, Misinterpretation and the Claims of History*, Bloomington: Indiana University Press.

Langer, L. (1991) *Holocaust Testimonies: The Ruins of Memory*, New Haven: Yale University Press.

Langford, M. (2008) *Suspended Conversations: The Afterlife of Memory in Photographic Albums*, Montreal and London: McGill-Queen's University Press.

Langford, M. (2006) 'Speaking the Album: An Application of the Oral-Photographic Framework', in A. Kuhn and K. E. McAllister (eds), *Locating Memory: Photographic Acts*, New York and Oxford: Berghahn, pp. 223–46.

Laub, D. and M. Allard (2002) 'History, Memory, and Truth: Defining the Place of the Survivor', in M. Berenbaum (ed.), *The Holocaust and History: The Known, the Unknown, the Disputed and the Reexamined*, Bloomington: Indiana University Press, pp. 799–812.

Lawler, S. (2008) 'Stories and the social world', in M. Pickering (ed.), *Research Methods for Cultural Studies*, Edinburgh: Edinburgh University Press, pp. 32–49.

Lazare, A. (2004) *On Apology*, New York: Oxford University Press.

Lazarus, R. S. and S. Folkman (1984) *Stress, Appraisal, and Coping*, New York: Springer.

LeCouteur, A. (2001) 'On saying sorry: repertoires of apologising to Australia's Stolen Generations', in A. McHoul and M. Rapley (eds), *How to Analyse Talk in Institutional Settings: A Casebook of Methods*, London: Continuum International, pp. 148–60.

Legerski, J. P. and S. L. Bunnell (2010) 'The risks, benefits, and ethics of trauma-focused research participation', *Ethics and Behavior*, 20 (6): 429–42.

Leitch, R. (2008) 'Creatively researching children's narratives through images and drawings', in P. Thomson (ed.), *Doing Visual Research with Children and Young People*, London: Routledge, pp. 37–58.

Levine, H. (1999) 'Reconstructing Ethnicity', *The Journal of the Royal Anthropological Institute*, 5 (2): 165–80.

Leys, R. (2000) *Trauma: A Genealogy*, Baltimore: Johns Hopkins University Press.

Liddington, J. and J. Norris (1978) *One Hand Tied Behind Us: The Rise of the Women's Suffrage Movement*, London: Virago; new edition London: Rivers Oram, 2000.
Lindlof, T. R. (1995) *Qualitative Communication Research Methods*, Thousand Oaks, CA: Sage.
Lowenthal, D. (1985) *The Past is a Foreign Country*, Cambridge: Cambridge University Press.
Lowenthal, D. (1997) 'European Landscape Transformations: The Rural Residue', in P. Groth and T. W. Bressi (eds), *Understanding Ordinary Landscapes*, New Haven: Yale University Press, pp. 180–8.
Luckhurst, R. (2003) 'Traumaculture', *New Formations*, 50: 28–47.
Luckhurst, R. (2008) *The Trauma Question*, London and New York: Routledge.
Lummis, T. (1987) *Listening to History*, London: Hutchinson.
Lynch, M. (1999) 'Archives in formation: Privileged spaces, popular archives and paper trails', *History of the Human Sciences*, 12 (2): 65–87.
Lynch, M. (2009) 'Ethnomethodology and history: documents and the production of history', *Ethnographic Studies*, 11: 87–101.
Lynch, M. and D. Bogen (1996) *The Spectacle of History: Speech, Text and Memory at the Iran-contra Hearings*, Durham, NC and London: Duke University Press.
Maccoby, E. E. and N. Maccoby (1954) 'The interview: a tool of social science', in G. Lindzey and G. Allport (eds), *The Handbook of Social Psychology*, Cambridge, MA: Addison-Wesley, vol. 1, pp. 449–87.
Mankekar, P. (1999) *Screening Culture, Viewing Politics: An Ethnography of Television, Womanhood and Nation in Postcolonial India*, Durham, NC: Duke University Press.
Marcus, G. E. (1995) 'Ethnography in/of the World System: The Emergence of Multi-Sited Ethnography', *Annual Review of Anthropology*, 24: 95–117.
Mark, J. (2010) *The Unfinished Revolution: Making Sense of the Communist Past in East-Central Europe*, New Haven: Yale University Press.
McAdams, D. P. (2001) 'The psychology of life stories', *Review of General Psychology*, 5 (2): 100–22.
McAdams, D. P. (2006) 'The redemptive self: Stories Americans live by', *Research in Human Development*, 3: 81–100.
McLaughlin, K. (2011) *Surviving Identity: Vulnerability and the Psychology of Recognition*, London: Routledge.
McLean, K. and M. Pasupathi (2010) *Narrative Development in Adolescence: Creating the Storied Self*, New York: Springer.
McLean, K., M. Pasupathi and J. Pals (2007) 'Selves creating stories creating selves: A process model of self-development', *Personality and Social Psychology Review*, 11 (3): 262–78.

McLeod, J. and R. Thomson (2009) *Researching Social Change*, London: Sage.
McNally, R. J. (2003) *Remembering Trauma*, Cambridge, MA: Harvard University Press.
McNaughton, P. R. (1988) *The Mande Blacksmiths: Knowledge, Power and Art in West Africa*, Bloomington: Indiana University Press.
Meier, A. J. (1998) 'Apologies: what do we know?', *International Journal of Applied Linguistics*, 8 (2): 215–31.
Middleton, D. (1997a) 'The social organisation of conversational remembering: Experience as individual and collective concerns', *Mind, Culture and Activity*, 4 (2): 71–85.
Middleton, D. (1997b) 'Conversational remembering and uncertainty: interdependencies of experience as individual and collective concerns in team work', *Journal of Language and Social Psychology*, 16 (4): 389–410.
Middleton, D. (2002) 'Succession and change in the socio-cultural use of memory: Building-in the past in communicative action', *Culture and Psychology*, 8 (1): 79–95.
Middleton, D. and S. D. Brown (2005) *The Social Psychology of Experience: Studies in Remembering and Forgetting*, London: Sage.
Middleton, D. and S. D. Brown (2007) 'Issues in the socio-cultural study of memory: Making memory matter', in J. Valsiner and A. Rosa (eds), *The Cambridge Handbook of Sociocultural Psychology*, Cambridge: Cambridge University Press, pp. 661–77.
Middleton, D. and D. Edwards (1990) *Collective Remembering*, London: Sage.
Mihelj, S. (forthcoming) 'The Persistence of the Past: Memory, Generation and "the Iron Curtain"', *Contemporary European History*.
Miller, B. (1999) *Narratives of Guilt and Compliance in Unified Germany: Stasi Informers and their Impact on Society*, London: Routledge.
Miller, B. (2003) 'Portrayals of past and present selves in the life stories of former Stasi informers', in R. Humphrey, R. Miller and E. Zdravomyslova (eds), *Biographical Research in Eastern Europe: Altered Lives and Broken Biographies*, Aldershot: Ashgate, pp. 101–14.
Miller, R. L. (ed.) (2000) *Biographical Research Methods*, London: Sage, vols I–IV.
Misztal, B. A. (2003) *Theories of Social Remembering*, Maidenhead: Open University Press.
Mjøs, O. J. (2011) 'Marriage of convenience? Public service broadcasters' cross-national partnerships in factual television', *International Communication Gazette*, 73 (3): 181–97.
Moran, James M. (2002) *There's No Place Like Home Video*, Minneapolis and London: University of Minnesota Press.
Morley, D. (1986) *Family Television: Cultural Power and Domestic Leisure*, London: Comedia.

Murphy, W. P. (1980) 'Secret Knowledge as Property and Power in Kpelle Society: Elders versus Youth', *Africa*, 50 (2): 193–207.
Nagel, J. (1994) 'Constructing ethnicity: Creating and recreating ethnic identity and culture', *Social Problems*, 41 (1): 152–76.
Nascimento, E. L. (2007) *The Sorcery of Color: Identity, Race and Gender in Brazil*, Philadelphia: Temple University Press.
Neal, A. G. (1998) *National Trauma and Collective Memory: Major Events in the American Century*, New York: M. E. Sharpe.
Neimeyer, R. A. (2004) 'Fostering posttraumatic growth: A narrative elaboration', *Psychological Inquiry*, 15 (1): 53–9.
Neisser, U. (1981) 'John Dean's memory: a case study', *Cognition*, 9 (1): 1–22.
Nelson, K. (1996) *Language in Cognitive Development*, Mahway, NJ: Erlbaum.
Nelson, K. and R. Fivush (2004) 'The Emergence of Autobiographical Memory: A Social Cultural Developmental Theory', *Psychological Review*, 111 (2): 486–511.
Newman, E. and D. G. Kaloupek (2004) 'The risks and benefits of participating in trauma-focused research studies', *Journal of Traumatic Stress*, 17 (5): 383–94.
Nguyen, N. (2008) 'Memory and silence in the Vietnamese Diaspora: the Narratives of two sisters', *Oral History*, 36 (2): 64–74.
Nicolson, H. N. (2001) 'Seeing How it Was?: Childhood Geographies and Memories in Home Movies', *Area*, 33 (2): 128–40.
Niessen, S. A. (1991) 'More to It than Meets the Eye: Photo-Elicitation amongst the Batak of Sumatra', *Visual Anthropology*, 4 (3–4): 415–30.
Nishida, M. (2003) *Slavery and Identity: Ethnicity, Gender and Race in Salvador, Brazil 1808–1888*, Indianapolis: Indiana University Press.
Nora, P. (1989) 'Between Memory and History: Les Lieux de mémoire', *Representations*, 26: 7–25.
Nora, P. (2002) 'Reasons for the current upsurge in memory', *Transit-Europäische Revue*, 22, <http://www.eurozine.com/articles/2002-04-19-nora-en.html> (accessed 18 January 2013).
Novick, P. (1999) *The Holocaust in American Life*, New York: Houghton Mifflin.
Olick, J. K. (1998) 'What Does it Mean to Normalize the Past? Official Memory in German Politics since 1989', *Social Science History*, 22 (4): 547–71.
Olick, J. K. (ed.) (2003) *States of Memory: Continuities, Conflicts, and Transformations in National Retrospection*, Durham, NC: Duke University Press.
Oliver, K. (2004) 'Witnessing and testimony', *Parallax*, 10 (1): 79–88.
Oral History Society (1972) 'Conference on 13 December 1969 at the British Institute of Recorded Sound', *Oral History*, 1 (1): 1.
O'Sullivan, T. (1991) 'Television Memories and Cultures of Viewing

1950–65', in J. Corner (ed.), *Popular Television in Britain: Studies in Cultural History*, London: BFI.
Owen, M. (1983) *Apologies and Remedial Interchanges*, New York: Mouton Publisher.
Parrott, L., G. Jacobs and D. Roberts (2008) *Stress and Resilience Factors in Parents with Mental Health Problems and their Children*, SCIE Research Briefing 23, London: Social Care Institute for Excellence.
Passerini, L. (1979) 'Work Ideology and Consensus under Italian Fascism', *History Workshop*, 8 (1): 82–108.
Passerini, L. (1987) *Fascism in Popular Memory: The Cultural Experience of the Turin Working Class*, Cambridge: Cambridge University Press.
Passerini, L. (1998) *Europe in Love, Love in Europe: Imagination and Politics in Britain Between the Wars*, London: I. B. Tauris.
Pasupathi, M. (2001) 'The social construction of the personal past and its implications for adult development', *Psychological Bulletin*, 127 (5): 651–72.
Patai, D. (1991) 'U.S. Academics and Third World Women: Is ethical research possible', in S. B. Gluck and D. Patai (eds), *Women's Words: The Feminist Practice of Oral History*, London: Routledge, pp. 137–53.
Payne, L. (2008) *Unsettling Accounts: Neither Truth nor Reconciliation in Confessions of State Violence*, Durham, NC: Duke University Press.
Pennebaker, J. W. (1997) *Opening Up: The Healing Power of Expressing Emotions*, New York: Guilford Press.
Pennebaker, J. W. and C. K. Chung (2007) 'Expressive writing, emotional upheavals, and health', in H. S. Friedman and R. C. Silver (eds), *Foundations of Health Psychology*, New York: Oxford University Press, pp. 263–84.
Pennebaker, J. W. and M. E. Francis (1996) 'Cognitive, emotional and language processes in disclosure', *Cognition and Emotion*, 10 (6): 601–26.
Personal Narratives Group (eds) (1989) *Interpreting Women's Lives: Feminist Theory and Personal Narratives*, Bloomington: Indiana University Press.
Peters, J. D. (2009) 'Witnessing', in P. Frosh and A. Pinchevski (eds), *Media Witnessing: Testimony in the Age of Mass Communication*, Basingstoke: Palgrave Macmillan, pp. 23–41.
Pickering, M. and E. Keightley (2008) 'Echoes and Reverberations: Photography and Phonography as Historical Forms', in S. Nicholas, T. O'Malley and K. Williams (eds), *Reconstructing the Past: History in the Mass Media 1890–2005*, London and New York: Routledge, pp. 153–68.
Pickering, M. and E. Keightley (2009) 'Trauma, Discourse and Communicative Limits', *Critical Discourse Studies*, 6 (4): 237–49.
Pinho, P. (2010) *Mama Africa: Reinventing Blackness in Bahia*, Durham, NC: Duke University Press.
Platt, J. (2001) 'The History of the Interview', in J. F. Gubrium and J. A.

Holstein (eds), *Handbook of Interview Research: Context and Method*, London: Sage, pp. 33–54.

Popular Memory Group (2006) 'Popular memory: theory, politics, method', in R. Perks and A. Thomson, *The Oral History Reader*, London: Routledge, 2nd edn, pp. 43–53; first published 1982.

Portelli, A. (1981) 'What makes oral history different?', *History Workshop*, 12: 96–107.

Portelli, A. (1991) *The Death of Luigi Trastulli and Other Stories: Form and Meaning in Oral History*, New York: State University of New York Press.

Portelli, A. (1997) *The Battle of Valle Giulia: Oral History and the Art of Dialogue*, Madison: University of Wisconsin Press.

Portelli, A. (1998) 'What makes oral history different?', in R. Perks and A. Thomson (eds), *The Oral History Reader*, London: Routledge, pp. 63–74.

Portelli, A. (2003) *The Order has been Carried Out: History, Memory and Meaning of a Nazi Massacre in Rome*, Basingstoke: Palgrave Macmillan.

Portelli, A. (2011) *They Say in Harlan County: An Oral History*, New York: Oxford University Press.

Potter, J. (2012) 'Re-reading *Discourse and Social Psychology*: transforming social psychology', *British Journal of Social Psychology*, 51 (3): 436–55.

Potter, J. and A. Hepburn (2005) 'Qualitative Interviews in Psychology: Problems and Possibilities', *Qualitative Research in Psychology*, 2 (4): 281–307.

Potter, J. A. and M. Wetherell (1987) *Discourse and Social Psychology: Beyond Attitudes and Behaviour*, London: Sage.

Potts, M. and R. Fido (1991) *'A Fit Person to be Removed': Personal Accounts of Life in a Mental Deficiency Institution*, Plymouth: Northcote House.

Presidência da República, Brasil (2003) LEI No. 10.639, <https://www.planalto.gov.br/ccivil_03/leis/2003/l10.639.htm> (accessed 15 February 2012).

Prosser, J. and D. Schwartz (1998) 'Photographs within the sociological research process', in J. Prosser (ed.), *Image-based Research: A Source Book for Qualitative Researchers*, London: Falmer Press, pp. 101–15.

Radley, A. and D. Taylor (2003) 'Images of recovery: A photo elicitation study on the hospital ward', *Qualitative Health Research*, 13 (1): 77–99.

Radstone, S. and K. Hodgkin (2003) 'Regimes of Memory: An Introduction', in S. Radstone and K. Hodgkin (eds), *Regimes of Memory*, London: Routledge, pp. 1–22.

Raine, C. (1994) *History: The Home Movie Project: A Novel in Verse*, New York: Doubleday.

Ramos, A. (2001) *The Predicament of Brazil's Pluralism: Beyond the Boundaries of the Old Geographies Conference*, Brasília: Departamento de Antropologia, Universidade de Brasília.

Reading, A. (2002) *The Social Inheritance of the Holocaust: Gender, Culture and Memory*, Basingstoke: Palgrave Macmillan.

Reavey, P. (1998) 'Child sexual abuse: professional and everyday constructions of women and sexuality', unpublished PhD thesis, Sheffield: Sheffield Hallam University.

Reavey, P. (2010) 'Spatial markings: memory, narrative and survival', *Memory Studies*, 3 (4): 314–29.

Reavey, P. (ed.) (2011) *Visual Methods in Psychology: Using and Interpreting Images in Qualitative Research*, London: Routledge.

Reavey, P. and S. D. Brown (2006) 'Transforming past agency and action in the present: Time, social remembering and child sexual abuse', *Theory and Psychology*, 16 (2): 179–202.

Reavey, P. and S. D. Brown (2009) 'The mediating role of objects in recollections of adult women survivors of child sexual abuse', *Culture and Psychology*, 15 (4): 463–84.

Redsell, S. and Hastings, A. M. (eds) (2010) *Listening to Children and Young People in Healthcare Consultations*, Oxford: Radcliffe Publishing.

Reissman, C. K. (2008) *Narrative Methods for the Human Sciences*, London: Sage.

Reiter, A. (2005) *Narrating the Holocaust*, London: Continuum.

Ricoeur, P. (1991) 'Life in quest of narrative', in D. Wood (ed.), *On Paul Ricoeur: Narrative and Interpretation*, London: Routledge, pp. 20–33.

Ritchie, D. A. (2003) *Doing Oral History: A Practical Guide*, 2nd edn, New York: Oxford University Press.

Ritchie, D. A. (2011) 'Introduction: The Evolution of Oral History', in D. A. Ritchie (ed.), *The Oxford Handbook of Oral History*, New York: Oxford University Press, pp. 3–19.

Robinson, J. D. (2004) 'The sequential organization of "explicit" apologies in naturally occurring English', *Research on Language and Social Interaction*, 37 (3): 291–330.

Rogoff, B. (1990) *Apprenticeship in Thinking*, New York: Oxford University Press.

Roper, M. (2005) 'Slipping Out of View: Subjectivity and emotion in gender history', *History Workshop Journal*, 59 (1): 57–72.

Rose, D. B. (2004) *Reports from a Wild Country: The Ethics of Decolonisation*, Sydney: UNSW Press.

Rose, G. (2010) *Doing Family Photography*, Farnham: Ashgate.

Roseman, M. (1999) 'Surviving memory: Truth and inaccuracy in Holocaust testimony', *Journal of Holocaust Education*, 8 (1): 1–20.

Rosenthal, G. (2004) 'Biographical Research', in C. Seale, G. Gobo, J. F. Gubrium and D. Silverman (eds), *Qualitative Research Practice*, London: Sage, pp. 48–64.

Rosser, S. V. and P. J. Miller (2000) 'Feminist theories: Implications for developmental psychology', in P. Miller and E. Scholnick (eds), *Towards a Feminist Developmental Psychology*, New York: Cambridge University Press, pp. 11–28.

Rothberg, M. (2000) *Traumatic Realism: The Demands of Holocaust Representation*, Minneapolis: University of Minnesota Press.

Rothberg, M. (2009) *Multidirectional Memory: Remembering the Holocaust in the Age of Decolonization*, Stanford: Stanford University Press.

Roulston, K. (2006) 'Close Encounters of the "CA" Kind: A Review of Literature Analysing Talk in Research Interviews', *Qualitative Research*, 6 (4): 515–34.

Rowe, S. M., J. V. Wertsch and T. Y. Kosyaeva (2002) 'Linking Little Narratives to Big Ones: Narrative and Public Memory in History Museums', *Culture and Psychology*, 8 (1): 96–112.

RTV Slovenija (2008) 'Lahovnik predlaga tehnično vlado', *RTV Slovenija*, <http://www.rtvslo.si/slovenija/lahovnik-predlaga-tehnicno-vlado/82510> (accessed 10 June 2012).

Rubin, D. C. (2006) 'The basic-systems model of episodic memory', *Perspectives on Psychological Science*, 1 (4): 277–311.

Rusinow, D. (1977) *The Yugoslav Experiment, 1948–1974*, Berkeley: University of California Press.

Sacks, H. (1992) 'Lecture 4: Storyteller as "witness;" Entitlement to experience', in H. Sacks, *Lectures on Conversation* (ed. G. Jefferson; introduction by E. A. Schegloff), Oxford: Blackwell, pp. 242–8.

Said, E. (2000) 'Invention, Memory and Place', *Critical Inquiry*, 26 (2): 175–92.

Sambri, C. (1970) *Una frontiera aperta: Indagini sui valichi italo–jugoslavi*, Bologna: Arnaldo Forti Editore.

Samuel, R. (1975) '"Quarry Roughs": life and labour in Headington Quarry, 1860–1920. An essay in oral history', in R. Samuel (ed.), *Village Life and Labour*, London: Routledge and Kegan Paul, pp. 139–263.

Sarkisova, O. and P. Apor (eds) (2008) *Past for the Eyes: East European Representations of Communism in Cinema and Museums after 1989*, Budapest: Central European University Press.

Schacter, D. (2001) *The Seven Sins of Memory: How the Mind Forgets and Remembers*, New York: Houghton Mifflin.

Schama, S. (1995) *Landscape and Memory*, New York: Knopf.

Schudson, M. (2004) 'Notes on scandal and the Watergate legacy', *American Behavioral Scientist*, 47 (9): 1231–8.

Schütz, A. (1967) *Collected Papers I: The Problem of Social Reality* (ed. M. A. Natanson and H. L. van Breda), Dordrecht: Martinus Nijhoff.

Schwartzman, L. F. (2007) 'Does money whiten? Intergenerational changes in racial classification in Brazil', *American Sociological Review*, 72 (6): 940–63.

Schweitzer, P. (2007) *Reminiscence Theatre: Making Theatre from Memories*, London: Jessica Kingsley.

Sclater, S. D. (2003) 'What is the subject?', *Narrative Inquiry*, 13 (2): 317–30.

Scott, T. (2008) 'It's all Alemannic to me! Ethnicity as an interpretive tool for cultural transformations', *Journal of the Australian Early Medieval Association*, 4: 175–85.

Sempik, J., J. Aldridge and S. Becker (2005) *Health, Well Being and Social Inclusion: Therapeutic Horticulture in the UK*, Bristol: The Policy Press.

Shaw, R. (2002) *Memories of the Slave Trade: Ritual and the Historical Imagination in Sierra Leone*, Chicago: Chicago University Press.

Shaw, R. and C. Kitzinger (2007) 'Memory in Interaction: An Analysis of Repeat Calls to a Home Birth Helpline', *Research on Language and Social Interaction*, 40 (1): 117–44.

Sheffer, E. (2011) *Burned Bridge: How East and West Germans Made the Iron Curtain*, Oxford: Oxford University Press.

Shopes, L. (2006) 'Oral history and the study of communities', in R. Perks and A. Thomson (eds), *Oral History Reader*, 2nd edn, London: Routledge, pp. 261–70, first published 1992.

Shotter, J. (1990) 'The social construction of remembering and forgetting', in D. Middleton and D. Edwards (eds), *Collective Remembering*, London: Sage, pp. 120–38.

Siegel, E. (2010) *Galleries of Friendship and Fame*, New Haven and London: Yale University Press.

Silverman, D. (2006) *Interpreting Qualitative Data: Methods for Analysing Talk, Text and Interaction*, London: Sage.

Simon, R. I. (1999) '"What happens when we press play?": Future research on the substance and use of Holocaust audiovisual testimony', *International Journal on the Audio-Visual Testimony*, 3: 103–11.

Simons, H. W. (2000) 'A dilemma-centered analysis of Clinton's August 17th apologia: Implications for rhetorical theory and method', *Quarterly Journal of Speech*, 86 (4): 438–53.

Simpson, R. and P. Lewis (2005) 'An investigation of silence and a scrutiny of transparency: Re-examining gender in organization literature through the concepts of voice and visibility', *Human Relations*, 58 (10): 1253–75.

Širok, K. (2009) 'Kolektivnospominjanje in kolektivnapozaba v obmejnemprostoru: SpomininaGorico, 1943–1947', PhD dissertation, Nova Gorica: Univerza v Novi Gorici.

Sitzia, L. and A. Thickett (2002) *Seeking the Enemy*, London: wORking Press.

Skeggs, B. and H. Wood (2012) *Reacting to Reality Television: Performance, Audience and Value*, London and New York: Routledge.

Skultans, V. (1998) *The Testimony of Lives: Narrative and Memory in Post-Soviet Latvia*, London: Routledge.
Sluga, G. (2001) *The Problem of Trieste and the Italo–Yugoslav Border*, Albany, NY: State University of New York Press.
Smith, D. (1999) *Writing the Social: Critique, Theory, and Investigations*, Toronto: University of Toronto Press.
Smith, G. (2010) *Oral History*, Historical Insights Focus on Research Series, Coventry: University of Warwick, Higher Education Authority and Institute of Historical Research, <http://www2.warwick.ac.uk/fac/cross_fac/heahistory/resources/rg_smith_oralhistory_20111015.pdf> (accessed 27 March 2012).
Smither, R. (2004) 'Why is so much television history about war?', in D. Cannadine (ed.), *History and the Media*, London: Palgrave MacMillan, pp. 52–66.
Social Services Inspectorate (2000) *A Jigsaw of Services: Inspection of Services to Support Disabled Adults in their Parenting Role*, London: Department of Health.
Sontag, S. (2003) *Regarding the Pain of Others*, London and New York: Penguin.
Sotgiu, I. and C. Mormont (2008) 'Similarities and differences between traumatic and emotional memories: Review and directions for future research', *Journal of Psychology: Interdisciplinary and Applied*, 142 (5): 449–69.
Spence, J. (1991) *Putting Myself in the Picture*, London: Virago.
Spence, J. and P. Holland (eds) (1991) *Family Snaps*, London: Virago.
Stacey, J. (1991) 'Can there be a feminist ethnography?', in S. B. Gluck and D. Patai (eds), *Women's Words: The Feminist Practice of Oral History*, London: Routledge, pp. 111–19.
Stein, A. (2007) 'Trauma stories, identity work and the politics of recognition', in J. M. Gerson and D. L. Wolf (eds), *Sociology Confronts the Holocaust*, London: Duke University Press, pp. 85–91.
Stephenson, N. and D. Papadopoulos (2006) *Analysing Everyday Experience: Social Research and Political Change*, Basingstoke: Palgrave.
Stewart, S. (1996) *On Longing*, Durham, NC and London: Duke University Press.
Stier, O. B. (2003) *Committed to Memory: Cultural Mediations of The Holocaust*, Amherst: University of Massachusetts Press.
Stoler, A. L. (2009) *Along the Archival Grain: Epistemic Anxieties and Colonial Common Sense*, Princeton: Princeton University Press.
Stoller, P. (1995) *Embodying Colonial Memories: Spirit Possession, Power and the Hauka in West Africa*, New York: Routledge.
Stone, D. (2006) *History, Memory and Mass Atrocity: Essays on Holocaust and Genocide*, London: Valentine Mitchel.

Stone, E. (1988) *Black Sheep and Kissing Cousins*, New York: Penguin.
Summerfield, P. (1998) *Reconstructing Women's Wartime Lives: Discourse and subjectivity in Oral Histories of the Second World War*, Manchester: Manchester University Press.
Šušmelj, J. (2005) 'Videmski sporazum', in J. Pirjevec, G. Bajc and B. Klabjan (eds), *Vojna in mir na Primorskem*, Koper: Založba Annales, pp. 307–22.
Sutton, L., N. Smith, C. Dearden and S. Middleton (2007) *A Child's-Eye View of Social Difference*, York: Joseph Rowntree Foundation.
Tavuchis, N. (1991) *Mea Culpa: A Sociology of Apology and Reconciliation*, Stanford: Stanford University Press.
Tedeschi, R. G. and L. G. Calhoun (2004) 'Posttraumatic growth: Conceptual foundations and empirical evidence', *Psychological Inquiry*, 15 (1): 1–18.
The Children Act (2004), <http://www.legislation.gov.uk/ukpga/2004/31/contents> (accessed February 2012).
Thompson, P. (1975) *The Edwardians: The Remaking of British Society*, London: Weidenfeld and Nicholson.
Thompson, P. (1978) *The Voice of the Past: Oral History*, Oxford: Oxford University Press.
Thompson, P. (2000) *The Voice of the Past: Oral History*, 3rd edn, Oxford: Oxford University Press.
Thompson, P. (1995) Letter published in *Oral History*, 23 (2): 27–8.
Thompson, P. and J. Bornat (1994) 'Myths and memories of an English rising: 1968 at Essex', *Oral History*, 22 (2): 44–54.
Thompson, P. and B. Corti (2008) 'Whose community?: The shaping of a collective memory in a volunteer project', *Oral History*, 36 (2): 89–98.
Thomson, A. (1994) *Anzac Memories: Living with the Legend*, Melbourne: Oxford University Press.
Thomson, A. (2006) 'Four Paradigm Transformations in Oral History', *Oral History Review*, 34 (1): 49–70.
Thomson, A. (2011) *Moving Stories: An Intimate History of Four Women across Two Countries*, Manchester: Manchester University Press.
Thomson, P. (2008) *Doing Visual Research with Children and Young People*, London: Routledge.
Thonfeld, C. (2011) 'Memories of former World War Two forced labourers – an international comparison', *Oral History*, 39 (2): 33–48.
Thorne, A. and K. C. McLean (2003) 'Telling Traumatic Events in Adolescence: A study of master narrative positioning', in R. Fivush and C. A. Haden (eds), *Autobiographical Memory and the Construction of a Narrative Self: Developmental and Cultural Perspectives*, Mahwah, NJ: Lawrence Erlbaum Associates, pp. 169–86.
Tileagă, C. (2008) 'What Is a 'Revolution'?: National Commemoration,

Collective Memory and Managing Authenticity in the Representation of a Political Event', *Discourse and Society*, 19 (3): 359–82.

Tileagă, C. (2009a) 'The social organization of representations of history: the textual accomplishment of coming to terms with the past', *British Journal of Social Psychology*, 48 (2): 337–55.

Tileagă, C. (2009b) '"Mea culpa": the social production of public disclosure and reconciliation', in A. Galasinska and M. Krzyzanowski (eds), *Discourse and Transformation in Central and Eastern Europe*, Basingstoke: Palgrave Macmillan, pp. 173–87.

Tileagă, C. (2011) '(Re)writing biography: Memory, identity and textually mediated reality in coming to terms with the past', *Culture and Psychology*, 17 (2): 197–215.

Tileagă, C. (2012) 'The right measure of guilt: Moral reasoning, transgression and the social construction of moral meanings', *Discourse and Communication*, 6 (2): 203–22.

Tilley, C. Y. (1994) *A Phenomenology of Landscape: Places, Paths, and Monuments*, Oxford: Berg.

Tilley, C. Y., W. Keane, S. Kuechler, M. Rowlands and P. Spyer (eds) (2006) *Handbook of Material Culture*, London: Sage.

Tismăneanu, V. (2008) 'Democracy and memory: Romania confronts its communist past', *Annals of the American Academy of Political and Social Science*, 617 (1): 166–80.

Todorova, M. (ed.) (2010) *Remembering Communism: Genres of Representation*, New York: Social Science Research Council.

Todorova, M. and Z. Gille (eds) (2010) *Post-communist Nostalgia*, Oxford: Berghahn Books.

Tonkin, E. (1992) *Narrating Our Pasts: The Social Construction of Oral History*, Cambridge: Cambridge University Press.

Tozzi, V. (2012) 'The epistemic and moral role of testimony', *History and Theory*, 51 (1): 1–17.

Trezise, T. (2001) 'Unspeakable', *The Yale Journal of Criticism*, 14 (1): 39–66.

Turner, G. (1997) 'Media Texts and Messages', in S. Cunningham and G. Turner (eds), *The Media in Australia: Industries, Texts, Audiences*, Sydney: Allen and Unwin, pp. 293–347.

Tusting, K., R. Crawshaw and B. Callen (2002) '"I Know, 'Cos I Was There": How Residence Abroad Students use Personal Experience to Legitimate Cultural Generalizations', *Discourse and Society*, 13 (5): 651–72.

UNESCO (no date) 'Brazil–Africa: Crossed histories programme', <http://www.unesco.org/new/en/brasilia/special-themes/ethnic-and-racial-relations-in-brazil/brazil-africa-project/> (accessed 13 February 2012).

Valsiner, J. and A. Rosa (eds) (2007) *The Cambridge Handbook of Sociocultural Psychology*, Cambridge: Cambridge University Press.

van Dijck, J. (2007) *Mediated Memories in the Digital Age*, Stanford: Stanford University Press.

van House, N. (2009) 'Collocated Photo Sharing, Story-telling, and the Performance of Self', *International Journal of Human–Computer Studies*, 67 (12): 1073–86.

van House, N. (2011) 'Personal Photography, Digital Technologies and the Uses of the Visual', *Visual Studies*, 26 (2): 125–34.

Velikonja, M. (2008) *Titostalgia: A Study of Nostalgia for Josip Broz*, Ljubljana: Peace Institute.

Verger, P. (1976) *Trade Relations between the Bight of Benin and Bahia from the 17th to the 19th Century*, Ibadan, Nigeria: Ibadan University Press.

Vidal-Naquet, P. (1992) *Assassins of Memory: Essays in the Denial of the Holocaust*, New York: Columbia University Press.

Vygotsky, L. S. (1978) *Mind in Society: The Development of Higher Psychological Processes*, Cambridge, MA: Harvard University Press.

Wagenaar, W. A. (1988) *Identifying Ivan: Case Study in Legal Psychology*, New York: Prentice Hall.

Wagenaar, W. A. and J. Groeneweg (1990) 'The memory of concentration camp survivors', *Applied Cognitive Psychology*, 4: 77–87.

Walker, A. and R. K. Moulton (1989) 'Photo Albums: Images of Time and Reflections of Self', *Qualitative Sociology*, 12 (2): 155–82.

Walker, M. U. (2006) *Moral Repair: Reconstructing Moral Relations after Wrongdoing*, New York: Cambridge University Press.

Walker, R., B. Schratz and P. Egg (2008) 'Seeing beyond violence: Visual research applied to policy and practice', in P. Thomson (ed.), *Doing Visual Research with Children and Young People*, London: Routledge, pp. 164–74.

Walkerdine, V. (1991) *Schoolgirl Fictions*, London: Verso.

Wang, Q. and M. Ross (2007) 'Culture and memory', in S. Kitayama and D. Cohen (eds), *Handbook of Cultural Psychology*, New York: Guilford Press, pp. 645–67.

Wanner, C. (1998) *Burden of Dreams: History and Identity in Post-Soviet Ukraine*, University Park, PA: The Pennsylvania University Press.

Waxman, Z. W. (2006) *Writing the Holocaust: Identity, Testimony, Representation*, Oxford: Oxford University Press.

Waxman, Z. W. (2010) 'Testimonies as sacred texts: The sanctification of Holocaust writing', *Past and Present*, 206 (5): 321–41.

Wengraf, T. (2001) *Qualitative Research Interviewing: Biographic Narrative and Semi-Structured Methods*, London: Sage.

Wertsch, J. (2002) *Voices of Collective Remembering*, Cambridge: Cambridge University Press.

Wertsch, J. (2007) 'Collective memory', in J. Valsiner and A. Rosa (eds), *The*

Cambridge Handbook of Sociocultural Psychology, Cambridge: Cambridge University Press, pp. 645–60.

Wetherell, M. (2003) 'Racism and the Analysis of Cultural Resources in Interviews', in H. van den Berg, M. Wetherell and H. Houtkoop-Steenstra (eds), *Analyzing Race Talk: Multidisciplinary Perspectives on the Research Interview*, Cambridge: Cambridge University Press, pp. 11–30.

Wideangle (2007) 'Brazil in Black and White: Introducing affirmative action in Brazil', 4 September 2007, <http://www.pbs.org/wnet/wideangle/episodes/brazil-in-black-and-white/introduction/965/> (accessed 18 January 2013).

Wieviorka, A. (2006) *The Era of the Witness*, New York: Cornell University Press.

Williams, B. (1989) 'A class act: Anthropology and the race to nation across ethnic terrain', *Annual Review of Anthropology*, 18: 401–44.

Wolfe, P. (2001) 'Land, Labor and Difference: Elementary structures of race', *The American Historical Review*, 106 (3): 866–905.

Wood, H. (2009) *Talking with Television: Women, Talk Shows, and Modern Self-Reflexivity*, Urbana and Chicago: University of Illinois Press.

Wooffitt, R. and S. Widdicombe (2006) 'Interaction in Interviews', in P. Drew, G. Raymond and D. Weinberg (eds), *Talk and Interaction in Social Research Methods*, London: Sage, pp. 27–49.

Wright, P. (2007) *Iron Curtain: From Stage to Cold War*, Oxford: Oxford University Press.

Wyness, M. (2006) *Childhood and Society: An Introduction to the Sociology of Childhood*, France: Lavoisier.

Yancey, W. L., E. P. Ericksen and R. J. Juliani (1976) 'Emergent Ethnicity', *American Sociological Review*, 41 (3): 391–403.

Yang, P. (2000) *Ethnic Studies: Issues and Approaches*, New York: State University of New York Press.

Yates, F. (1966) *The Arts of Memory*, London: Routledge and Kegan Paul.

Young, H. (2007) 'Hard Man, New Man: Re/composing masculinities in Glasgow, c. 1950–2000', *Oral History*, 35 (1): 71–81.

Young, J. E. (1988) *Writing and Rewriting the Holocaust: Narrative and the Consequences of Interpretation*, Bloomington: Indiana University Press.

Young, J. E. (1993) *The Texture of Memory: Holocaust Memorials and Meaning*, New Haven: Yale University Press.

Young, J. E. (1997) 'Between history and memory: The uncanny voices of historian and survivor', *History and Memory*' 9 (2): 47–58.

Yow, V. R. (1997) '"Do I like them too much?" Effects of the Oral History Interview on the Interviewee and Vice-Versa', *Oral History Review*, 24 (1): 55–79.

Yow, V. R. (2005) *Recording Oral History: A Guide for the Humanities and Social Sciences*, 2nd edn, Walnut Creek, CA: AltaMira Press.

Zabaki, R. and L. Camargo (2007) 'Raçasnãoexiste', *Veja*, 6 June 2007, <http://veja.abril.com.br/060607/p_082.shtml> (accessed 5 December 2011).

Zelizer, B. (1995) 'Reading the Past against the Grain: the Shape of Memory Studies', *Critical Studies in Mass Communication*, 12 (2): 214–39.

Žerdin, A. (2004) 'Kotaleči se mejni kamni', *Mladina*, 20 February 2004, <http://www.mladina.si/94291/kotaleci-se-mejni-kamni/> (accessed 10 June 2012).

Zhang, E. and W. L. Benoit (2009) 'Former Minister Zhang's discourse on SARS: Government's image restoration or destruction', *Public Relations Review*, 35 (3): 240–6.

Zimmerman, P. R. (1995) *Reel Families: A Social History of Amateur Film*, Bloomington and Indianapolis: Indiana University Press.

Zukas, M. (1993) 'Friendship in Oral History: a feminist psychologist's view', *Oral History*, 21 (2): 73–9.

Notes on Contributors

Jo Aldridge is Professor of Social Policy and Criminology in the Department of Social Sciences at Loughborough University. She is also Director of the Young Carers Research Group (YCRG), which is known internationally for its pioneering and innovative research on young carers. Jo's most recent research study was a photographic participation investigation (funded by the Economic and Social Research Council) of children who care for parents with serious mental health problems. She is also currently working with Manchester Carers Forum and Child and Adolescent Mental Health Services on a project that looks at the psychological impact of caring on children and young people.

Paul Basu is Reader in Material Culture and Museum Studies in the Institute of Archaeology at University College London. He is a social anthropologist specialising in cultural heritage, memory, and museums in diasporic contexts and in West Africa. His recent publications include *Highland Homecomings: Genealogy and Heritage Tourism in the Scottish Diaspora* (2007), *Exhibition Experiments* (co-edited with Sharon Macdonald, 2007), and a special issue of the journal *Mobilities* on the theme of 'Migrant Worlds, Material Cultures' (co-edited with Simon Coleman, 2008). He is currently a managing editor of the *Journal of Material Culture*. His recent work has focused on cultural heritage and memory in Sierra Leone, where he also acts as a consultant on behalf of the British Museum's Africa Programme.

Joanna Bornat is Emeritus Professor of Oral History in the Faculty of Health and Social Care at the Open University. She has researched and published edited collections, articles and book chapters in the area of oral history and ageing and has a particular interest in remembering in later life. Her most recent ESRC-funded research activities include 'The Oldest Generation', a joint project in the Timescapes programme, and an investigation into the experiences of South Asian overseas-trained doctors and their contribution to the development of the geriatric specialty. She has been an editor of the journal *Oral History* for over thirty years and is a long-standing member of the UK Oral History Society.

Steve Brown is Director of the Centre for Philosophy and Political Economy at Leicester University. His research interests are around social remembering, constructionism and social theory. Recent work includes *The Social Psychology of Experience: Studies in Remembering and Forgetting* (with David Middleton, Sage 2005) and *Psychology Without Foundations* (with Paul Stenner, Sage 2006). He is Associate Editor of the *British Journal of Social Psychology*.

Jovan Byford is Senior Lecturer in Psychology at the Faculty of Social Sciences, Open University. He is the author of *Denial and Repression of Antisemitism: Post-Communist Remembrance of the Serbian Bishop Nikolaj Velimirović* (CEU Press 2008) and *Teorija zavere: Srbija protiv 'novog svetskog poretka'* [Conspiracy theory: Serbia vs. the 'New World Order'] (Beogradski centar za ljudska prava, 2006). In addition to the two books, Jovan has published articles on conspiracy theories, the Christian Right and antisemitism in Serbia, as well as on Holocaust memory in that country. He is currently working on a project on the changing role of (and attitudes towards) survivors and survivor testimonies in Yugoslav/Serbian historiography and commemorative culture after 1945.

Chris Dearden was a Research Fellow in the Centre for Research in Social Policy (CRSP) and a member of the Department of Social Sciences' Young Carers Research Group, both at Loughborough University. She has extensive experience of conducting in-depth qualitative research with vulnerable groups, including adult and young carers, children of recently divorced or separated parents, adults with severe mental health problems, ex-prisoners, and low income households. Along with Jo Aldridge and other colleagues, she has done much to raise the profile of young carers, a group that has existed for centuries but, hidden within a culture of 'private' family relationships and assumptions about family and familial responsibilities, had hitherto remained silent and neglected in policy discussions and practical support.

Robyn Fivush is the Samuel Candler Dobbs Professor of Psychology and Chair of the Department of Psychology at Emory University, Atlanta, Georgia. She received her PhD from the Graduate Center of The City University of New York in 1983, and was a post-doctoral fellow at the Center for Human Information Processing, University of California at San Diego from 1982 to 1984. She joined the Emory faculty in 1984, where she is a core faculty member at the Emory Center for Myth and Ritual in American Life, associated faculty member with the Department of Women's Studies, and a Senior Fellow in the Center for the Study of Law and Religion. She has published over 100 books, articles and chapters. Her work focuses on autobiographical memory with an emphasis on the social construction of autobiographical memory and the relations among memory, narrative, trauma, and coping.

Ann Gray is Professor of Cultural Studies in the Lincoln School of Media, University of Lincoln, and co-director of the Centre for European Cultural Studies. She was the Principal Investigator for the AHRC Televising History 1992–2010 project and has published, with Erin Bell, the edited collection *Televising History: mediating the past in post-war Europe*. They are currently working on their book, *History on Televison*, for Routledge. Her book, *Research Practice for Cultural Studies*, was published by Sage in 2003, and she recently co-edited two volumes of *CCCS Selected Working papers in Cultural Studies*, published by Routledge in 2007. Her next project will address the uses of history.

Amanda Kearney is a Senior Lecturer in Anthropology in the School of Social Science and International Studies at the University of New South Wales. She has published in relation to indigenous Australian anthropology, emotional geography, and intangible cultural heritage. Most recently, her work involves a comparative analysis of emerging and resurging ethnicity in the post-colonial spaces of Australia and Brazil. Her book, *Before the Old People and Still Today: Yanyuwa narratives of engagement* (Australian Scholarly Publishing) focuses on the emotional geographies of indigenous homelands in northern Australia and how this articulates across the lives of younger and older generations of indigenous people. Amanda's work is characterised by a research philosophy that brings together theory and praxis through ethnographic research with indigenous groups in Australia and inter-ethnic groups in Brazil.

Emily Keightley is Senior Lecturer in Communication and Media Studies in the Department of Social Sciences at Loughborough University. She has published in relation to both conceptual and methodological issues in memory studies. Her recent journal articles include 'Remembering Research: Memory and Methodology in the Social Sciences' (*International Journal of Social Research Methodology*, 2010), and 'Trauma, Discourse and Communicative Limits' (*Critical Discourse Studies*, 2009, with Michael Pickering). Her recent book, co-written with Michael Pickering, *The Mnemonic Imagination*, published by Palgrave Macmillan (2012), explores and reconceives the relationship between memory and imagination. Her recent edited collection *Time, Media and Modernity* has also been published by Palgrave Macmillan in 2012.

250 NOTES ON CONTRIBUTORS

Sabina Mihelj is Lecturer in Media, Communication and Culture in the Department of Social Sciences at Loughborough University. Her recent research focuses on issues of collective identity, nation-building, mass communication, Cold War culture, and memory, with particular reference to the Western Balkans and more broadly Eastern and Central Europe after 1945. She has written over thirty journal articles and book chapters on these topics and is currently completing a book manuscript on media, modernity and nationalism (due to be published by Palgrave in 2011).

Michael Pickering is Professor of Media and Cultural Analysis in the Department of Social Sciences at Loughborough University. He has published in cultural studies and the sociology of art and culture, media and communication studies, and social and cultural history. His recent books include *History, Experience and Cultural Studies* (1997); *Researching Communications* (1999/2007), co-written with David Deacon, Peter Golding and Graham Murdock; *Stereotyping: The Politics of Representation* (2001); *Creativity, Communication and Cultural Value* (2004), co-written with Keith Negus; *Beyond a Joke: The Limits of Humour* (2005), co-edited with Sharon Lockyer; *Blackface Minstrelsy in Britain* (2008), *Research Methods for Cultural Studies* (2008), *Popular Culture*, a four-volume edited collection (2010), and *Rhythms of Labour: The History of Music at Work in Britain* (2013), co-written with Marek Korczynski and Emma Robertson. His recent book, co-written with Emily Keightley, is *The Mnemonic Imagination*, published by Palgrave Macmillan (2012).

Paula Reavey is Senior Lecturer in Psychology at London South Bank University. Her research interests are around embodiment, social remembering and feminist theory. Recent work includes a co-edited volume (with Sam Warner, Routledge 2003), *New Feminist Stories of Child Sexual Abuse: Sexual Script and Dangerous Dialogues*, and a number of article on child sexual abuse, sexuality and embodiment, using discourse analysis, visual methods and memory work. She is Associate Editor of *The Psychology of Women Section Review*.

Cristian Tileagă is Senior Lecturer in Social Psychology the Department of Social Sciences at Loughborough University. Cristian's main research interests are in political discourse analysis, collective memory, and social representations of history. Drawing on discursive psychology, his current research explores how the official political imaginary and histories of the (Romanian) communist/post-communist past are constructed in talk and text. He is particularly interested in the social production of public disclosure and reconciliation with the past in accounts of 'collaboration' with the Securitate, and the social organisation of collective memory and social representations of history in the context of how post-communist democracies reckon with former regimes (with a special focus on the 'Tismăneanu Report' condemning communism in Romania).

Index

Abrams, Lynn, 29–30, 31, 42
agency, 7, 34, 57, 137, 139, 146, 165, 170, 175, 177, 194
Alderman, Derek H., 136, 139
Alderson, Priscilla, 167
Allen, Matthew, 59
Amery, Jean, 205
analogue/digital, 105
anti-Semitism, 160–1
apologia, 8, 185–99
Appadurai, Arjun, 116–18
archives, 40, 42, 82, 83, 86–9, 91, 93, 98, 104, 117, 119, 122, 126, 128, 138, 193, 194, 196, 198
Australia, 36, 132–3, 137

Banks, Marcus, 172
Banks of Green Willow, 110
Bartlett, Frederick, 26, 27
Batchen, Geoffrey, 111
Bauer, Yehuda, 204
BBC, 83–9
Bell, Erin, 79, 95
BenEzer, Gadi, 156, 161
Benoit, William L., 187, 198
Berdahl, Daphne, 73
Bergson, Henri, 51
Berliner, David, 136
Bhowmick, Bimal, 36
Blitz, 83

Bodnar, John, 61, 73, 75
Bogen, David, 214
Bok, Sissela, 198
Borland, Katherine, 38
Born, Georgina, 93
Bourdon, Jerome, 81
Brandt, Bill, 102
Brassaï, George, 102
Brazil, 132–5, 137, 140–8
Britzman, Deborah P., 170
Brown, Steven D., 50–1, 53–4, 58–9, 189–90, 198, 214
Brownie cameras, 100
Browning, Christopher, 202–4, 214
Bruner, Jerome, 28
Buchanan, 51
Butterworth, George, 110

Caldwell, John T., 93
Campbell, Sue, 54–5
Capa, Robert, 84–5
Carrier, Peter, 115
Caruth, Cathy, 154, 164, 166
Chalfen, Richard, 99–100, 112n
Chambers, Deborah, 103–4
Chanan, Michael, 87, 89
Chandler, Michael J., 26
change, 26, 32, 80, 101, 138
Channel 4, 82, 89–92
Chapman, James, 83, 86–7

INDEX

Chicago School, 31
child sexual abuse, 22, 26, 55–7, 151, 153
childhood/youth, 8, 22, 24, 35, 91, 99, 110, 151, 159–64, 167–84
Chung, Cindy K., 28
Churchill, Winston, 65
cine cameras, 98
collective memory, 4, 6, 8, 13, 34, 82, 115, 189, 208
Collier, John Jr, 181
Collier, Malcolm Carr, 181
Commaroff, Jean, 140
Commaroff, John L., 140
commemoration, 61, 80–1, 83, 115, 117, 133, 140, 153
community, 4, 6, 19, 29, 36, 39, 42, 80, 89, 100, 106, 115, 124, 127, 132, 147, 162, 198, 211
confession, 8, 186, 188, 190, 191–2, 195–6
Connerton, Paul, 140
Conway, Martin, 28
Crace, John, 89
Crawford, Robert Copland, 119, 121–4
Crusenberry, Sudie, 35
Cubitt, George, 181
cultural studies, 2, 13, 18, 41, 152

Dale, Richard, 86–8
Dangerous Films, 84, 86
D-Day 6.6.1944, 82–9
Dean, John, 49
Deleuze, Gilles, 53
Dewey, John, 46, 50, 55
di Bello, Patrizia, 103, 111
digital, 31, 39, 40, 41, 79, 84
Dijck, José van, 111, 112n
Dillon, Brian, 162–4
discourse analysis, 6, 49, 58, 93, 95, 102, 133–4, 186, 190–6, 198
discursive psychology, 46–51, 58–9, 188–9, 198
Dunkirk, 83

Edgeron, Gary R., 79, 95
Edkins, Jenny, 153
Edwards, Derek, 47–50, 59, 214
Eisenhower, Dwight, 84–5
elicitation techniques, 17–18, 106–7, 129, 130, 158, 170–3, 189
empathy, 88, 94, 133, 156, 207
Empires's Children, 82, 89–92
Erll, Astrid, 116
Ethics, 5–6, 22, 40, 41, 57, 62, 72, 74, 75, 87, 89, 92, 109, 133, 152, 156–7, 168, 176–7, 181, 182, 187, 191, 202–4, 211
ethnicity, 7, 34, 37, 38, 41, 94, 132–47
ethnography, 31, 38, 93, 100–1, 105, 111, 118, 128–30, 132–5, 144–6, 147–8, 199
Europe, 65–6, 74, 80, 117, 200
European Union, 66
Evans, George Ewart, 31–2

family, 7, 15, 17, 36, 45, 48, 63, 65, 81, 82, 88, 89, 90–2, 95, 97–100, 102–6, 110–11, 116, 126, 133, 135, 136, 141, 157, 159, 163–4, 168, 170–3, 178, 185
family albums, 89, 91, 101–7, 111, 135, 170, 172
Fanima, 119–23
Felman, Shoshana, 166, 214
Feminism, 14, 18, 20, 26, 37–8, 42, 103
First World War, 34, 153
Foucault, Michel, 53
Francis, Martha E., 24
Frisch, Michel, 39–40
Frosh, Paul, 214
Fulton, Missouri, 65

gender, 18, 22, 29, 34, 35, 37, 38, 41, 61, 94, 102, 105, 106, 157, 200
generations, 29, 30, 36, 39, 72, 84, 89, 97, 99, 104, 106, 117, 125, 141, 153, 157, 159, 166, 208
Ginzburg, Carlo, 203
Gluck, Sherna Berger, 38

Goodchild, Tim, 86
Gray, Ann, 79, 95
Green, Anna, 34
Grele, R., 33
Groot, Jerome de, 95

Halbwachs, Maurice, 13, 47, 51, 115, 139, 151
Harrison, Brian, 31
Hartley, Leslie Poles, 145–6
Hartman, Geoffrey, 205–6
Hay, James Shaw, 119
Hepburn, Alexa, 75
Heywood, Colin, 167
Hirsch, Marianne, 103, 111
Historiography, 34, 200, 202, 204, 208
history, 2, 29, 33–4, 41, 63, 70, 79–80, 82, 85–7, 91, 135, 142–5, 152, 154, 190, 202–3, 205–6, 208, 213
History Workshop movement, 33
Hodgkin, Patricia, 116
Hoelscher, Stephen, 136, 139
Holocaust, 8–9, 151, 157, 159, 161, 200–14
home movies, 99–101, 111
home-mode media, 6–7, 99–102, 106–7, 111
Human Body, The, 86
Hungary, 159
Hutton, Lord Patrick, 83
Huyssen, Andreas, 80

identity, 2–3, 7, 8, 13, 29, 36, 38, 39, 45, 70, 73, 80, 82, 83, 89, 90, 92, 94, 95, 102, 115, 118, 132–4, 136–47, 153, 157, 160–1, 186–8, 190–200, 205, 213
individual memory, 2, 4–6, 8, 9, 13, 16, 27, 29, 47, 50, 80, 95, 97, 132, 157, 195–7
interviewing, 6–7, 18, 22, 30, 31–5, 37–9, 41, 56, 60–4, 67, 74, 75, 93–4, 100, 104–6, 108–9, 134, 111, 157–8, 205, 208–9
Iron Curtain, 64–73

Israel, 190
Italy, 42, 64–7, 69, 72–3

James, William, 46
Janesick, Valerie, 129–30
Janša, Janez, 67
Joanou, Jamie Patrice, 181
Jowell, Tessa, 83

Kansteiner, Wulf, 152, 166
Kelly, Dr David, 83
Knutsford, Lord, 119
Kodak, 98
Kuhn, Annette, 103, 172–3, 175

Lakoff, Robin Tolmach, 198
Landsberg, Alison, 88–9
Langer, Lawrence, 208, 214
Langford, Martha, 103, 104, 111
Largo, 119–24
Laub, Dori, 166, 214
Lawson, Nigel, 59
Levine, Hal B., 138
Leys, Ruth, 166
Liddington, Jill, 31–2
Ljubljana, 65
loss, 101, 151, 163–4
Loughborough University, 105
Lowethal, David, 115
Luckhurst, Roger, 166
Lynch, Michael E., 214

Maccoby, Eleanor E., 38
Maccoby, Nathan, 38
Mackay, H. B., 119–24
Mackiah, 119–24
Mandingo, 125–6
Marcus, George, 118, 128, 130
Mark, James, 75
McAdams, Dan P., 16
McLeod, Julie 39
media, 1–2, 7, 54, 58, 80, 85, 93, 97–9, 101, 105–9, 111–12, 125, 129, 134, 146, 158, 173, 181, 190, 201, 214
media studies, 2, 81, 93, 152

Meier, A. J., 198
memory
  autobiographical memory, 4, 6, 13–28, 103, 107–8, 159–64
  individual memory, 2, 4–6, 8, 9, 13, 16, 27, 29, 47, 50, 80, 95, 97, 132, 157, 195–7
  public memory, 1–2, 4, 6, 30, 35, 41, 61–2, 73, 74–5, 80, 95, 97, 115, 153, 157, 162
  social memory, 2, 79, 135, 142, 143
  vernacular memory, 60–75, 97–112
memoryscapes, 7, 116, 130
Middleton, David, 46–9, 50–1, 53–4, 58–9, 198, 214
Moran, James, 99
Moulton, Rosland Kimball, 103
music, 36, 82, 105–7, 109–12, 144, 158

national memory, 3, 6, 61–4, 75, 79, 81–3, 91, 95, 116
Neisser, Ulrich, 49
Nora, Pierre, 80, 88, 115
Norris, Jill, 31–2
Nova Gorica, 62, 64–7, 72, 75
Novick, Peter, 204

oral history, 4, 6, 29–42, 98–105, 107, 128–9, 136, 157, 200–1, 206–7

painful pasts, 8, 109, 151–66
Parnham, Peter, 86
Passerini, Luisa, 33–4, 42
Patai, Daphne, 38
Pennebaker, James W., 24, 28
People's War, The, 83–4
Perks, Rob, 42
personal memory, 13, 95, 112, 193, 199
Personal Narratives Group, 37–8
photography, 6–8, 39, 48, 98–109, 111, 158, 162–3, 170–7, 181–2
Pinchevsky, Amit, 214
Pinho, Patricia de Santana, 147
Polaroid cameras, 100
Popular Memory Group, 33, 37

Portelli, Allejandro, 33–5, 42, 201
Potter, Jonathan, 47–50, 59, 75, 189, 214
Prosser, Jon, 172
Proulx, Travis, 26
psychiatry, 152
psychoanalysis, 93, 152, 201, 206

Radstone, Joanna, 116
Raine, Craig, 174
Ramos, Alcida Rita, 142–3
Reading, Anna, 157
Reavey, Paula, 59
Reiter, Andrea, 211
Rollins, Peter, 95
Romania, 190
Rose, Gillian, 104–5, 111
Rothberg, Michael, 166
Roulston, Kathryn, 75

Sack, Harvey, 53, 57
Samuel, Raphael, 31
Schacter, Daniel, 135
Schindler's List, 210
Schudson, Michael, 188
Schwartz, Dona, 172
Scott, 137
self-interviews, 107–12, 158
Sempik, Joe, 170
Serbia, 212, 210
shell-shock, 153
Siegel, Elizabeth, 103, 111
Sierra Leone, 117–29
Simons, Herbert W., 187–8
Slovenia, 62, 64, 66–7, 73, 75
Smith, Sydney, 1
Smither, Roger, 88
social psychology, 2, 6, 49–50, 58, 185, 187, 198
sociology, 1, 2, 31, 32, 41, 45, 147, 152, 167, 200, 213
Spence, Jo, 103, 111
Stacey, Judith, 38
Stier, Oren Baruch, 207
Stoler, Ann, 128
Sutton, Liz, 170

Tavuchis, Nicholas, 198
television, 7, 41, 79–95, 97, 190, 201
testimony, 8, 36, 49, 83, 85, 87–8, 167–70, 177, 199, 200–14
Thompson, Paul, 29, 31–3, 42, 206
Thomson, Alistair, 31, 34, 36, 39, 42
Thomson, Pat, 170, 172, 175, 177, 181
Thomson, Rachel, 39
Tileagă, Cristian, 202
Tonkin, Elizabeth, 125
Tozzi, Veronica, 205
Trauma, 4, 8, 16–17, 21–2, 26, 37, 139, 142, 147, 152–66, 200, 201, 205–12

UK video, 6–7, 98–9, 101, 107, 111, 170, 174, 205, 207, 214
United Kingdom, 31–2, 37, 39, 41–2, 80, 86, 94, 95, 117, 119, 126, 159–60, 168–9, 179
United States of America, 26, 84, 98–100, 105, 117, 198, 200, 206, 212
University of Essex, 31

Walker, Andrew, 103
Walker, Rob, 174–6
Walkerdine, Valerie, 103
Watergate, 49
Wetherell, Margaret, 49
Who Do You Think You Are?, 89–92
Wieviorka, Annette, 214
Winston, Robert, 86
witnessing, 8, 30, 82, 84–5, 87–9, 132, 133–5, 137, 153–4, 194–5, 200–14
Wood, Helen, 94

Yang, Philip Q., 147
Yates, Frances, 115
Young carers, 8, 167–84
Young, James, 128
Yow, Valerie, 42
Yugoslavia, 65–7, 70, 73

Zelizer, Barbie, 82
Zimmerman, Patricia, 98–9

EU Authorised Representative:
Easy Access System Europe Mustamäe tee 50, 10621 Tallinn, Estonia
gpsr.requests@easproject.com

Printed and bound by CPI Group (UK) Ltd, Croydon, CR0 4YY
17/02/2026
02054585-0002